Happy Christmas '97
with all our love April + [...]
x [...]

www.active-unafe.com.

CARRIER COMBAT

CARRIER COMBAT

DAVID WRAGG

SUTTON PUBLISHING

First published in the United Kingdom in 1997 by
Sutton Publishing Limited · Phoenix Mill
Thrupp · Stroud · Gloucestershire · GL5 2BU

British Library Cataloguing in Publication Data
A catalogue record for this book is available from the British Library

ISBN 0 7509 1397 5

ALAN SUTTON™ and SUTTON™ are the
trade marks of Sutton Publishing Limited

Typeset in 10/13pt Sabon.
Typesetting and origination by
Sutton Publishing Limited.
Printed in Great Britain by
Butler & Tanner Ltd, Frome, Somerset.

CONTENTS

PART FIVE: TAKING THE WAR TO JAPAN

PART SIX: CARRIER WARFARE IN PEACE

FOREWORD

I have always had the greatest admiration for those who fight for their country, and especially for those who do this flying from a ship at sea, or struggling to maintain and operate aircraft in often less than ideal weather conditions. In *Carrier Combat*, I have tried to give carrier warfare the human perspective, using accounts of those who have experienced this highly effective and most flexible form of warfare.

Obviously, I have been heavily dependent on those who have recorded their experiences in books or in other media, but in addition my gratitude is also due to those who contacted me after *Navy News* published a notice asking for help, including the Reverend Donald Farquharson-Roberts,

Dennis Sutton, Frank Taylor, Harry Wharton and many others.

Thanks are also due to the Sound Archive and Photographic Archive at the Imperial War Museum, to the Photographic Archive of the Fleet Air Arm Museum, marked as FAAM in the captions, to the United States Naval Institute, to Austin Brown at the Aviation Picture Library and Robert F. Dorr in Washington for help with USN and US National Archive material, and last but not least to Frank B. Mormillo in California for his superb colour photographs, one of which graces the front cover of this book.

David Wragg
South Queensferry
August 1997

LIST OF PLATES

PART ONE

THE MAKING OF THE AIRCRAFT CARRIER

THE MAKING OF THE AIRCRAFT CARRIER

1918–1939

BORN OUT OF NECESSITY

The aircraft carrier was the product of warfare, and of a dawning realization of the importance of naval aviation. It also reflected the discovery that the hydro-aeroplane, sometimes called the floatplane or seaplane, had its limitations and could not be expected to carry the warload needed by an effective bomber, or possess the rate of climb and the agility of a successful fighter. Combat conditions had already demonstrated these weaknesses. There was dissatisfaction too with the aircraft capacity of the seaplane carriers, although, to be fair, none of those in use during the First World War had been purpose-built. The early seaplane carriers were old colliers and packets, or ferries as we would now call them, converted for wartime operation. The exception was the French *La Foudre*, converted from a cruiser. For the most part, they were too small and often too slow to keep up with the fleet.

The potential for naval aviation to do more than simply act as an extension of the eyes and guns of the fleet was recognized early enough. On Christmas Day 1914 seven British seaplanes left the seaplane carriers *Engadine*, *Riviera* and *Express* for a raid on the German airship hangars at Nordholz, near Cuxhaven.

An improvement on the standards of seaplane carrier also came as the war progressed. The Cunard liner *Campania*, 18,000 tons, was requisitioned by the British

Admiralty and joined the fleet in 1915 with a 200-foot wooden deck built over the ship's forecastle, so that the new Fairey seaplane, also called the Campania, could take off from the wooden deck using wheeled trolleys placed under the floats. In 1916, the ship's fore-funnel was divided to allow the take off platform to be lengthened. Even so, the *Campania* was still too slow to keep pace with the rest of the fleet. As for the Fairey Campania, cruising speed was a sedate 80 m.p.h. and the operational ceiling was just 2,000 feet, although the three hour endurance must have had some value for reconnaissance purposes.

Naval airmen were well aware of the advances in performance being made as the war progressed, with the RNAS during the early part of the conflict being tasked with the air defence of the United Kingdom using landplanes to counter the growing German Zeppelin menace.

The take-off platform aboard *Campania* had already proven its usefulness. Perhaps with landplanes and a ship that was both larger and faster, naval air power could take another step forward. The obvious candidate for conversion had to be one of a class of three battlecruisers, larger than cruisers, but faster and less heavily armoured than battleships. The class which the Admiralty had in mind was of unusual design, and was known in naval circles as the 'Outrageous class', because of their light construction. They had been built as shallow draft vessels to take the war to

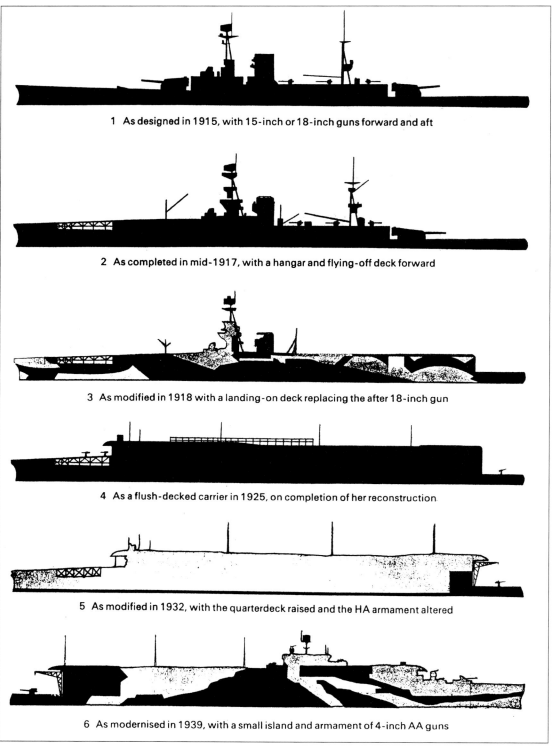

1 As designed in 1915, with 15-inch or 18-inch guns forward and aft

2 As completed in mid-1917, with a hangar and flying-off deck forward

3 As modified in 1918 with a landing-on deck replacing the after 18-inch gun

4 As a flush-decked carrier in 1925, on completion of her reconstruction

5 As modified in 1932, with the quarterdeck raised and the HA armament altered

6 As modernised in 1939, with a small island and armament of 4-inch AA guns

Uncertainty over the way forward in carrier design can be seen from this drawing showing the evolution of *Furious* from battlecruiser to aircraft carrier.

Germany in the Baltic. Fast, at 32.5 knots, the first of these ships, *Furious*, had some of the largest guns ever fitted to a British warship, at 18 inches, but these weapons were a liability, since the relatively thin battlecruiser hulls used to ripple when they were fired. One officer who served aboard *Furious* used to relate that in his cabin when the guns fired, 'it was like being in the middle of a blizzard,' except that instead of snowflakes, rivets went flying around! Her sisters, *Glorious* and *Courageous*, had 15-inch guns.

The 22,000-ton *Furious* was still under construction when the decision was taken to remove her forward turret and build a flight deck forward, while retaining a single turret aft. In this form she joined the fleet in mid-1917.

Despite take-offs from warships before the war, first in the United States and then in Britain, no one had landed an aircraft on a ship underway at sea. On 2 August 1917 Squadron Commander (the RNAS equivalent of Lieutenant-Commander) E.H. Dunning RN, flew a Sopwith Camel past the funnel and superstructure of *Furious*, and then cut his engine as the aircraft hovered at stalling speed over the now all too short flight deck, while some of his fellow officers attempted to grab the toggles hanging from the trailing edges of his biplane's lower wing. They were successful, so that Dunning had the distinction of being the first man to land on a ship underway at sea. Sadly, when he attempted a repeat performance a few days later, the aircraft was blown over the side of the ship and poor Dunning was drowned. No more attempts were allowed.

The *Furious* then underwent further rebuilding, with her aft turret removed and a landing deck built at her stern. The deck continued around on either side of the funnel so that aircraft could be manoeuvred from the landing deck to the flight deck. The after-deck was also used on occasion to carry a reconnaissance airship. On landing, aircraft would catch arrester wires, at first running fore and aft, with hooks on the undercarriage spreader bar, and as a last resort there was a large safety net.

Rebuilt in this way, *Furious* launched the first successful attack from an aircraft carrier when, on 19 July 1918, seven Sopwith Camels attacked the airship sheds at Tondern in northern Germany, destroying the airships L.54 and L.60.

THE SEARCH FOR A DEFINITIVE DESIGN

There were no further significant naval air operations during the First World War. After the war, *Furious* was rebuilt twice, with a period of lay-up between 1919 and 1922. She eventually rejoined the fleet in 1925 as a flush-deck aircraft carrier without super-structure, although a fairly low super-structure was added during a further refit in 1937–8, when the flying-off deck was removed from the upper hangar and the hangar closed off at the same time.

Even while the *Furious* was newly com-missioned with her flying-off and landing decks, an Italian liner still under construction was requisitioned by the Admiralty and completed as a second aircraft carrier, the *Argus*. Smaller and slower than the *Furious*, the *Argus* displaced 15,775 tons and with a speed of 29 knots, she joined the Fleet in September, 1918, only a couple of months before the Armistice and did not see action in the First World War. *Argus* was in fact the first flat-top, with the wheelhouse and bridge positioned on a lift, which made manoeuvring difficult during flying operations. Boiler room smoke was expelled through ducts at the stern, which could make landing difficult.

There was still some uncertainty over the right layout for an aircraft carrier. Early experience with *Furious* at her interim stage with separate decks had shown that turbulence from the superstructure was a problem. A third aircraft carrier, the *Eagle*,

Converted from a liner while still under construction, *Argus* was known to the Royal Navy as the 'Flat Iron'. (IWM FL941)

was put in hand, using the incomplete Chilean battleship *Almirante Cochrane*, on which work had been suspended at the outbreak of war in 1914. The resultant aircraft carrier was the first with the now familiar starboard side 'island' for the funnels, bridge and flying control, but was unusual for the time in having two funnels. Delays for the results of various trials with deck landing meant that the *Eagle*, 22,600 tons, was not commissioned until February 1924. Her other claim to fame was to be the first ship to introduce the cambered 'round down', so distinctive of British carrier design, to reduce the effect of turbulence from the ship on aircraft landing on, and something which was to persist as inter-war British naval aircraft tended to be less robust than their American counterparts.

The fourth vessel of the Royal Navy's initial quartet of aircraft carriers was the first to be laid down as an aircraft carrier. This was the small *Hermes*, just 10,850 tons, laid down in January, 1918, but again not completed for some years while the design questions were clarified, so that she entered service with the fleet within a few days of the *Eagle*. Despite her small size, *Hermes*, with her hull plated up to flight deck level and her single large funnel, had what might be regarded as a modern appearance.

So why do aircraft carriers have a starboard island? Well, for a start, there were many exceptions which lacked an island altogether, and this included many Japanese ships. The Japanese also built two aircraft carriers, the *Akagi* and the *Hiryu*, with a port-side island. Nevertheless, the starboard island is

The first ship to be laid down as an aircraft carrier, *Hermes*. (FAAM Carrier H/130)

more usual. Trials showed that on most occasions, for some reason no one really fully understands, pilots in trouble tend to veer to port. A starboard island means that there are no obstacles in their way and an accident might be avoided, or if not, at least the chances of survival are increased and those of damaging the ship reduced.

Some suggest, with justification, that since ships were, centuries ago before the advent of the wheel, steered by a large oar on the starboard, or 'steerboard', side this is why aircraft carriers have adopted this layout. Nevertheless, the two Japanese port islands resulted in many more accidents landing on. The Japanese chose this perverse layout simply because they had plans to operate pairs of ships with starboard and port islands, so that their aircraft could use different approach patterns without confusion or congestion.

The Americans and the Japanese were also keen to put aircraft carriers into service.

The United States Navy converted a collier, the *Jupiter*, to produce her first aircraft carrier, the *Langley*, 11,500 tons with a maximum speed of 14 knots, which entered service in March 1922. The USN also had a seaplane tender by this time, the *Wright*. The choice of these names owed much to Samuel Langley's predilection for launching his unsuccessful aeroplane design from the roof of his houseboat. The *Langley* introduced the American, and now universal, designation for aircraft carriers, CV. This is because she was designated CV.01, or cruiser, heavier-than-air, No. 1.

The first Japanese aircraft carrier was also a conversion from a tanker, although the conversion started while the ship was still on the slipway. The new carrier, *Hosho*, was completed in late 1922, but did not join the

The impracticability of a separate flying-off deck is clearly shown as *Courageous* takes a heavy sea. (FAAM Carrier C/209)

fleet until February 1923. Completed with a starboard island, and three funnels, the island proved unpopular with pilots and was soon removed, probably because there was no room since the ship displaced just 7,470 tons. For the rest of her service with the Imperial Japanese Navy, *Hosho* was navigated from a position below the forward end of the flight deck at hangar deck level.

Most of these early carriers were soon fitted with catapults, or accelerators as they were more usually called, which were hydraulically operated. Using trolleys, seaplane launches were commonplace.

THE RUSH TO CONVERT BATTLECRUISERS

The next stage in defining the aircraft carrier came with the Washington Naval Treaty of 1922, which limited the size of individual ships to 27,000 tons and stipulated that their armament be limited to guns with a maximum calibre of 8 inches. In one sense this reinforced the carrier/cruiser connection, since a heavy cruiser was defined as having 8-inch guns, and a light cruiser as having 6-inch guns, irrespective of tonnage, which for a cruiser was to be a maximum of 10,000 tons.

Under the terms of the Washington Naval Treaty, the United States and the United Kingdom were limited to a maximum aircraft carrier tonnage of 135,000 tons each, out of a maximum fleet tonnage of 525,000 tons each, while Japan was limited to 81,000 tons of aircraft carriers out of a maximum of 315,000 tons fleet tonnage. Italy and France were limited to 60,000 tons of aircraft carrier tonnage apiece, out of national fleet limits of 175,000 tons. The *Langley* was exempted from these limits since she was accepted as an experimental ship. The Treaty limits had an indirect effect on the growth of aircraft carrier fleets, as Britain, the United States and Japan all had battlecruisers in excess of their Treaty limits for this category of ship, and

immediately set about converting some of these to aircraft carriers!

The American battlecruisers, *Saratoga* and *Lexington*, were incomplete while the Treaty was at the draft stage, and the decision to convert was actually taken before the Treaty was signed. There were some exceptions to the blanket limits for ship sizes set out in the Treaty, and these two sister ships both took advantage of a clause allowing two aircraft carriers of up to 33,000 tons each, and a further clause allowing 3,000 tons of armour plating against bomb attack, as opposed to the nominal carrier limit of 27,000 tons! The armoured flight decks of these two ships were unusual features for American aircraft carriers, even for those completed during the Second World War. While aircraft sizes were to increase considerably after the entry of these two ships into service in November and December 1927, they could each take ninety aircraft of the day, and even range all of them at once on the 888-foot-long flight decks!

The size and design limitations of *Furious'* two sister ships, *Courageous* and *Glorious*, meant that the decision to convert these was also taken while the Treaty was at draft stage. Despite being new vessels, both were already laid up. As battlecruisers they had differed from their sister ship *Furious* in having the more usual 15-inch guns rather than the 18 inch with which *Furious* was fitted. Once converted, these two 'Treaty' carriers reflected the now orthodox carrier design, with starboard islands and single large funnels. Of just 22,500 tons each, one feature which they shared with *Furious* was that they lacked full-length flight decks in favour of having a separate take-off deck leading from the hangar. However, as aircraft sizes increased, the take-off decks proved insufficient in length and had a relatively short life. The *Courageous* entered service in May 1928, and was followed by the *Glorious* in March 1930. Both ships had a maximum speed of around 30 knots, and were later fitted with accelerators to assist aircraft taking off.

The Japanese had been receiving considerable assistance from the Royal Navy, as a result of having been an ally of both Britain and the United States during the First World War. Relations started to cool, however, as Japan objected to many of the restrictions of the Treaty, wanting a far larger tonnage allocation. Japan also had to make the best of the situation, and started to convert two uncompleted battlecruisers, the *Amagi* and *Akagi*, into aircraft carriers. The *Amagi* was severely damaged by an earthquake while still on the slipway and had to be scrapped, so the battleship *Kaga*, still fitting out when the Treaty was signed, was converted instead.

The *Akagi* was most unusual, lacking an island and having not one, but two, flying-off decks. The upper one was just 60 feet in length, leading from the upper hangar and was for use by fighters, while the lower one led from the lower hangar, was 100 feet long, and was for use by torpedo-bombers and other heavier aircraft. She had a maximum speed of 31 knots.

By comparison, the *Kaga* was relatively conventional, although lacking an island she had just one flying-off deck. As a converted battleship, she was slower, being capable of 27 knots. Both ships exceeded the Treaty limits, with *Akagi* at 30,000 tons and *Kaga* just slightly smaller.

Both ships were rebuilt during the 1930s, with full-length flight decks, while the *Kaga* received a starboard island and the *Akagi* received her unusual port island, albeit with a single downward-pointing starboard funnel!

The French also undertook conversion of a major capital ship, the battleship *Bearn*, although this move was not dictated by France's Treaty obligations. Originally laid down in 1914, work had been suspended on

Kaga was a converted battleship – the waste of hangar deck space on many Japanese carriers can clearly be seen. (IWM MH6489)

Bearn for most of the First World War, and she was not completed until 1920. Trials with a wooden flight deck on the quarterdeck followed, and in 1923 work started on her conversion to an aircraft carrier, in which form she rejoined the fleet in 1925. The large single funnel and starboard island were conventional, but it appears as if the conversion was skimped, with the flight deck continuing over the former forward gun turret positions with a considerable open wasted space below. This may have accounted for her small aircraft complement, just twenty-five in a ship of 22,146 tons. More serious still was her speed, or the lack of it, with a maximum of just 21 knots.

THE ARMS RACE

Despite the good intentions of the Washington Naval Treaty, by 1930 the scene was set for an arms race, although few in the democracies were able to recognize this. The London Naval Conference in that year saw Japan insist on an increase in her permitted tonnage, and after this was refused, she eventually renounced the Treaty in 1934.

Before this, in an attempt to keep within the Treaty restrictions, Japan introduced her first purpose-built aircraft carrier, the *Ryujo*, which entered service with a displacement of just 10,600 tons in May 1933. Despite her small size, she could accommodate as many as forty-eight aircraft, although this figure dropped to thirty-six for operations. She had been designed for a much lower tonnage, but problems with stability meant that enlarged torpedo bulges had to be fitted, although the extra weight was compensated to some extent by the removal of the six twin 5-inch gun turrets. Although two downward pointing smokestacks were positioned to starboard, this was another aircraft carrier without an island. Although no provision was made for a separate take-off deck, the flight deck and hangar did not run the full length of the ship,

with a substantial open forecastle area wasted. Worse, by the time war broke out in 1941, only her after lift was capable of handling aircraft of Second World War size.

Freed from the constraints of the Washington Naval Treaty, two much more substantial ships were laid down, the *Soryu* in 1934 and the *Hiryu* soon afterwards. The *Soryu*, at 15,900 tons, had a starboard island, but again had two funnels ducting downwards. Unusually, she had three lifts, and a very narrow beam which contributed to a maximum speed of 34.5 knots. Again, the hangar did not run the full length of the ship, although the flight deck almost did so, with an open quarterdeck and fo'c'sle. With a capacity of 60 aircraft, she entered service in December 1937. In common with *Ryujo*, she lacked any armour.

The other new carrier, the *Hiryu*, joined the Imperial Fleet in July 1939. Clearly the Japanese were feeling their way forward, for this ship displaced 17,300 tons, and while she had the same turn of speed and aircraft accommodation as *Soryu*, she was broader in the beam, providing much needed extra stability, and had a wider radius of action. For the last time, the Japanese had also built a carrier with a port-side island and starboard funnels!

Just as the Germans and Italians had the experience of the Spanish Civil War to test their equipment and battle-harden their men, the Japanese advances into China during the late 1930s provided the same opportunity for the Imperial Japanese Navy. Japanese Naval Air Force and Japanese Army Air Force aircraft were sometimes outclassed by Chinese aircraft flown by American volunteers. The *Kaga* saw operations in the China campaign, although often seemed to be used as an aircraft transport.

The Americans had also been considering the best way of increasing their carrier fleet, albeit within the Treaty limitations. The first purpose-built American aircraft carrier

Ranger was an American attempt to squeeze as many carriers as possible out of their Washington Naval Treaty limits – but they soon realized that bigger was better. (IWM FL18153)

entered service in 1934. This was the *Ranger*. In an attempt to see how many small carriers could be fitted into the Treaty limitations, she displaced just 14,500 tons. The USN would have liked to see five 13,800-ton carriers, but the *Ranger* convinced them that this was not feasible. Originally designed as a pure flat-top, a starboard island was added before completion. No fewer than six funnels were used, with three on each side towards the stern, and these could be folded into the down position for flying operations. No fewer than seventy aircraft of the day could be accommodated, while the flight deck extended over the open forecastle. Although capable of 30 knots as a result of her narrow beam, later, in service, the *Ranger* had to be withdrawn from operations in the Pacific because her small tonnage made operational flying difficult.

Far more successful were the next two American carriers, the Yorktown class, consisting of the *Yorktown* and the *Enterprise*. These displaced 19,800 tons each, had a starboard island, and could steam at 33 knots. They could each accommodate eighty aircraft, and had three lifts and two catapults. Unusual features included arrester wires placed forward to allow aircraft to land over the bows in a strong wind, and catapults angled to allow aircraft to be flown off at an angle to port or starboard through the hangar deck side apertures – none of these features proved to be of great practical value and they were eventually removed.

Perhaps one of the most attractive features of these two ships was that they were not paid for out of the defence budget, but out of a separate public works programme designed to stimulate employment in the depressed shipbuilding industry. The *Yorktown* joined the fleet in September 1937, followed by her sister eight months later. A third vessel of this class, the *Hornet*, was laid down as war broke out in Europe, but before this, another small carrier, the *Wasp*, had been built to an improved design based on the *Ranger* tonnage.

The British were not simply content to keep within the Treaty limits, but also wished to see the maximum size of aircraft carriers reduced from 27,000 tons to 22,000 tons. For this reason, their next aircraft carrier, the purpose-built *Ark Royal*, which entered service in November 1938, displaced just 22,000 tons. Nevertheless, the designers ensured that weight was reduced, through using welding as far as possible, although they also reduced the armour plating, apart from some armouring of the hangar. The flight deck extended beyond the hull fore and aft to provide the maximum space, with the hull and stern plated up to flight deck level. Unusually for British carriers, three lifts were fitted. Two accelerators, as catapults were known to the Admiralty at that time, were fitted at the forward end of the flight deck. The ship could manage a relatively high speed, 32 knots, and up to 72 aircraft could be carried, although this was reduced as aircraft sizes increased, and for operations, 60 was a more realistic number.

With remarkable foresight, given the turn of events in the war in the Pacific, the next six British aircraft carriers were not simply further versions of the *Ark Royal*. The first four ships were ordered in 1936, and two more in 1937, while a variant of the design was ordered the following year as a fleet maintenance carrier, to enable the fleet to operate away from base for extended periods. Originally intended as replacements for the *Argus*, *Furious*, *Eagle* and *Hermes*, it was soon realized that the new ships would be an expansion of the fleet as the danger of war in Europe became more apparent.

Distinguishing features of the new carriers were the armoured flight deck and hangar deck, in effect an armoured box capable of withstanding a great deal of punishment and, unusually for British warships, triple screw propulsion on the six fast carriers, the Illustrious class, which consisted of *Illustrious* herself, and *Victorious*, *Formidable*, *Indomitable*, *Implacable* and *Indefatigable*. The seventh carrier, the *Unicorn*, differed from her sisters in having just twin screws and more headroom in the hangar to facilitate heavy maintenance work. The displacement of the first six ships rose to 23,000 tons, while aircraft accommodation was almost a third less than that of the *Ark Royal*.

Another advantage of the new ships was that they introduced the barrier landing system to the Royal Navy. Aircraft which missed the arrester wires would be brought to a stop by the crash barrier, which protected aircraft already landed. Those aircraft which landed safely, catching the arrester wires, would have the barrier lowered in front of them and taxi forward, ready to be struck down into the hangars while the barrier was raised behind them for protection. Aircraft hitting the barrier were usually badly damaged since many aircraft, including the Seafire and the Corsair which had a longer nose, would pitch forward onto their propeller. Injury to the pilot was also common in such circumstances. Nevertheless, this was preferable to running into parked aircraft with fuel in their tanks and often still holding munitions. The barrier system enabled aircraft to land on at a faster rate – some have claimed as many as four a minute, but two seems to have been more probable. Under combat conditions, this must have been a welcome improvement as aircraft returned from operations, often with little fuel remaining.

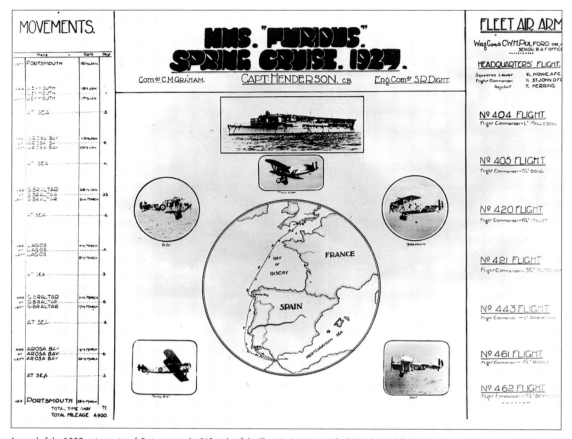

A record of the 1927 spring cruise of *Furious*, note the RAF ranks of the Fleet Air Arm personnel. (FAAM Carrier F/168)

At the same time, in 1938, the British Admiralty received Parliamentary approval for a 300 per cent increase in Fleet Air Arm funding.

THE NEED FOR TRUE NAVAL AIRCRAFT

The problem was, as we shall see, that the Royal Navy was close to getting some of the finest ships possible within the constraints of size and the technology of the day, but the aircraft were a different matter.

The problem for the British was that on 1 April 1918, they had merged naval and army aviation, creating the first autonomous air force, the Royal Air Force. After the war

ended, the new RAF was slimmed down, so that at one stage it had just twelve squadrons. Given the austerity measures applied to public spending during the Depression, the new service struggled to create an effective strategic air arm with fighter and bomber elements. Naval aviation was not seen as a priority by the RAF's leaders, and funds for developing naval aircraft designs were limited. The Royal Navy itself could take some of the blame, since its senior officers were ambivalent about naval air power, and indeed such attitudes were also commonplace among admirals of the old school in both the United States Navy and the Imperial Japanese Navy.

Fortunately, the Royal Navy regained control of naval aviation in 1937, and progressively RAF air and ground crew were displaced from the squadrons embarked aboard the aircraft carriers.

Throughout the period of RAF control, a few naval officers had remained as fliers in the Royal Navy, wearing the British naval aviator's wings on their sleeve, but being confined to flying amphibians or seaplanes from cruisers and battleships. One of these officers, Charles 'KP' Keighly-Peach, later a Captain, joined the staff of the then Rear Admiral Destroyers in the Mediterranean in 1935. The Rear Admiral, none other than Andrew 'ABC' Cunningham, looked at Keighly-Peach with distaste and asked him, 'Do you intend to keep that thing on your sleeve while on my staff?'

KP recalled that, 'somewhat abashed, I said yes, I did; that it was the recognized uniform for the FAA.'[1]

In Japan, the young Mitsuo Fuchida, who later led the attack on Pearl Harbor, was offered a choice of specializations for his future career, including navigation and gunnery, but not aviation. His superiors tried to discourage him from opting for the Japanese Naval Air Force, as a bad career move!

Not the least of the problems engendered by these attitudes was that both services were to be hampered in the future by a lack of senior officers with naval aviation experience.

Whatever the problems faced by these navies, they were nothing compared to those of the German Navy. The Germans wanted naval aviation, and on the outbreak of war in 1939, an aircraft carrier, the *Graf Zeppelin* was being built, while a second, the *Peter Strasser*, was also planned. Arguments over whether the aircraft embarked aboard these ships would be operated by the Luftwaffe or the Navy meant that work was delayed and the *Graf Zeppelin* never went to sea.

The French, who had belatedly realized that naval aviation had something to offer, but that the *Bearn* would not be up to it, had two carriers of advanced design under construction at the fall of France. These two ships, the *Joffre* and the *Painleve*, have sometimes been credited with having an early version of the angled flight deck, but it is now generally accepted that in fact the flight deck was offset to port, as far away as possible from any turbulence from the starboard island, and possibly also increasing the deck parking available during flying.

[1] *Daily Telegraph*, 8 March 1995.

PART TWO

WAR IN EUROPE

BACKGROUND

READY FOR WAR?

The outbreak of the Second World War in Europe found none of the participants really ready for it. The United Kingdom had made the best of the breathing space created by the Munich Agreement in 1938, but it was not enough. In France, industry had been disrupted by political action, including the nationalization of the aircraft industry, which meant that many promising aircraft designs were not in full production when so desperately needed. Even in Germany, many had been planning on not having to fight Britain until 1945, and the Kriegsmarine was not prepared for battle so soon. The new battleships *Bismarck* and *Tirpitz* were not completed, and Germany's first aircraft carrier was still under construction, with the debate between the Kriegsmarine and the Luftwaffe over who should operate her aircraft unresolved. In fact, the ship would never be completed.

As already mentioned, the Fleet Air Arm had good ships on order at the time, and plans for these to replace the Royal Navy's older carriers were abandoned as it soon became clear that every ship would be needed. Aircraft were the problem, with the Royal Navy lacking good high performance aircraft designed for carrier use. This problem was to persist for some time.

There were to be other difficulties as well. Years of RAF control of naval aviation meant that a whole generation of senior officers familiar with the strengths and needs of naval air power had been missed. The Royal Navy had aircraft carriers and enthusiasm at operational level, but these ships were not part of the strategy for fighting and winning the war. Whether attitudes would have been different with aircraft capable of defending the fleet from enemy attack remains an unanswerable question.

Reactions to the outbreak of war among naval aviators varied. One officer under training at the time listened to Prime Minister Neville Chamberlain's famous radio broadcast, and recalled that there were a few weak cheers among his peers, 'but most of us felt depressed'.

The Conservative MP, the late Ronald Bell, who served aboard a seaplane carrier during the war, once said that 'in wartime at sea, everything is either all right, or an absolute disaster'.[1] Many would agree with that. Even if not under attack at the time, vigilance is essential and not only because of the enemy; war at sea is often a battle with the elements as well. This was to be the case, especially in the North Atlantic and in the Arctic.

[1] Interview with the author, 1973.

WHAT 'PHONEY WAR'?

FIRST LOSSES AND SUCCESSES

On 1 September 1939, Germany and the Soviet Union invaded Poland, in defiance of a British and French ultimatum, which led to these two countries declaring war on Germany two days later. The first winter of the Second World War has often been referred to as the 'phoney war', without large-scale land operations and with much of the air operations involving leaflet-dropping. For the navies, however, there was no such thing.

SHIPS AND AIRCRAFT

Two aircraft carriers featured in operations during the first month of the Second World War, *Courageous* and *Ark Royal*, both of which have already been described.

The aircraft demonstrated much that was wrong with the state of British naval aviation at the end of the thirties. The two aircraft types could certainly not be described as modern.

The Fairey Swordfish had been first flown in 1934. Most Swordfish, known affectionately to the Fleet Air Arm as 'Stringbags', were three-seat aircraft with an observer and telegraphist-air-gunner, or TAG, although to enhance the range on occasion one of these would be omitted in favour of a fuel tank which fitted between the pilot's and crewman's positions in the open cockpit. The TAG spent most of his time on operation standing in the open cockpit, secured to the aircraft by a single strap. The Swordfish was versatile, and could be used as a torpedo aircraft or a dive-bomber, but its top speed of 140 m.p.h. was difficult to achieve. It was happier flying at 100 knots, or less, using a 690 h.p. Bristol Pegasus radial engine. Later models had radar between the landing gear.

The other aircraft was the Blackburn Skua, a two-seat dive-bomber monoplane powered by a single 830 h.p. Bristol Perseus engine. In service for just 3 years, 165 were built and saw relatively little action apart from the Norwegian campaign. Officially termed by the Admiralty as a 'fighter dive-bomber', one of its pilots later described it as being '90 per cent dive-bomber, 10 per cent fighter'. A development of the Skua was the Roc, which had no forward-firing guns at all, but instead had a turret behind the cockpit with four guns. The weight and drag of the turret meant that the aircraft could not even catch up with a bomber, and its service life was extremely short.

INTO ACTION

On 17 September, the British aircraft carrier, *Courageous*, was sunk by a salvo of three torpedoes from the German submarine, *U-29*, in the Western Approaches, south-west of Ireland. The irony of the situation was that *Courageous* was operating as part of a U-boat hunting unit in a technique soon abandoned by the Admiralty.

The day's searching over, the last Swordfish had landed on the aircraft carrier, the crew thankful that their fuel, now so very low, had been just enough. With her aircraft being struck down into her hangar, protection for *Courageous* consisted of two Asdic-equipped destroyers.

Gloster Gladiators were the RAF's last biplane fighter, and the Sea Gladiator variant served with the Fleet Air Arm. (FAAM Gladiator/2)

An unknown photographer on one of the two destroyers escorting *Courageous* took this photograph of her sinking after being torpedoed by *U–29*.

Charles Lamb was the pilot of the final Swordfish to land on *Courageous*. He headed for the wardroom with his observer:

'I said to him: "What are you going to have?" but he had not time to answer because at that moment there were two explosions, a split second apart, the like of which I had never imagined possible. If the core of the earth exploded, and the universe split from pole to pole, it could have been no worse. Every light went out immediately and the deck reared upwards. . . . In the sudden deathly silence which followed I knew the ship had died.'[1]

Courageous sank twenty minutes later, taking 500 men with her, having been attacked in broad daylight. The U-boat, *U-29*, escaped unscathed.

Despite this inauspicious start, the first German aircraft to be shot down by the British during the war was by a Fleet Air Arm aircraft.

On 26 September, 1939, two Fairey Swordfish on patrol over from the aircraft carrier, *Ark Royal*, sighted three Dornier Do.18 flying-boats of Kustenfliegergruppe 506. *Ark Royal* launched nine of her Blackburn Skua 'fighter-torpedo-bombers' and one of these, flown by Lieutenant B.S. McEwen, shot down one of the flying-boats, which force-landed in the sea and later its four-man crew was taken prisoner aboard a British destroyer.

---

[1] Charles Lamb. *War in a Stringbag*, Cassell, 1977.

Action Off Norway

Germany Strikes North

To secure their supplies of iron ore from neutral Sweden, the Germans decided to invade Denmark and Norway, starting at midnight on the night of 8/9 April 1940. During the morning of 8 April, the Royal Navy had been laying mines at strategic points, but these had little impact on the subsequent invasion. The invading troops met no resistance in Denmark, but heavy fighting followed the invasion of Norway. Even so, by 10 April all of the airfields and the main ports were in German hands, partly because of a mistake by the British Admiralty which left the Vestfjord approach to Narvik without a British patrol. Plans to send British and French troops to help defend Norway were bungled, and the troops were still ashore in Scotland at the time the German invasion was starting. Nevertheless, the Germans lost ten destroyers in Narvik Fjord in actions by British destroyers on 10 and 13 April with the operation on 13 April reinforced by the veteran, but extensively modernized, battleship, *Warspite*.

Ships and Aircraft

Three British aircraft carriers took part in the Norwegian campaign, first of all *Furious*, soon followed by *Ark Royal* and *Glorious*, sister ship of *Courageous*. Before conversion to an aircraft carrier, both had been sister ships of *Furious*, albeit with a more orthodox armament.

The carrier-borne aircraft included two single-engined biplanes, the Gloster Sea Gladiator, a modified version of the standard RAF fighter, and the Fairey Swordfish, as well as the Blackburn Skua monoplane. Both the Swordfish and the Skua are described in the previous chapter.

The other aircraft involved came aboard the *Glorious*, and were RAF Gloster Gladiator and Hawker Hurricane fighters. The Gladiator was the RAF's last biplane fighter, capable of 270 m.p.h., and the wonder is that it was still in production at the time of the Norwegian campaign, having entered production in 1937, albeit to a 1930 specification. Powered by a single 830 h.p. Bristol radial engine, the aircraft boasted an enclosed cockpit!

The Hurricane alone of these three aircraft was reasonably modern, being Hawker's first monoplane fighter. The production version first flew in late 1937. The Hurricane used the Rolls-Royce Merlin engine, and had a maximum speed in excess of 300 m.p.h. At the time, most Hurricanes would have been equipped with machine-guns, the four 20-mm cannons were introduced in 1941. A variant of the Hurricane for carrier use was the Sea Hurricane.

The Operation

The first aircraft carrier on the scene was the *Furious*, which arrived on 10 April. North-west of Trondheim, *Furious* made the first air torpedo attack in naval warfare at 04.00 on 11 April, expecting to find the cruiser,

Admiral Hipper. However, the ship had sailed and her Swordfish attacked three destroyers left in the harbour at Trondheim. Unfortunately, the torpedoes dropped by the Swordfish grounded in the shallow water, hitting an unexpected sandbar, and the attack was unsuccessful. A Swordfish bombing raid a few days later, in appalling weather with snow and low cloud, was also unsuccessful.

British troops started landing in Norway on 14 April, followed by further troops on the following days, and the first French troops arrived on 19 April.

Francis Smith was a telegraphist-air-gunner, or TAG, in a Swordfish flying from Furious on a raid over Narvik. It was looking for German destroyers in very low cloud, flying through the fjords with mountains on either side. The aircraft carried a fuel tank instead of a navigator, and Smith had had no navigational training. He recalls, '. . . I kept a check of the compass courses that we were steering, because I was wondering how the hell we were going to find our way out, after two hours of flying up these fjords. . . . But eventually we ran into such blinding snow that there was no way we could go on . . . communication in those days, there was no RT, you had Gosport tubes . . . your pilot blew into his, and it came into your ears; and you blew into yours . . . so communication is not all that good, very distorted as well.'[1]

Smith's pilot decided to turn back, and eventually they found the ship as darkness fell, but his pilot had no experience of 'landing on' in darkness. They decided that they should ditch their bombs, not being sure whether or not this was the right thing to do, although later an instruction was given that unused bombs and depth charges should be ditched before landing on.

'He hit the deck with his starboard wheel, then hit the deck with his port wheel, and his port wing-tip, and then cartwheeled over the side, into the water. And that was it. And the ship gave two or three blasts on her siren, and vanished into the darkness. So when the aircraft surfaced again he's still strapped in this cockpit – I pulled the toggle that was supposed to release the dinghy, and the cover came off the dinghy stowage, and the dinghy still lay there, all nicely folded up . . . then the aircraft sunk.

'I could swim, but it wouldn't have been much use . . . when I was doing a deck landing, day or night, I blew up my Mae West . . . we didn't have automatic Mae Wests, you had to blow them up . . . knowing how difficult it was to blow them up in the water, when you're struggling in the water, I always used to blow mine up on take–off and landing.

'. . . as the aircraft sunk I walked up to the tail of the aircraft . . . and I floated off in the water.'[2]

Both Smith and his pilot were rescued, by a boat from a destroyer.

Landing on was difficult in daylight and in good weather, and even experienced naval pilots could get it wrong.

The *Ark Royal* and *Glorious* arrived later, when the operation was well under way. In addition to mounting attacks against the enemy with the Swordfish, the carriers' Gloster Sea Gladiator fighters and Blackburn Skuas mounted combat air patrols over the fleet. Eight Skuas from the *Ark* shot down seventeen German aircraft during the campaign, while the ship's four Rocs were completely unsuccessful.

The campaign in Norway came at a time when the Allies were under intense pressure. The Low Countries and France were invaded by Germany, with defeat for Britain and France, culminating in the British Expeditionary Force being evacuated from Dunkirk in late May, early June. At this time, the decision was taken to evacuate the British Expeditionary Force from Norway.

Aircraft from *Glorious* had flown anti-submarine patrols and also helped in

[1] Imperial War Museum Sound Archive.

[2] Imperial War Museum Sound Archive.

reconnaissance and spotting for *Warspite* and her destroyers.

On 7 June, RAF Gloster Gladiator and Hawker Hurricane units ashore in Norway were ordered to destroy their aircraft, which lacked the range to be ferried back to the UK. One of the units affected by this order was No. 46. One of the squadron's pilots, Patrick 'Jamie' Jameson, who later became an Air Commodore, and his squadron commander, the then Squadron Leader 'Bing' Cross (later an Air Chief Marshal), were appalled at the instruction. They decided that they would attempt to fly their aircraft to one of the aircraft carriers, realizing the importance of saving their precious fighters and that they did not have the range to fly to Scotland. *Glorious* was the first choice, despite the fact

that her flight deck was 100 feet shorter than that of *Ark Royal*, because her lifts were larger than those of *Ark Royal*, and the aircraft would not need to have their wings removed before striking down into the hangar. The carrier's commanding officer reluctantly agreed to accept the RAF fighters.

The first aircraft to fly out to *Glorious* were ten Gloster Gladiators of No. 262 Squadron. Then came the first of the Hurricanes, with Jameson taking the first flight of three aircraft that evening.

'We left at 00.45 hours,' Cross wrote to a friend, 'dead beat; and as we left we were pleased to see the Skuas of the Fleet Air Arm coming in to cover the embarkation of our troops who had a destroyer standing by for them at a little fishing village seventeen miles

Glorious turns away from an escort on the afternoon before she was sunk. The RAF Hurricanes can be seen clearly ranged aft on her flight deck, but they were later struck down into the hangar. The Carley floats which can be seen on her stern were painted in camouflage, and were difficult to spot from the air, leading to the deaths of many who survived her sinking.

away. We were navigated out to sea by a Swordfish at 100 knots and the old Hurricanes had to do some fairly hearty zigzagging to get behind. It wasn't a nice feeling knowing that if we couldn't get on the deck there was no way out.'[3]

The Hurricanes had no carrier arrester gear, but pinned their hopes on the efficacy of the 14-lb sandbag that Jameson had placed under each tailplane, allowing the aircraft to use their full braking power without tipping forward onto the nose. All of the aircraft landed safely, even though none of the pilots had ever landed aboard a carrier before.[4]

The Hurricane pilots had done the Fleet Air Arm a great service, proving that high performance aircraft could land on an aircraft carrier.

After their flight to the carrier, which had been preceded by several days of intense flying against an increasingly strong and confident enemy, the RAF pilots were exhausted.

The morning of 8 June dawned bright and clear.

'When Cross woke up late that forenoon and went on deck he was puzzled by the lack of activity. In contrast to his previous stay in the ship, when there had been anti-submarine patrols and CAPs flying almost around the clock, the flight deck was silent and deserted. There was no flying and there had been none since the *Glorious* detached to proceed home independently. One Swordfish and a section of three Sea Gladiators were at ten minutes' notice, but they were not ranged on the flight deck.

'It seemed that risk of attack by surface ships had been completely discounted, but there were still other dangers. "When I woke up I went to the island," said Cross. Everybody not on watch was sitting in corners. I saw in the Plot the line [on the chart] from where we were, straight to Scapa. "We're short of fuel," somebody told me. We were 200 miles off the Norwegian coast. Exactly right

for the Luftwaffe! . . . I said, "Have we got a search up?" And whoever it was said, "No, we're doing seventeen knots and that's too fast for any submarine to torpedo us."'[5]

Cross saw that his Hurricanes had been stowed in the hangar, well towards the stern, leaving the forward part of the hangar and the forward lift clear. The ship was still perfectly capable of flying-off her own aircraft for CAP, reconnaissance or any other activity. The real problem was that everyone seemed to have wound down, and there was an atmosphere which Cross was to describe later as a 'curious lassitude'[6], which he thought was a reaction to the intense activity of the previous few days. There was also a high level of excitement at being on the way home, and the Sea Gladiator and Hurricane pilots had a sense of real satisfaction at having saved their aircraft.

One of the ship's own Fleet Air Arm pilots, Petty Officer Pilot Dick Leggott, had been flying Gloster Sea Gladiator CAP patrols, and then had been on standby until the early hours of the morning. 'We were to report at our aircraft in the hangar at 09.00. Our CO and the CO of 823 appeared some twenty minutes later, having conferred with the Captain. One of our pilots noticed that warheads were being removed from torpedoes and other armaments that were normally in "ready–use" stowages when we were in the war zone were being struck down or stowed away. The Chief Torpedo Instructor, in reply to one of our squadron, said with a happy smile that they were getting a "lap ahead" to get ready for giving leave. This seemed very wrong to some of us.'[7]

The ship had not had radar fitted, but the weather was good. As a further indication of the ship's sudden dropping of her guard, there was no lookout in the crow's nest. Shortly after 16.00, while many of those aboard were having tea, *Scharnhorst* and *Gneisenau* opened

[3] John Winton. *Carrier Glorious*, Leo Cooper, 1986.
[4] *Daily Telegraph*, 3 October 1996.
[5] John Winton. *Carrier Glorious*, Leo Cooper, 1986.
[6] John Winton. Op cit.
[7] Ibid.

fire. Only then did the aircraft carrier take evasive action and shortly afterwards the call came over the tannoy for first one, then two, and then all Swordfish aircraft to be ranged. One of the great advantages enjoyed by British and American warships during the Second World War was the use of radar – on this occasion a major unit of the British fleet hadn't got it, but both its German opponents had!

The two German battlecruisers opened fire at 28,000 yards with their 11–inch guns, outgunning the carrier's own weapons. Frantic attempts were made to range the five remaining Swordfish, and one airman, a TAG, actually climbed into his aircraft, although he got out again to look for the rest of the crew. Shortly after 16.15, the Germans scored their first hit, crashing through the recently vacated Swordfish and one other, penetrating the flight deck and exploding among the Hurricanes parked below, still with fuel in their tanks and ammunition: within seconds the hangar deck was an inferno, with fires almost out of control. The flight deck was torn and splintered like matchwood.

Further hits followed, even though the aircraft carrier had restarted boilers which had closed down and was working up to full speed, reaching 27 knots quickly. A salvo at around 17.00 destroyed the bridge, by which time the ship was, according to the Germans, 'a pillar of smoke and flame'.

The carrier's two escorting destroyers, *Ardent* and *Acasta*, were sunk while making a desperate torpedo attack on the *Scharnhorst*, which, unknown to the Admiralty at the time, crippled her.

By 18.00 it was all over. It is estimated that as many as 900 out of the 1,500-strong crew from *Glorious* were able to abandon ship, many of them suffering from burns or serious wounds including missing limbs, but of these just thirty-nine survived two days in the cold water, without food or drink.

Cross and Jameson were among the survivors after spending two days on a Carley float, using a miniature escape compass which was hidden in one of Jameson's tunic buttons.

The great air success of the Norwegian campaign had already been flown by naval aircraft, but from a shore base at Hatston, just outside Kirkwall in Orkney. On 10 April, the day following the start of the German invasion, sixteen Blackburn Skuas of 800 and 803 naval air squadrons attacked the cruiser *Königsberg*, which had been damaged by Norwegian shore batteries. The Skuas had to fly more than 600 miles to Bergen, at the extreme limit of their range, each carrying just one 500-lb armour-piercing bomb.

The Skuas arrived in perfect visibility at 8,000 feet, catching the ship completely by surprise, with the sole resistance coming from a single gunner. The aircraft scored three direct hits and five near misses, including some between the ship and the jetty, which was also hit. The ship caught fire, turned over and sank. One Skua was lost, with its crew, a pilot and observer.

Later, another of the pilots was to have a lucky escape. Leslie 'Skeets' Harris, of the Royal Marines, later Major, was shot down on 16 May while flying from the carrier *Ark Royal*. He wrote, 'a bullet splattered through my windscreen and into my shoulder after several head-on attacks and I parked in a fjord off Narvik. The Skua, sedate to the end, waddled to the sea bed. Luckily, the Royal Navy had had a ringside seat and after a remarkably short but very cold bath they picked up my observer and myself.'[8]

Five days after the loss of *Glorious*, fifteen aircraft from *Ark Royal* took off to attack the *Scharnhorst*, moored at Trondheim. Dive-bombing the ship through heavy AA fire, eight of the aircraft were shot down. Only one of the bombs struck the ship, and that failed to explode. One can only reflect that, just possibly, if *Glorious* had flown off her five Swordfish, it might have made little difference to the outcome.

[8] *Daily Telegraph*, 30 June 1995.

The Blackburn Skua played an important role in the Norwegian campaign, sinking the German cruiser *Königsberg*. (FAAM Skua/50)

ACES

No carrier fighter aces emerged from the Norwegian campaign, but 'Skeets' Harris received the DFC for his daring raids. The sinking of the *Königsberg* in no way compensated for the later loss of the *Glorious*, but it did show that naval air power could potentially change the way in which battles could, and indeed would, be fought.

COMMENT

The Norwegian campaign was a brave attempt to help a small but gallant nation which had been determined to maintain its neutrality. It was of strategic importance from the outset, to become even more so once Russia changed sides. The massive supply operation required resulted in great losses to Allied merchant vessels, which would have been much less had Norway not been occupied by the Germans.

At this early stage, British forces were hindered by inadequate equipment and were not strong enough for the many demands placed upon them. There were too few good airfields in Norway, and a stronger carrier force with first-class fighters and bombers could have done much to complement the successful actions of the surface vessels.

There can be no accounting for the lack of activity aboard *Glorious* on 10 June. The other aircraft carrier withdrawing from Norway, *Ark Royal*, had reconnaissance and CAP, and it is hard to understand why the CO of *Glorious*, Captain D'Oyly-Hughes, had not ordered such activity to continue aboard his ship. The shortage of fuel, which meant that she was steaming at just 17 knots, was probably beyond his control, although had she been able to steam faster, it is unlikely that the German battlecruisers would have been able to catch a carrier with a good turn of speed.

DISARMING VICHY FRANCE: THE BATTLE OF MERS EL-KEBIR

VICHY FRANCE WAS A LOOSE CANNON

After the Vichy Government of France had concluded an armistice with Germany on 22 June, the British were concerned that French warships which had fled to British ports or to French colonies in North and West Africa would return to France and might be available to the Germans, with or without their crews. There was also a French squadron sharing Alexandria with the British Mediterranean Fleet. On 3 July, the Royal Navy seized those French warships, including two battleships and some smaller vessels, in British ports, while the squadron at Alexandria was neutralized.

The bulk of the French fleet remaining outside France was in harbour at Mers El-Kebir, or Oran, in Algeria.

SHIPS AND AIRCRAFT

The aircraft carrier *Ark Royal* was involved, and she has been described earlier. She was operating Fairey Swordfish at the time, and these have also been described.

THE ACTION

Reluctant to enter battle with the forces of a country which had, until recently, been an ally, Vice-Admiral Somerville, commanding Force H, presented the French admiral, Admiral Gensoul, commanding the forces at Oran, with an ultimatum, demanding that the warships be handed over or neutralized. He sent one of his officers, Captain Holland, commanding officer of *Ark Royal*, to receive the French response. Holland was flown in a Fairey Swordfish seaplane from a battlecruiser. On receiving the French rejection of the ultimatum, Holland flew straight back to Force H, and his pilot had to land his Swordfish aboard the *Ark Royal*, despite the absence of a wheeled undercarriage. My father, Leading Air Mechanic (later Lieutenant) S.H. 'Harry' Wragg saw the preparations for the Swordfish's landing: 'Prior to landing the arrester wires were disconnected and laid along the edge of the flight deck. It was a perfect landing; the only damage being to the keels of the floats.'[1] Earlier in the campaign, while radio silence was being observed, he had caught a lead weighted message bag dropped by the Swordfish as it made a pass over *Ark Royal*.

The low speed of the Swordfish and the skill of the pilot saved the day, and the aircraft was soon wheeled out of the way by the flight deck party.

The British attack on the French fleet followed soon afterwards. A single burst of gunfire from one of the battleships blew an Army barracks off the crest of a hill, but the main target was the harbour and the fleet. In just fifteen minutes, the British battleships, with an attack by aircraft from *Ark Royal*, managed to blow up the old French battleship *Bretagne*, and crippled

[1] Interview, 29 March 1997.

A sequence of photographs by an unknown seaman shows Captain Holland returning to *Ark Royal* with news of the French rejection of Britain's ultimatum – the Swordfish seaplane landed safely, probably just as well for the onlookers!

the battlecruiser *Dunkerque* and the battleship *Provence*, both of which were run aground to save them from sinking. The battlecruiser *Strasbourg*, accompanied by six destroyers, managed to escape to Toulon. The British fleet suffered no loss or damage.

A similar attack took place five days later, when the *Hermes* and two heavy cruisers attacked Dakar, in West Africa, damaging the battleship *Richelieu*. In late September, there was to be a further attempt by the British to seize or destroy the French fleet at Dakar, which resulted in heavy damage to both sides.

COMMENT

The decision to attack the French warships led to much ill-feeling on the part of the French. While it seems ignoble to turn upon a former ally, the fall of France and Italy's entry into the war made the British position very vulnerable, especially in the Mediterranean and in North Africa, with direct threats to Malta and the Suez Canal and, perhaps, Cyprus as well. In German hands, or with Vichy France actively allied with Germany, these ships could have swung the balance of seapower even more heavily against the British.

OPERATION JUDGEMENT: THE ATTACK ON THE ITALIAN FLEET AT TARANTO

THE MEDITERRANEAN IN 1940

The risk of the war spreading to the Mediterranean was recognised early, and Italy's entry into the war on 10 June 1940 was not a big surprise to the British, who had seen Mussolini's North African ambitions manifest themselves during the late 1930s and were, of course, aware of the political similarities between the Italian and German leadership.

Obviously, Italy posed a major threat to British interests, threatening Malta and the Suez Canal, as well as communications across the Mediterranean. Italian involvement also made the position of Yugoslavia and Greece far less secure.

There were other worries. Britain was anxious that Spain should not enter the war. Recovering from a bloody civil war, the Spanish economy was in no fit state for more conflict, and much of the equipment used by the armed forces at that time was obsolete. Even so, Spain could provide bases for German aircraft and ships, while the major British base at Gibraltar would be difficult to defend against a determined attack.

Another possible threat could have come from Turkey, who had been an ally of Germany and the Austro-Hungarians during the First World War, and who was perceived as being within the German sphere of influence.

The main British base in the Mediterranean for much of the war had to be Alexandria. Gibraltar was too small to be much more than a transit point, and indeed it was only the necessities of wartime that led to the territory receiving its first airfield, on the racecourse. Malta had everything the British needed, except security. The small islands were too close to Italy for comfort and British forces on the main island had been reduced to the absolute minimum before Italy's declaration of war. Before the war, the RAF and the British Army had declared that Malta could not be defended against sustained attack. The Admiralty rejected this advice and insisted that Malta's extensive dockyard facilities should at least be available for light forces and submarines. At one time, the air defence of Malta was left to just three Gloster Sea Gladiator biplanes, nicknamed Faith, Hope and Charity, left behind by a carrier, and flown by a scratch team of RAF pilots.

Malta was not short of airfields. Imperial Airways, by this time the British Overseas Airways Corporation, BOAC, had been developing a base at Ta Kali, while there were other airfields at Luqa, for the RAF, and, in the south of the island, at Hal Far, used by the Fleet Air Arm. Nearby was a well established flying-boat and seaplane base at Kalafrana.

Admiral Sir Andrew Cunningham commanded the Mediterranean Fleet at the time of Taranto. (FAAM PERS/315)

THE THREAT POSED BY THE ITALIAN FLEET

The Royal Navy was hard pressed to demonstrate its supremacy in the Mediterranean. The Italian Navy had a substantial fleet of modern vessels, and the Regia Aeronautica was able to exercise aerial supremacy. The British Mediterranean Fleet was under the command of Admiral Sir Andrew Cunningham, known as 'ABC' to his colleagues. The state of naval aviation in 1940, despite the successful attack on the *Königsberg*, was poor. Captain, later Rear Admiral, Denis Boyd, the commanding officer of *Illustrious*, recalled later that, 'The state of the Fleet Air Arm in 1939 was terrible – we had only taken control of our own aviation in 1937. There was no radar on the carriers. Carriers and their aircraft were regarded as second rate to the rest of the fleet.'[1]

Illustrious, when she entered service in 1940, was to change all of this. Even so, when Cunningham called his commanders to a conference, Boyd feared that 'ABC' might want the carriers, at that time *Illustrious* and *Eagle*, to leave the Mediterranean altogether. He needn't have worried. Cunningham's opening remarks were: 'Gentlemen, I have called you together for I want your advice on how we can best annoy the enemy.'[2]

Many believe that the *Königsberg* attack had given the Fleet Air Arm the idea of a raid on Taranto. In fact, this idea had its origins in a plan prepared during the Abyssinian crisis of 1935, when the League of Nations had attempted to curb Italy's North African ambitions. If the idea of a strike at the Italian fleet in its main base at Taranto belonged to any single author, it was Captain Lister, commanding officer of the aircraft carrier

[1] Imperial War Museum Sound Archive.

[2] Imperial War Museum Sound Archive.

Illustrious at sea with Fairey Swordfish on deck. (FAAM Carrier 1/6)

Glorious in 1935. Lister was a great proponent of night flying, in which the Fairey Swordfish crews of *Glorious* became proficient. They also trained hard for an attack on Taranto, but the crisis evaporated and no action was taken.

These plans were now dusted off and updated, aided by the fact that Lister was by now Cunningham's Rear Admiral Carriers.

The initial plan for the operation, code-named Operation Judgment, was to use aircraft from both *Illustrious* and *Eagle*, but the older ship was forced to remain at Alexandria for repairs to damage received from Italian aerial attack, which had badly damaged her aviation fuel system. It had also been the intention to launch the attack on 21 October, the anniversary of Nelson's great victory at the Battle of Trafalgar. The crews trained in night torpedo tactics, but a serious hangar fire aboard *Illustrious* meant

that the ship could not be ready in time. Although two aircraft were destroyed in the fire, the remaining aircraft were doused with water and had to be completely stripped down. Since the operation was planned for a moonlit night, and the next full moon was not until 11 November, this set the timetable.

SHIPS AND AIRCRAFT

The aircraft carrier used on the Taranto raid was *Illustrious*, the first of the Royal Navy's new 23,000-ton fast armoured carriers. The aircraft was the trusty Fairey Swordfish, mentioned in the Norwegian campaign. For the raid on Taranto, extra fuel was carried and the aircraft operated with a pilot and observer, regarded as important for night navigation, rather than the TAG.

Fairey Swordfish had an extra fuel tank fitted in place of the TAG, telegraphist-air-gunner, for the raid on Taranto. (FAAM Taranto/31)

THE ACTION

Illustrious left Alexandria on 6 November 1940, with a cruiser and destroyer escort. The departure of major units of the Mediterranean Fleet was always noticed and the British always suspected that the information quickly reached the enemy. One advantage of the delay was that the departure of the force coincided with the need to operate a convoy of reinforcements to Greece, which had just entered the war against the Axis powers, and another convoy of supplies to Malta. The presence of a major aircraft carrier on an undertaking of this kind was not unusual – this was well before the advent of the escort carrier.

It had originally been the intention to use thirty aircraft from the two carriers, but without *Eagle* this plan had to be modified. Several of *Eagle*'s Swordfish were transferred to *Illustrious* to join the ship's 815 Squadron, giving a total of twenty–four aircraft for the operation. Unfortunately, the day before the attack one Swordfish had to ditch in the sea with a fuel failure, and on the day of the attack, the same thing happened again. These

ill omens led to much consternation aboard the carrier, and after some investigation, it was discovered that one of the ship's aviation fuel tanks had been contaminated with sea water. This meant that all of the aircraft earmarked for the operation had to have their fuel systems drained and refuelled.

Meanwhile, at noon on 11 November, a cruiser force was detached from the main force and sent on a reconnaissance mission towards the Straits of Otranto. Six hours later, Cunningham signalled Lister to take *Illustrious* and her escorts and proceed in 'execution of previous orders'.[3] The operation was on. By 20.00 the carrier was 170 miles from Taranto.

The raid was led by Lieutenant-Commander Kenneth Williamson, with the then Lieutenant Norman 'Blood' Scarlett-Streatfeild as his observer. The first wave consisted of twelve aircraft, and the second wave had nine. Climbing through thick cloud, the first wave broke up, with three of the four dive-bombers having disappeared along with one torpedo-bomber. Fortunately, the two flare-droppers had managed to maintain formation.

[3] Imperial War Museum Sound Archive.

Illustrious parts company with the 3rd Cruiser Squadron ready for the raid on Taranto, from a painting by the Admiralty war artist, Lieutenant Rowland Langmaid, RN. (IWM A9763)

Navigation towards the target was simplified after the port's anti-aircraft defences opened up, shooting at a patrolling RAF Short Sunderland flying-boat. As they arrived over Taranto, Williamson detached the two flare-droppers, who moved away to drop their flares, with the torpedo Swordfish following so that they could strike at the warships while these were silhouetted against the light.

Hugh Janvrin was an observer in one of the two flare-droppers: 'We had a grandstand view so we didn't go down to sea level. We dropped our flares at about 8,000 feet. And in fact we were fired at considerably. We had a fair amount of ack-ack fire and most extraordinary things that looked like flaming onions . . . one just sort of went through it and it made no great impression. One didn't think they would ever hit you.

'. . . there was fear but I think in the same way that one always had butterflies in the tummy beforehand, but when things were actually happening you don't seem to notice the butterflies much.

'. . . the torpedo aircraft went down and they attacked in two sub flights. The leader took his sub flight of three and went down and attacked. And he . . . attacked a Cavour-class battleship, launched his torpedo, which hit and was shot down immediately afterwards . . .

'. . . we had bombs as well, and we dive-bombed some more fuel tanks . . . and then we returned to the carrier . . .'[4]

Charles Lamb was one of the pilots charged with the flare-dropping. He recalls:

'. . . flying into the harbour only a few feet above sea level – so low that one or two of them actually touched the water with their wheels as they sped through the harbour entrance.

'Nine other spidery biplanes dropped out of the night sky, appearing in a crescendo of noise in vertical dives from the slow moving glitter of the yellow parachute flares.'[5]

Williamson had sunk the *Conte di Cavour* in shallow water, but in turning in the middle of the harbour to escape, the Swordfish came

[4] Imperial War Museum Sound Archive.

[5] Charles Lamb. *War in a Stringbag*, Cassell, 1977.

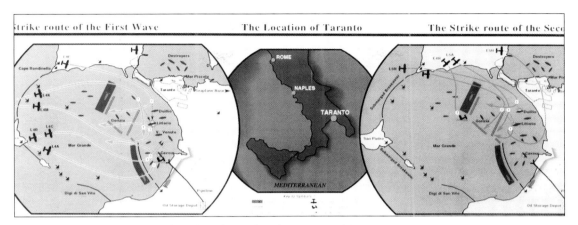

The location of Taranto and the routes of the first and second waves of aircraft. (FAAM Taranto/42)

to grief, although even those aboard were not sure if this was due to Italian AA fire or an accident – as Scarlett-Streatfeild relates, 'We put a wing tip in the water. I couldn't tell. I just fell out of the back into the sea. We were only about 20 feet up. It wasn't very far to drop. I never tie myself in on these occasions.

'Then old Williamson came up a bit later on and we hung about by the aircraft, which still had its tail sticking out of the water. Chaps ashore were shooting at it.

'The water was boiling, so I swam off to a floating dock and climbed on board that. We didn't know we'd done any good with our torpedo. Thought we might have because they all looked a bit long in the face, the Wops.'[6]

One other aircraft, together with its crew, Lieutenants Bayley and Slaughter, did not survive the attack. Yet, for the loss of just two aircraft, the Fleet Air Arm had inflicted more damage on an enemy than Jellicoe's battleships and battlecruisers had managed at Jutland. The battleships *Littorio*, *Conte di Cavour* and *Caio Duilio* were sunk, although the *Conte di Cavour* was refloated and repaired at the end of the war. No less important, fuel tanks ashore were damaged. The cruiser *Trento* had a lucky escape, with a

bomb crashing through the ship and out through the bottom of the hull without exploding. The Italian Navy made no further use of Taranto for the duration of the war.

The crews were jubilant as they returned to *Illustrious*. As the *Illustrious* and cruisers rejoined the *Warspite* at daylight on 12 November, Cunningham ordered a hoist of flags conveying a message, remarkable even for him for understatement, yet somehow fitting the occasion. It said briefly, '*Illustrious* manoeuvre well executed'.[7]

The overwhelming feeling among the aircrew was for a repeat raid the following night, but as the weather worsened, Cunningham vetoed this.

Speaking to the aircrew after debriefing, Captain Denis Boyd recalled that most of them mentioned the Italian AA fire. One pilot said, 'I didn't take it personally, sir, until they started hitting my aircraft, and then I didn't like it much!'[8]

Amused, Boyd thought that this was 'One for the Line Book' (a large scrap book usually decorated with a carrier's badge in which rivalry between the ship's company and the embarked air squadrons, or between squadrons, was often reflected). He went to

[6] *Daily Telegraph*, 22 October 1993.

[7] S.W.C. Pack. *Cunningham the Commander*, B.T. Batsford, 1974.

[8] Imperial War Museum Sound Archive.

Captain Denis Boyd, commanding officer of *Illustrious* for the Taranto raid. (FAAM Pers/314)

see the aircraft, with its fabric hanging in ribbons, and promptly decided that it wasn't.

Later, *Illustrious*' angry sailors were to tear down from the ship's notice-boards the first list of awards for this valiant effort, with six medals, including a DSC for Scarlett-Streatfeild. Given the inadequacy of their aircraft and the well-defended target, the sailors could be excused for expecting that the aircrew would have received far higher awards, including the Victoria Cross.

ACES

Given the extreme heroism of the aircrew and the elderly aircraft, it would be wrong to highlight any one member of the attacking force for special mention. If there were to be an ace, the leader of the raid and commander of 815 Squadron, Lieutenant-Commander Kenneth Williamson deserves this accolade, along with Scarlett-Streatfield, whose navigational skills and torpedo aiming contributed to the victory.

COMMENT

At the time, few appreciated the success of the Fleet Air Arm. No warship in British naval history so lived up to her name as did the *Illustrious* on that night. Even Cunningham, whose fault it was that the awards were so meagre, was later full of praise for the achievements of 815 Squadron and her reinforcements from *Eagle*, but confessed that he had not realized at the time what a 'tremendous stroke' it was.

He was not alone. Churchill, Britain's wartime Prime Minister, was later to say that 'before El Alamein [the major battle giving the Allies a desert war victory in North Africa] nothing had gone right, afterwards everything did'. He had overlooked Taranto, and a number of other achievements by naval airmen.

Apart from the damage to the Italian fleet and the port itself, the operation may well have signalled to Spain and Turkey that British seapower was a force to be reckoned with, since Spain in particular was under pressure to join the Axis forces.

OPERATION EXCESS:
ILLUSTRIOUS UNDER ATTACK

10 JANUARY 1941

MALTA'S PLIGHT

Despite the victory at Taranto, the situation on Malta continued to be serious, and indeed was to become very much worse before the situation eased later in the war. Malta was short of fuel, food and munitions and was under almost constant aerial bombardment first from the Regia Aeronautica and then from the Luftwaffe. This was not the only area in the Mediterranean under pressure. The land war in North Africa was going badly for the British after initial successes against the Italians brought reinforcements in the form of

Vice-Admiral Sir James Somerville, commander Force H in the Mediterranean. (IWM A3509)

Rommel's Afrika Korps, and the Allies were on the defensive in Greece. The Malta convoys were known to the Royal Navy as 'club runs'.

In January 1941, a small convoy, Operation Excess, was sent eastwards across the Mediterranean from Gibraltar, with four fast merchantmen, one for Malta and three for Alexandria. Force H, under Vice-Admiral Somerville, was responsible for escort and air cover, using the carrier *Ark Royal*, as far as the Straits of Sicily, where the Mediterranean Fleet, with Admiral Cunningham aboard the battleship *Warspite*, accompanied by the battleship *Valiant* and the aircraft carrier *Illustrious*, waited to take over.

At the height of the war, small convoys for Malta were usual. The situation did not permit the large and relatively slow-moving convoys of the North Atlantic, as long as the Axis powers had control of the air. Indeed, supplies for Malta were often rushed in by fast minelayers, capable of 40 knots, such as the *Manxman*, since these were the only ships which could hope to dodge enemy air attack.

SHIPS AND AIRCRAFT

Once again we have the fast armoured British carrier, *Illustrious*. On this occasion, the aircraft of note was not the Fairey Swordfish, but the other aircraft embarked aboard, the Fairey Fulmar. The Fulmar was intended to be the naval equivalent to the Supermarine Spitfire and Hawker Hurricane, but her performance fell well short of their standards because of the need for the aircraft to carry a second crew member, the observer, rather than risk a lone pilot navigating with the primitive equipment of the day over the sea, often for lengthy periods. The aircraft was a low-wing monoplane with eight machine-guns and was powered by a single Rolls-Royce Merlin engine, giving a maximum speed of around 280 m.p.h. The Fulmar had mixed reports, some saying that Italian bombers could outpace it and that it could only succeed in downing another aircraft if it had the element of surprise. On the other hand, Cunningham, who had had to be won over to the cause of naval aviation, felt that Fulmar squadrons did their job and rarely let the fleet down.

THE ACTION

Shortly after 12.30 on 10 January, forty-three Ju.87 Stuka dive-bombers in two groups, 11/St G2 led by Major Enneccerus and 1/St G1 under Hauptmann Hozzel, attacked the main units of the Mediterranean Fleet near Malta. Diving from 12,000 feet, ten aircraft attacked the two battleships, but most of the force concentrated on the carrier.

Cunningham wrote later that, 'One was too interested in this new form of dive-bombing attack to be frightened, and there was no doubt that we were watching complete experts. . . . We could not but admire the skill and the precision of it all. The attacks were pressed home at point blank range, and as they pulled out of their dives some were seen to fly along the flight deck of the *Illustrious* below the level of the funnel.'[1]

The Stukas released their bombs as they passed down through 1,200 to about 800 feet. Within just a few minutes, the dive-bombers scored six direct hits and three very near misses on *Illustrious*. The carrier had a 3-inch armoured deck which was designed to withstand a direct hit from a 500-lb bomb,

but at least some of the Stukas were armed with 1,000-lb armour-piercing bombs, and any armour capable of withstanding such a blast would have been so thick that it would have made the ship top-heavy and unstable.

Neither of the first two 1,000-lb bombs hit the flight deck itself. One hit a gun position, while the other plunged through several decks and set fire to a paint store. It seems that it was the smaller 500-lb bombs, which the armoured flight deck of *Illustrious* could resist, that did the damage. One hit the unarmoured after lift, and blew the lift platform down into the hangar. Another 500-lb bomb followed the first down into the same lift well, exploding inside the hangar, where it set fire to several aircraft. Yet another bomb struck the forward lift directly, again causing serious damage so that the sixth and final bomb, one of the 1,000-lb armour-piercing bombs penetrated the flight deck and exploded into the hangar.

Hugh Janvrin was aboard *Illustrious*, after a spell at a shore base, when the attack began: 'We were having lunch in the wardroom at the time. And action stations went . . . action stations for unemployed air crew were, unwisely as it turned out, in the hangar by their aircraft . . . my first indication that anything untoward was happening was when there was a great . . . explosion aft, by the after lift well. I was forward . . . and half the after lift which was up at the time seemed to buckle . . . you could see the daylight through it.

'And then there was a considerable amount of mayhem and we felt the shudder of near misses and the ship increasing speed and keeling over [as she turned] . . . I remember that there were a number of casualties in the after end of the hangar and I went to my Swordfish and was just unzipping the first aid kit which was on the outside of the aircraft . . . with the vague idea of going . . . to do something with it . . . when there was a considerable explosion and a great blast. And the Swordfish and myself were lifted up in the

---

[1] Admiral of the Fleet Sir Andrew Cunningham, *A Sailor's Odyssey*, Hutchinson, 1951.

Illustrious under heavy aerial attack from Luftwaffe Ju.87s and Ju.88s (FAAM I/145)

Smoke streams from *Illustrious* after taking several hits. (IWM A4160)

air and moved about twenty yards down the hangar . . . this was a 1,000-lb armour-piercing bomb which had come straight into the centre of the flight deck just by me.

'The vagaries of the blast of a bomb are extraordinary because people down the far end of the hangar were killed by this bomb and yet I was really one of the closest people to it on my aircraft. And I was just lifted with the aircraft bodily and transported about twenty feet . . .

'And I got down from the aircraft . . . and I remember that my left leg collapsed and I couldn't understand why that I couldn't walk on it . . . a sailor came along and said, "Let me help you, sir." And I put one arm over his shoulders and he lugged me along . . . he said, "Excuse me, sir, you've got something in your side." And he bent down and plucked something out and he dropped it with an oath . . . it was a white-hot piece of metal . . . a fragment from the bomb . . . that had lodged in my side . . . but I didn't feel the pain at all.'[2]

The ship was now blazing from numerous fires, with her hangar an inferno. The mining

Damaged equipment by the island. (FAAM Carrier 1/37)

Illustrious under attack, showing the shattered aft lift. (FAAM Carrier 1/43)

effect of near misses and the repercussion of those that had exploded put the steering out of action, a problem aggravated by the flooding of the steerage flat, caused by the numerous hoses of the fire-fighters and sprinklers.

Some have argued that the Royal Navy would have been better served by more carriers of the same pattern as *Ark Royal*, but the *Ark Royal*, so lacking in armour, would not have survived such a crippling attack. Hugh Janvrin's bomb would not have been the first to penetrate the flight deck, and instead would probably have penetrated the hangar floor, perhaps wrecking the boilers or machinery, or igniting the fuel tanks.

Thanks to her armoured flight and hangar decks, at no time during this action were the ship's machinery spaces damaged, which left her pumps and fire-fighting mains operational, while her speed never fell below 18 knots. Throughout the bombardment, the ship's AA guns continued to fire. The hull

[2] Imperial War Museum Sound Archive.

remained intact and the huge tanks of aviation fuel were undamaged. The damage control parties toiled effectively in uncomfortable and dangerous conditions. Eventually, at first by using the engines for steering, control of the ship was regained. Far below the blazing hangar decks, the temperature in the boiler rooms rose to 140°F.

A combination of the ship's AA defences and the Fulmar fighters saw four of the Stuka dive-bombers shot down. Of course, after the attack, the Fulmars could not land on the aircraft carrier, and running short of fuel, they had to head for Malta, where for a while they reinforced the RAF Hurricane fighters.

Shortly after the last of the Stukas had left, high-level bombers made an unsuccessful attack on the ship, which was forced to put into Malta for emergency repairs and to put out the fires, as well as burying her dead. While in Malta, she continued to attract the attention of high-level bombers, but nine of these were shot down by the Fulmars and Hurricanes. Leaving Malta on 23 January, the carrier had to be repaired in the USA, and was not operational again until late in the year, although many of her less well-armoured contemporaries would not have survived such an attack.

ACES

There can be little doubt that both Major Enneccerus and Hauptmann Hozzel led an attack which was both precise and valiant, since the Stuka was generally regarded as obsolescent on the outbreak of the Second World War. When diving, the Stuka was vulnerable to well-placed AA fire and to fighter attack.

COMMENT

The severe damage to the *Illustrious* meant her withdrawal from service for most of the year, but she was not sunk and was able to resume operations and continue until the end of the war. The temporary respite from the attentions of her aircraft which this afforded the Axis powers was of little benefit to them. The Swordfish were a diminishing asset now that German fighters were more often to be seen in the skies over Italy, while the Fulmars were ashore in Malta, helping the RAF.

On the other hand, it can be seen just how effective the Stuka would have been for naval operations if the Luftwaffe and the Kriegsmarine had been able to resolve their differences and the *Graf Zeppelin* had been completed. The Germans would have had the same problems as the British over a naval fighter, with the Messerschmitt Bf.109 suffering from the range and undercarriage problems which also afflicted the Seafire, and perhaps having a weaker tailplane as well, but the robust Stuka would have been ideal for carrier operations. The Focke-Wulf Fw.190, when it entered service, would have been a frighteningly effective fighter had it been able to get to sea.

As for the Royal Navy, comparing this action with those in the Pacific underlines the necessity to have sufficient air power at sea when intensive airborne attack is likely, which means that a single carrier is vulnerable. Yet again it stresses the importance of naval fighter aircraft able to prove a match for land-based opponents.

BATTLE OF CAPE MATAPAN

CONTROLLING THE MIDDLE SEA

The Royal Navy was close to dominating the Mediterranean, although the hold was fragile without domination of the air. The British wished to take advantage of the Italian fleet's weakness and lack of confidence by reinforcing British and Commonwealth forces fighting in Greece, but the Germans were anxious to see the situation reversed, both to help their campaign in Greece and to ease the situation for their convoys from Italy to North Africa. The Germans managed to convince the Italians that the British had just one battleship fit for action in the Mediterranean, encouraging them to consider operations by the battleship *Vittorio Veneto* and her cruiser escort.

In fact the Royal Navy had three Queen Elizabeth class battleships, the *Warspite*, flagship of Admiral Sir Andrew Cunningham, *Valiant* and *Malaya*, and the new Illustrious-class aircraft carrier, *Formidable*, with the new Fairey Albacore biplane torpedo-bomber and Fairey Fulmar fighters. Many naval officers have questioned Cunningham's commitment to naval aviation earlier in the war, but whether or not he was, as some suggest, committed even before the outbreak of war, there was little doubt of his advocacy of strong carrier-borne air power by this time. The arrival of *Formidable* to replace the battered *Illustrious* can be seen as proof of his commitment. *Formidable* had arrived in Alexandria by the 'back door', coming through the Suez Canal after a voyage around Africa, rather than sailing across the Mediterranean.

Fairey Fulmar in flight. (FAAM Fulmar/82)

45

Fairey Albacore torpedo-bombers, most with wings folded, ranged on the flight deck of *Formidable* before taking off to attack the Italian fleet in the build up to the Battle of Cape Matapan. (IWM HU67447)

SHIPS AND AIRCRAFT

An Illustrious class aircraft carrier, *Formidable* needs no introduction herself, but she did bring a new aircraft into the war, the Fairey Albacore, a biplane intended as a replacement for the Swordfish, which in practice could only supplement the earlier aircraft. In common with the Swordfish, the Albacore was a three-seat single-engined biplane, albeit this time with a covered cockpit. The aircraft could carry a 1,600-lb torpedo or bombs up to 2,000 lbs. Defence was provided by three machine-guns. Early versions had a 1,065 h.p. Bristol Taurus engine, but on later aircraft the power output was increased to 1,130 h.p. About 800 were built.

THE ACTION

British reconnaissance aircraft had detected the Italian fleet at sea, and Cunningham was anxious to bring the Italians to a decisive engagement.

Nevertheless, Alexandria was supposed to be full of Italian agents – which seems odd considering the Italians' apparent ignorance of the condition of the British Mediterranean Fleet – and subterfuge had to be resorted to in order to maintain an element of surprise.

On 27 March, Cunningham went ashore during the afternoon with a suitcase, so that an observer would assume that the Admiral would be spending the night ashore. He returned to the *Warspite* immediately after dark and the fleet sailed at 19.00. Brownrigg, master of the fleet, wrote:

'We intentionally sent principal staff officers away by air during the day so as to allay all the Italian agents' apprehension; we also kept our awnings spread, and the Admiral invited people to dinner. As soon as it was dark we furled our awnings, the officers returned, and the dinner was cancelled.'[1]

[1–3] S.W.C. Pack. *Cunningham the Commander*, B.T. Batsford, 1974.

46

Having played games with the supposed enemy agents, operations began early the following morning, 28 March. By 06.00 there was sufficient light for *Formidable* to fly off aircraft for reconnaissance, fighter combat air patrol and for anti-submarine patrols.

In his book, *Cunningham the Commander*, S.W.C. Pack, one of *Formidable*'s senior officers, wrote, 'At 07.20 our aircraft reported four cruisers and four destroyers in 34 degrees 22' North, 24 degrees 47' East steering 230 degrees. Another reported that 07.39 she had sighted four cruisers and six destroyers steering 220 degrees in 34 degrees 05' North, 24 degrees 26' East. When it became known that Pridham-Wippell had been ordered to rendezvous at 06.30 south of Gaudo Island, the conviction spread that his own force must have been the subject of the two separate reports from aircraft. . . . At 09.39 Cunningham had ordered the *Formidable* to fly off the six Albacores that had been ranged on the flight deck for the last hour, His aim was to attack the Trieste cruisers now being shadowed by Pridham-Wippell. . . . The attack saved the British cruisers.'[2]

This was no exaggeration. The problem was that Pridham-Wippell's cruiser and destroyer force was in trouble, being pursued by the Italians with their heavy cruisers who were gaining on him, and within range of the heavy guns of the *Vittorio Veneto*. The fleeing light cruisers made smoke, although this did not protect the cruiser *Gloucester* until a destroyer, *Hasty*, managed to shield her with her own smokescreen.

At 11.27, *Formidable*'s striking force appeared, escorted by Fulmar fighters which were able to shoot down one of two Junkers Ju.88 fighter-bombers and drive another one off. In the face of determined Italian AA fire, the six Albacores of *Formidable*'s 826 Squadron pressed home a torpedo attack, but failed to hit their target, although they did force the *Vittorio Veneto* to break off the action.

A second strike of three Albacores and two Swordfish, of 829 Squadron, was flown off before the first strike returned, in part to clear the decks for the aircraft needing to land on. No sooner had the aircraft from the first strike landed on at 12.44 than two Italian S.79s made a torpedo-bombing attack on the carrier, which managed to avoid being hit.

'*Formidable*'s log for this day shows that flying operations were conducted on twenty-one separate occasions. Each operation might occupy only a few minutes but required an alteration of course into the wind which was upsetting when the whole fleet had to conform to these movements to ensure that the destroyer screen would remain effective. Essential routine operations severely limited the number of aircraft that could be made ready for the big strikes. She had a total of only 27 aircraft on board: 13 Fulmars, 10 Albacores (of which only 5 were fitted with long-range tanks), and 4 Swordfish. These had to cover all routine requirements, such as fighter protection and anti-submarine patrol in addition to the shadowing, mass reconnaissance, and offensive strikes needed in battle: a pitiably small force when compared with the large forces available in carriers in the Pacific Campaign of 1945.'[3]

During the afternoon, Royal Air Force Blenheim bombers operating from bases in Greece made four attacks on the *Vittorio Veneto* and her cruiser force, using high altitude bombing which resulted in a number of near misses but no direct hits. The second wave of aircraft from *Formidable* meanwhile had arrived over the *Vittorio Veneto*, with Lieutenant-Commander Dalyell-Stead leading aircraft of 829 Squadron. Machine-gunning the bridges and superstructure by fighters surprised the battleship's look-outs and gunners, allowing three Albacores to press home their attack. The lead aircraft dropped its torpedo 1,000 yards ahead of the ship as she turned to starboard to take evasive action, while the aircraft in turn suffered the ship's concentrated AA fire, blowing it out of the sky. The torpedo hit the *Vittorio Veneto* almost immediately after the aircraft crashed, striking just above the port outer screw and 15 feet below the waterline, so that a massive volume of water was shipped and within minutes the engines had stopped.

Damage control parties worked quickly on the ailing battleship, which was now settling by the stern and listing to port. The two starboard engines were restarted, and at 17.00, 90 minutes after the attack, the ship was managing 15 knots. At 17.35, Lieutenant-Commander Gerald Saunt flew off with six Albacores of 826 Squadron and two Swordfish of 829 Squadron, while *Warspite*'s own Swordfish seaplane spotted the ship at 18.20. At dusk, *Formidable*'s aircraft, augmented by two Swordfish from the naval air station at Maleme in Crete, attacked the Italian fleet, hitting the heavy cruiser *Pola* which immediately lost speed and drifted out of her position. It took an hour for the Italian Admiral, Iachino, to become aware of the problems with *Pola* and, not expecting a night battle, he sent the two heavy cruisers *Zara* and *Fiume*, with four destroyers to provide assistance.

Iachino later described the Fleet Air Arm aircraft: 'They looked like giant vultures, flying around their prey until a favourable moment should present itself to descend.'[4]

In the confusion, Cunningham, preparing a night action, mistook the radar trace of *Pola* for *Vittorio Veneto*, but as his ships prepared to open fire, the *Zara* and *Fiume*, with destroyers, blundered across the path of the British fleet. The three British battleships opened fire with massive 15-inch broadsides after the Italian force had been illuminated by a searchlight from the destroyer, *Greyhound*. In the ensuing battle, both the Italian cruisers and two of the Italian destroyers were sunk, as was the crippled *Pola*, by torpedoes from two British destroyers. At the height of what must have been a confusing night battle, *Warspite*'s searchlights picked up *Formidable*, and the officer in charge of the battleship's secondary 6-inch guns was training his armament upon her and was only prevented from opening fire with seconds to spare.

The following morning, the British picked up 900 Italian survivors, before German aircraft forced them to withdraw – notwithstanding this, Cunningham directly communicated the position of the remaining survivors in the water to Rome, thus saving many more Italian lives.

COMMENT

Matapan was an unqualified British success, damaging a battleship and sinking three Italian cruisers and two destroyers, with no British losses. The action did little to prevent the loss of Greece to the Axis forces. On 25 May, *Formidable* was badly damaged by Luftwaffe Stuka dive-bombers during the battle for Crete, but only after the ship had carried out an effective attack on the Luftwaffe airfield at Scarpanto in the east of the island. Evacuation of British and Commonwealth forces first from Greece and then from Crete would not have been possible without the victory at Matapan. Naval aviation helped in locating the Italian fleet and then in delaying its withdrawal, crippling two major warships, one of which was later sunk.

---

[4] *Daily Telegraph*, 26 August 1996.

SINK THE *BISMARCK*!

VULNERABILITY OF THE UNITED KINGDOM

In any major war, the United Kingdom has always been vulnerable to attack on its extended shipping routes. Traditionally, the country has been a net importer of food, and dependent, until recent years, on imported oil. The country has very little in the way of metal-bearing ore. The Germans exploited this weakness in both world wars, both by the use of submarines and by surface commerce raiders. During the winter of 1940–41, the commerce raiders were much in evidence in both the Atlantic and the Indian Oceans. The key to successful commerce raiding was to avoid contact with British naval forces and the risk of serious damage to the raider, which would often be very far from its base, all the time seeking softer prey. Apart from the merchant shipping losses, commerce raiding forced the Royal Navy to support convoys with ever larger warships, while convoys themselves hampered the free flow of materials, since they inevitably proceeded at the speed of the slowest vessel, and time was wasted waiting for convoys to assemble, so that supplies arrived spasmodically.

The loss of the *Königsberg* not withstanding, the Kriegsmarine was confident that it had relatively little to fear from aerial attack.

Germany had not got all of her planned fleet available for service on the outbreak of war in 1939. They might not have felt that this mattered. Two other explanations do exist. The first is that the British were far more successful at putting their economy and armed forces on a war footing, making the most of

the breathing space afforded by the Munich Agreement in 1938. The other is that many senior German officers were not expecting to have to fight the United Kingdom until 1945.

Two battleships which entered service early in the war were the *Bismarck* and her sister ship, the *Tirpitz*. *Bismarck* was first in service, and together with the heavy cruiser, *Prinz Eugen*, put to sea under the command of Admiral Gunther Lutjens on 18 May 1941, leaving the German port of Gotenhafen. Seeking a passage north of Iceland, well away from British maritime reconnaissance and the Home Fleet's northern base at Scapa Flow in Orkney, the ship called at Korsfjord, south of Bergen, in German-occupied Norway. Lutjens called this first raiding cruise of the *Bismarck* and *Prinz Eugen* 'Operation Rhine Exercise'.

One of the ship's officers, Baron Burkard von Mullenheim-Rechberg, was the Fourth Gunnery Officer and Adjutant, as an Oberleutnant, on this the first voyage of the ship. He recalls his surprise that, on leaving Gotenhafen, the *Bismarck*'s fuel tanks were not completely full – a hose had given way during the final stages, interrupting fuelling. He was further surprised when the ship did not replenish her tanks during the call at Korsfjord.

Once at sea, the *Bismarck* was shadowed by two British heavy cruisers, *Suffolk* and *Norfolk*, which maintained contact, despite bad weather, using their radar. Vice-Admiral Holland took the battlecruiser *Hood* and the new, and still not fully operational, battleship, *Prince of Wales*, to confront the two German ships. On 24 May, the British ships

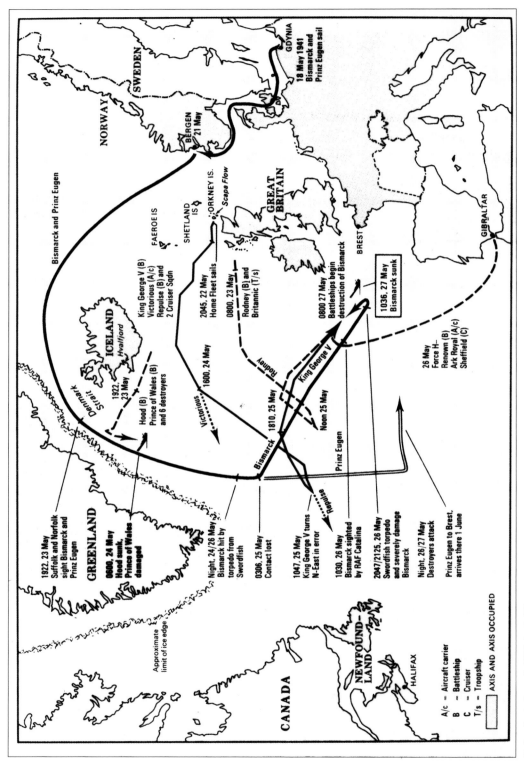

The hunt for the *Bismarck*. (FAAM Cars B/81)

18 May 1941
Bismarck and
Prinz Eugen sail

Bismarck and Prinz Eugen

BERGEN
21 May

GDYNIA

NORWAY

SWEDEN

FAEROE IS.

SHETLAND
IS

ORKNEY IS.
Scape Flow

GREAT
BRITAIN

BREST

GIBRALTAR

ICELAND
Hvalfjord

King George V (B)
Victorious (A/c)
Repulse (B) and
2 Cruiser Sqdn

2045, 22 May
Home Fleet sails

0800, 23 May
Rodney (B) and
Britannic (T/s)

0800 27 May
Battleships begin
destruction of Bismarck

1036, 27 May
Bismarck sunk

Denmark Strait

1922,
23 May

Hood (B)
Prince of Wales (B)
and 6 destroyers

1600, 24 May

Victorious

1810, 25 May

Noon 25 May

Rodney

King George V

Bismarck

Prinz Eugen

26 May
Force H–
Renown (B)
Ark Royal (A/c)
Sheffield (C)

1922, 23 May
Suffolk and Norfolk
sight Bismarck and
Prinz Eugen

GREENLAND

0600, 24 May
Hood sunk,
Prince of Wales
damaged

Night, 24/26 May
Bismarck hit by
torpedo from
Swordfish

0306, 25 May
Contact lost

1047, 25 May
King George V turns
N–East in error

1030, 26 May
Bismarck sighted
by RAF Catalina

2047/2125, 26 May
Swordfish torpedo
and severely damage
Bismarck

Night, 26/27 May
Destroyers attack

Prinz Eugen to Brest,
arrives there 1 June

Repulse

Approximate
limit of ice edge

CANADA

NEWFOUND–
LAND

HALIFAX

A/c = Aircraft carrier
B   = Battleship
C   = Cruiser
T/s = Troopship

AXIS AND AXIS OCCUPIED

intercepted the German force, and a classic naval gun battle broke out, during the course of which, the *Hood*, with Holland aboard, exploded, with the loss of some 1,500 men, leaving just three survivors. The *Prince of Wales* was forced to retire after receiving several hits from the two German ships. The action was not entirely one-sided, however, since the *Bismarck* was hit three times, causing a fuel leak which forced Lutjens to break company with the *Prinz Eugen* and attempt to head for St Nazaire, with Brest as an alternative, in occupied France. His fuel problems were to become critical, since not only was fuel being lost through the leak, but connections with the forward fuel tanks in the forecastle were severed. The leaking fuel also made tracking the ship much easier.

SHIPS AND AIRCRAFT

Once again we have the venerable Fairey Swordfish, while the aircraft carrier *Ark Royal* has already been described and the other carrier in this action, *Victorious*, belongs to the Illustrious class.

The *Bismarck* had a net displacement of 46,000 metric tonnes and a full-load displacement of 50,955 tonnes, although a post-war United States Navy assessment suggested that this was nearer 53,000 tonnes, with a broad beam to provide greater stability as a gun platform in a seaway. The ship was heavily armoured, but was fast for her type, with a maximum speed of 30 knots using three screws. She had two twin 38-cm, approximately 15-inch, turrets forward, and

Fairey Swordfish taking off from *Victorious* to attack *Bismarck*.

the same again aft. Four single-engined Arado Ar.196 floatplanes were carried, and these low-wing monoplanes could be used for reconnaissance or as light fighters. At the time of the action, 2,200 men were aboard, consisting of her wartime complement, the Admiral's staff, and German war correspondents.

THE ACTION

The *Prince of Wales* and the heavy cruisers *Suffolk* and *Norfolk* continued to track the *Bismarck* throughout 24 May. That evening, at around 22.30 British Summer Time, 21.30 GMT, nine Fairey Swordfish biplanes from the new aircraft carrier, *Victorious*, found the *Bismarck* and launched a torpedo attack.

Von Mullenheim-Rechberg had what almost amounted to a ringside seat: 'Aircraft alarm! In seconds every anti-aircraft gun on the *Bismarck* was ready for action. One after the other, the planes came towards us, nine Swordfish, torpedoes under their fuselages. Daringly they flew through our fire, nearer to

After the first torpedo strike, *Bismarck* leaked a tell-tale streak of oil. (IWM C2456)

the fire-spitting mountain of the *Bismarck*, always nearer and still nearer. Watching through my director, which, having been designed for surface targets, had a high degree of magnification but only a narrow field, I could not see all of the action. . . . But what I could see was exciting enough.

'Our anti-aircraft batteries . . . fired into the water ahead of the aircraft, raising massive water spouts. To fly into one of those spouts would mean the end. And the aircraft: they were moving so slowly that they seemed to be standing still in the air . . . the pilots pressed their attack with suicidal courage.'[1]

The *Bismarck* increased her speed to 27 knots and began to zigzag to avoid the torpedoes. Those aboard thought that this was an impossible task since the Swordfish pilots had planned their attack so that torpedoes were heading for the ship from several different directions, and to avoid one meant putting the ship in the way of another.

'All at once the sharp, ringing report of an explosion punctuated the roar of our guns and the *Bismarck* gave a slight shudder . . . what I supposed was a torpedo hit . . . launched at close range, it could not possibly have reached its set depth . . . but had probably struck in the area where our armour belt was strongest: at the waterline amidships.'[2]

The torpedo had killed a warrant officer, and injured six engineers.

After the aerial attack, a brief gunnery exchange with the *Prince of Wales* followed, but was broken off in the fading light.

The following day, Vice-Admiral Somerville left Gibraltar with Force H, which included the aircraft carrier *Ark Royal*, as well as the battlecruiser, *Renown*, and two cruisers. Contact with the *Bismarck* was lost in the early hours of 26 May, but during the morning an RAF Consolidated Catalina flying-boat discovered her position.

[1–4] Baron Burkard Von Mullenheim-Rechberg. *Battleship Bismarck*, Triad, Grafton Books, London, 1982.

Damage to the cruiser *Sheffield* during the engagement. (IWM A4096)

During the early afternoon, in rough weather, fifteen Swordfish took off from the *Ark Royal*, while the cruiser *Sheffield* was ordered to maintain contact with the *Bismarck*. Unfortunately, the Swordfish aircrew had been told that the only ship they would see would be the *Bismarck*, and dropping out of the clouds they attacked *Sheffield* by mistake, until they recognized her. Prompt evasive action by the *Sheffield* and high speed enabled her to miss the few torpedoes which didn't explode on contact with the sea due to defects in their magnetic detonators.

Meanwhile, Admiral Tovey, commander-in-chief of the Home Fleet, was at sea with the new battleship *King George V*, and another battleship, *Rodney*, with escorting destroyers. Nevertheless, Tovey had to signal Somerville that, unless the *Bismarck*'s speed could be reduced by midnight, *King George V* would have to withdraw to refuel, leaving *Rodney* on her own.

Again, at 19.15 with low cloud and poor visibility, a further strike by fifteen Swordfish was launched from *Ark Royal*. On this occasion, the torpedoes had contact detonators, more reliable than the magnetic detonators but needing a direct hit. The Swordfish appeared again over the *Sheffield*, which directed them to the *Bismarck*, but thirty minutes later the aircraft were back over the *Sheffield* having failed to find their target. New directions were given and the aircraft went in search of their target once again. This time those aboard *Sheffield* knew that the aircraft had the *Bismarck* because of the sound of heavy anti-aircraft fire!

Von Mullenheim-Rechberg again: 'They approached even more recklessly than the planes from the *Victorious* had done two days earlier. . . . Every pilot seemed to know what this attack meant to Tovey . . .

'Once more, the *Bismarck* became a fire-spitting mountain. The racket of her anti-aircraft guns was joined by the roar from her main and secondary turrets as they fired into the bubbling paths of oncoming torpedoes, creating splashes ahead of the attackers. . . . The antique-looking Swordfish, fifteen of them, seemed to hang in the air, near enough to touch. The high cloud layer, which was especially thick directly over us, probably did not permit a synchronized attack from all directions, but the Swordfish came so quickly after one another that our defence did not have it any easier. . . . They flew low, the spray of the heaving seas masking their landing gear. . . . It was as though their orders were, "Get hits or don't come back!"'[3]

Once again, *Bismarck* weaved this way and that, attempting to avoid the torpedoes. Von Mullenheim-Rechberg had a rudder indicator in his position, and he could see it moving frantically, while the engine room was constantly bombarded with orders to stop, or to increase speed, or even move astern, as Captain Lindemann attempted to save his ship. Waiting for the sound and shock of a torpedo striking the ship, Von Mullenheim-Rechberg thought that the attackers were attempting to hit the twin rudders or the triple screws, none of which were far from his position.

'We had been under attack for perhaps fifteen minutes when I heard that sickening sound. Two torpedoes exploded in quick succession, but somewhere forward of where I was. Good fortune in misfortune, I thought . . . . The attack must have been almost over when it came, an explosion aft! My heart sank. I glanced at the rudder indicator. It showed 'left 12 degrees'. . . . It stayed at 'left 12 degrees'. Our increasing list to starboard soon told us that we were in a continuous turn. The aircraft attack ended as abruptly as it had begun.'[4]

Rumours soon started to circulate throughout the ship that seven of the attackers had been shot down, but they had in fact all returned to *Ark Royal*.

The damage was serious. The rudder was jammed and had to be cut or blown off so that the ship could manoeuvre either on engine power or by putting a temporary rudder in position – the hangar door was considered for this, but rough seas were making action difficult. The impact of the torpedo had closed the safety valve in the starboard engine room,

For *Ark Royal*, victory was relatively short-lived, being torpedoed by *U-81* off Gibraltar on 13 November 1941. (IWM A6334)

shutting down the engines, but this fault was quickly remedied. Nevertheless, the hole in the hull proved to be so big that the steering rooms were flooded. Then the pumps which could have pumped out the steering rooms failed as water flooded their starter motors. Even when a hand rudder was coupled to the rudder yoke, some time later, and men ordered to man it, they weren't able to get to it.

The *Ark Royal* and the *Renown* had had a close shave, unknown to them. Both ships had passed close to the submarine *U-556*, whose Kapitanleutnant, Herbert Wohlfarth, could have torpedoed both ships, one with his forward tubes and the other with his tubes aft, but for the fact that he was at the end of a mission and had already expended all of his torpedoes.

British destroyers carried out a torpedo attack on the *Bismarck* that night, but without scoring any effective hits.

The following morning, the battleships *Rodney* and *King George V* engaged the *Bismarck*, which was soon hit several times and after ninety minutes had fires burning fiercely. Two cruisers made a torpedo attack. A further strike by *Ark Royal*'s Swordfish also flew off from the carrier, but had to turn back because of the danger of pressing home the attack under the intense fire provided by the two battleships.

Eventually, the order was given to abandon ship. A large number of those aboard made it into the water, although many were badly wounded. The British cruiser, *Dorsetshire*, arrived to pick up survivors, one of whom told his rescuers that U-boats were coming, causing *Dorsetshire* to move away, leaving men in the water. Whether or not the German seaman's remarks were intended in good faith, believing that U-boats in the area would be coming, or he simply wanted to wait for a German rescuer to avoid becoming

a prisoner-of-war, no one knows, but the ruse backfired as most of those in the water perished, leaving just 115 survivors out of the 2,200 men who had been aboard.

COMMENT

The *Bismarck* was the pride of the Kriegsmarine and could have done untold damage to the merchant vessels providing a lifeline to the United Kingdom. The operation tied down a substantial part of the available forces, but failure to do so would have had serious consequences. No one seems to understand why the ship could not shoot down the attacking aircraft – it has been surmised that the AA guns were set to deal with a minimum approach speed, and that since the Swordfish could not manage this the aircraft were virtually invulnerable. Von Mullenheim-Rechberg does not speculate too much on why the aircraft were not shot down, but his comments about the work of the men in the signals office suggest that not all of the crew were as proficient as might have been expected, and so one can speculate on whether or not this was the reason.

This was a clear example of just how vulnerable even the most powerful surface vessels were to the reconnaissance and striking abilities of even carrier-borne aircraft. The inability to put a balanced fleet to sea, with carriers as well as battleships, was the Kriegsmarine's undoing. On the other hand, had they had more aircraft and perhaps ones with superior performance, the Royal Navy might not have lost the *Hood*. This ship was known to be vulnerable to attack, although paradoxically she was lost when just within her zone of invulnerability, where she was safe from falling shellfire. Perhaps the Admiralty should have converted the *Hood* to an aircraft carrier!

THE NEED TO DO SOMETHING: RAIDS ON PETSAMO AND KIRKENES

GERMANY TURNS ON THE SOVIET UNION

On 22 June 1941 in Operation Barbarossa, Germany attacked the Soviet Union, which had been its ally in the invasion and partition of Poland in September 1939. The campaign had originally been planned for April, but had been delayed by German intervention in Yugoslavia in support of Italy. After the invasion, the Soviet Navy made no offensive move against German forces in the Baltic. The initial German advance was so rapid that the major naval bases at Kronstadt and Leningrad were surrounded by the autumn, while the Gulf of Finland was closed by dense minefields. The only route for supplies from Russia's new allies in the west was around the northern part of Norway, well above the Arctic Circle.

After the invasion, there was political pressure on the Royal Navy to, in effect, 'do something'. The area was well outside the operational radius of RAF bombers, even if flight over heavily defended German airspace in itself had been feasible, and there was nowhere for the British Army to intervene. There was no choice but to use sea power.

The reluctant Commander-in-Chief, Home Fleet, Sir John Tovey, was urged by Britain's wartime prime minister, Winston Churchill, to carry out an attack as 'a gesture in support of our Russian allies to create a diversion on the enemy's northern flank'.[1]

The Soviet Union had already been pressing for attacks on German shipping, which was using the two former Finnish ports of Petsamo and Kirkenes.

SHIPS AND AIRCRAFT

The small force which could be spared for this operation consisted primarily of the two aircraft carriers, *Victorious* and *Furious*, both of which have been described.

The aircraft in use were the Fairey Albacore and Swordfish torpedo-bombers, and the Fairey Fulmar fighter.

THE ACTION

Victorious was to launch twenty Fairey Albacore torpedo-bombers of 827 and 828 Naval Air Squadrons, escorted by Fairey Fulmar fighters of 809 Squadron, at Kirkenes, while Petsamo was to be attacked by nine Fairey Swordfish of 812 Squadron and nine Fairey Albacores of 817 Squadron, also escorted by Fulmars, in this case from 800 Squadron.

The raid was conducted in broad daylight, rather than during the short Arctic summer night, affording the attackers little protection. Worse still, before the aircraft flew off in mid-afternoon, they were spotted by a German reconnaissance aircraft. Not surprisingly, German fighters were waiting for both strikes.

[1] *Daily Telegraph*, 30 October 1996.

For the raid on Kirkenes, *Victorious* had Fairey Fulmar fighters of 809 squadron to escort her Albacores. (FAAM Fulmar/83)

Serving as a telegraphist-air-gunner on one of the Albacores of 828 Squadron from *Victorious* was Francis Smith, who recalled that the aircrew were assured that there would be very little fighter opposition, and that only training aircraft would be encountered, even though they were only a few miles from the frontline between Russian and German forces! Nor was the German reconnaissance aircraft their only problem, since they were warned not to attack a hospital ship which they would encounter en route to the target. Not surprisingly, some of the aircrew did not like this, arguing that there was nothing to stop a hospital ship from warning those ashore.

Petty Officer Francis Smith recalls, '. . . eventually we get to the fjord leading into Kirkenes . . . we went in one side of Kirkenes Bay, and 827 Squadron went in the other side. And all of a sudden, there's flaming onions and God knows what coming down at us – because we're flying up the fjord, and the Germans are firing down, from the cliffs with light ack-ack. Not funny at all.

'So we go in so far, and we have to climb over the end of the fjord . . . over the mountain and down into the bay. And there's all this mass shipping – about four little ships. And before anything can happen, there were 110s and Stukas all over the place – they're all airborne . . . they're there, waiting for us.

'And they start. . . . By now the ack-ack has stopped firing, they've left it to the Stukas and the 110s, and they're blasting away with cannon-shells and God knows what. Well, almost immediately, my last sub-flight all got shot down. . . . Everyone jettisoned their torpedoes . . . nobody got a chance to fire at any ship.'[2]

2 Imperial War Museum Sound Archive.

A deck full of Albacores. (FAAM ALB/22)

The aircraft turned to make their escape, flying back the way they had come, with the German aircraft in hot pursuit. Smith watched more aircraft being shot down, and had to look out for aircraft for his pilot, the squadron CO.

'And the only protection you had in Albacores, or Swordfish, was to go down on the water and wait . . . see the cannon shells hitting the water, and at the last second, yell out to the pilot, "hard a-starboard" or "hard a-port". With which . . . he spun left or right and the cannon shells went by you. . . . In this case, it worked, and they didn't hit us. But I did see the cannon shells going by.

'When we got back to the ship, we couldn't land on . . . because there was an aircraft on the flight deck, bent in two – broken its back on landing – we found out afterwards he hadn't broken his back, he was just shot in two, and the telegraphist-air-gunner was dead

in the back – he'd been cut in two, more or less, by cannon shells.

'So while we're circling, there was five of 827 come back. Now one of them . . . his lower main plane was just flapping in the breeze, it was in tatters and streamers, where he'd been shot up.'[3]

Meanwhile, at Petsamo, aircraft from the *Furious* had found no ships at all, and so they had loosed their torpedoes at the wharves.

Victorious lost thirteen of her aircraft at Kirkenes. Petsamo was less heavily defended, and just three of the aircraft from *Furious* were lost. Altogether, forty-four aircrew were lost, seven of them killed.

Intelligence about both harbours had been minimal, and there was little shipping for the attackers, whose score at Kirkenes amounted to one 2,000-ton freighter sunk, another set on fire, and four enemy aircraft shot down – a tribute to the skill of the Fulmar pilots.

[3] Imperial War Museum Sound Archive.

Tovey reported, 'The gallantry of the aircraft crews, who knew before leaving that their chance of surprise had gone, and that they were certain to face heavy odds, is beyond praise.' He added, pointedly, 'I trust that the encouragement to the morale of our allies was proportionately great.'[4]

COMMENT

Apart from the great courage and airmanship of those involved, it is hard to believe that this was the same navy that triumphed at Taranto. Where was the planning, the training, the intelligence, the reconnaissance, the common sense? This was a waste of aircraft and most of all, airmen, hard to replace at the best of times. Worse, the two aircraft carriers and their squadrons could have been elsewhere, where they might have made a difference.

Operation Barbarossa had started late. Perhaps, the British and the Americans should have stood aside and waited for the Russian winter to do its worst. The heavy cost of the Arctic convoys to Russia was also not worth it. There was evidence still that the Soviet Union was not the kind of ally one would choose. Keeping Russia supplied as the war progressed might have tied down many German divisions, but the equipment and munitions supplied could have been better used elsewhere, as could the men and ships lost in the Arctic convoys.

[4] *Daily Telegraph*, 30 October 1996.

CONVOY OPERATION PEDESTAL

AN ALL-OUT EFFORT TO RE-SUPPLY MALTA

The difficulties of sending convoys across the Mediterranean have already been covered. By 1942, the situation on Malta had been desperate for some time, and the small number of ships which had got through could never have been adequate to feed those on the Maltese islands as well as supply ammunition, fuel and spares for the forces based there. The Italians also had their problems. The First Battle of Syrte in December 1941, had resulted from a British attempt to disrupt an Italian convoy to Tripoli. The Second Battle of Syrte in March 1942 arose when the Italians attempted to destroy a British Malta-bound convoy from Alexandria. In June, two convoys had left for Malta, one from Alexandria and the other from Gibraltar, with the former having to return after being ravaged by light forces, U-boats and aircraft, while the latter lost four out of the six merchantmen intended for Malta. For their part, the Italians lost a cruiser, and the battleship *Littorio* was hit by torpedoes and bombs from aircraft based on Malta.

By this time, the Germans had become more heavily committed in the Mediterranean theatre. Despite a large Italian submarine force at Italy's entry to the war, the Italian successes in submarine warfare came from daring use of midget submarines and 'human torpedoes', and not from deploying submarines to make life even more difficult for British ships. The Germans sent U-boats into the Mediterranean, while heavy air attacks by Fliegerkorps II during April made Grand Harbour and Sliema Creek almost unusable for the British, sinking three destroyers, three submarines and several other ships.

AIRCRAFT AND SHIPS

What made the convoy of 10–15 August 1942 so special was the sheer size of it. Operation Pedestal had no fewer than fourteen merchant vessels – usually Malta convoys consisted of no more than half-a-dozen ships. By this time, the situation was desperate, and no doubt the British realized that not all of the ships would survive the nightmare passage. The escorting force was even larger and more powerful than usual. Vice Admiral Syfret commanded a fleet with the battleships *Nelson* and *Rodney*, which, with their 16-inch guns in three triple turrets forward, had been the two most powerful warships in the Royal Navy before the outbreak of war, and the aircraft carriers *Eagle*, *Furious*, *Indomitable* and *Victorious*, as well as seven cruisers and twenty-seven destroyers. *Furious* was carrying fighters for the defence of Malta. *Indomitable* and *Victorious* were sister ships of *Illustrious*.

The aircraft embarked aboard these ships included forty-two Supermarine Spitfires aboard *Furious*, which was delivering these much needed fighters to Malta. They would make a big difference to the island's defences, provided that there was enough fuel for them when they arrived!

The backbone of the fleet's fighter defences were Hawker Sea Hurricanes, which by this time were obsolescent in the fighter role,

The Malta convoy of August 1942, 'Operation Pedestal', about to enter the Mediterranean. Although born out of desperation, from then on the situation in the Mediterranean started to move in favour of the Allies. (IWM A11151)

although continuing to provide good service as ground-attack aircraft in North Africa. Between them, the carriers had forty-three Sea Hurricanes. The other fighters were Fairey Fulmars and Grumman Martlets, as the F4F Wildcat was known to the Fleet Air Arm. The number of aircraft available for anti-shipping duties was limited, since air attack was seen as the main threat. The Italian Fleet by this time rarely ventured out to sea, but submarine attack from German U-boats had become a major hazard in the Mediterranean. The anti-shipping striking power of the carriers was left with twenty-eight Fairey Albacores, supposedly the successors to the Swordfish, although some Swordfish remained in service well after the Albacore was eventually retired.

Victorious had sixteen Fulmars of 809 and 884 Naval Air Squadrons, five Sea Hurricanes of 885 and twelve Albacores of 832 Squadrons. *Indomitable* had nine Martlets in 806 Squadron, twenty-two Sea Hurricanes in 800 and 880 Squadrons, and sixteen Albacores in 827 Squadron. *Eagle* had sixteen Sea Hurricanes in 801 Squadron and another four in 813. *Furious* had aboard four Albacores of 823 Squadron as spares.

THE ACTION

If secrecy was not something which the naval planners could always count on during the Second World War, in the Mediterranean the situation was almost impossible. At one end, Alexandria was teeming with spies for the

Two 885 Squadron Sea Hurricanes ranged aft on *Victorious* while an Albacore of 827 Squadron takes off from the *Indomitable*. *Eagle* is next in line, with *Furious* just visible astern. (IWM A15961)

Axis powers, while at the other end, regardless of the loyalty of the Gibraltarians, the Straits of Gibraltar were so narrow – just eight miles at one point – that shipping movements could be observed from Morocco and Spain, or Spanish territory at Ceuta and Melilla. Spain's sympathies lay with the Germans and Italians, whose support in the Civil War had aided a Nationalist victory.

Although the main Italian fleet was confined to harbour because of fuel shortages, the convoy was attacked by submarines, motor torpedo-boats and from the air.

Passing Gibraltar on the night of 10/11 August, the convoy suffered its first loss at 13.15 on 11 August, when the German submarine *U-73* fired four torpedoes at the elderly carrier, *Eagle*.

George Aymes was an air mechanic aboard *Eagle* during Operation Pedestal. He had been on 'club runs' across the Mediterranean before, originally in *Argus* delivering aircraft to Malta, and then during the hard-fought 'Harpoon' convoy in June in *Eagle*. Below decks at the time, he heard 'four distinct detonations and the ship lurched . . . but I had not realized the ship had been torpedoed, I thought that we had hit a school of whales.'[1] He was soon disabused of this notion as the ship rapidly started to list to port, and he ran up to the flight deck, where he could see that the crew were already starting to jump into the water. He saw 'two marines jump, but they hit the ship's torpedo blisters and the impact drove their legs up into their torsoes, killing them'.[2] *Eagle* sank in just four minutes, taking with her 160 out of her total ship's company of 953.

In common with many of the survivors, Aymes spent some time in the water before a destroyer could risk stopping to pick them up.

Eagle had a four aircraft patrol of Sea Hurricanes in the air at the time, sharing this duty with both *Victorious* and *Indomitable*.

The attack was witnessed by those aboard the other ships in the convoy, including a Sea Hurricane pilot strapped in his cockpit aboard *Indomitable*.

'The wind was chancy, and we were to be boosted off. I was in position on the catapult, engine running. The flight deck engineer waggled the ailerons to draw my attention to something or other, and I looked out over the port side to see what he wanted. And, as I did so, I stared in shocked surprise beyond him to where *Eagle* was steaming level with us, half-a-mile away. For as I turned, smoke and steam suddenly poured from her, and she took on a heavy list to port, and the air shook with a series of muffled explosions.

'There had hardly been time to assimilate the fact that she had been hit before she had capsized and sank; and when I took off a few minutes later, my mind was still numbed by what I had seen. It was as if, at any moment, our own ship might stagger and lurch and list, and our aircraft go slithering down the deck into the sea.'[3]

Eagle had been considered too slow for frontline operations, and had spent the earlier part of the war escorting troop convoys from Australia to North Africa, before ferrying aircraft to Malta; 183 fighter planes reached the island safely, having been flown off her flight deck.

Later that day, at 20.45, came the first air attack by thirty-six Luftwaffe aircraft flying from bases in Sardinia, followed by another air attack at 09.15 on 12 August, this time by twenty Luftwaffe aircraft, before a combined Luftwaffe and Regia Aeronautica force of seventy aircraft attacked at noon. The Luftwaffe's Junkers Ju.87 Stuka dive-bombers and Ju.88 bombers were the real threat to the convoy and its escorts.

The fleet's fighters were either in the air or kept ready for action. Lieutenant B. Ritchie of 800 Squadron, embarked aboard *Indomitable*,

---

[1,2] Imperial War Museum Sound Archive.

[3–5] Peter Smith. *Pedestal: The Malta Convoy of August 1942*, William Kimber, 1970.

The last moments of *Eagle* as she sinks after being torpedoed during Operation Pedestal – one of the escorts is dropping depth charges in an unsuccessful attack on *U-73*. (IWM A11355)

had just taken off when he saw a Stuka dive-bomber at 400 feet, having just carried out its attack. He chased it for a mile through the thick flak thrown up by the fleet's anti-aircraft guns before carrying out a beam attack at 100 yards. Part of the Stuka's engine cowling broke off, and as he closed on the aircraft he saw the rear-gunner double up, and the aircraft started to dive, belching smoke and flame, before one wing dropped and it crashed into the sea from 200 feet, leaving no survivors.

The convoy's escorts managed to sink a U-boat at around 16.00, before another combined strike of 100 aircraft attacked around 19.00, sinking one ship and seriously damaging the aircraft carrier *Indomitable*, putting her out of action.

Arthur Lawson was a leading telegraphist aboard the carrier.

'Round about 19.30, the attacks were being concentrated on the carriers and *Indomitable* was under continuous bombing, while fighting tooth and nail. Suddenly the ship shuddered from stem to stern and one had the strangest feeling of great resistance being exerted by the whole vessel to stop herself from being pressed under water. A strange hush prevailed immediately following the hits, followed by the bedlam of the damage control parties going about their grisly work. My most vivid memory of that moment was seeing an officer finishing a drink he was having with half his head blown away!'[4]

Victorious had to recover those of *Indomitable*'s aircraft which were in the air at the time.

Life aboard the carriers was stressful, especially for the fighter pilots and those on the flight deck and in the hangars supporting them. An engineer aboard *Victorious* described the scene.

'The pilots snatched meals as they could and rushed back on deck to take their places on the revolving wheel of readiness. And in the hangar the maintenance crews worked like men possessed to make the aircraft serviceable as they were struck down. They were coming in now with battle damage to be repaired as well as the normal trouble of oil leaks, coolant leaks, sprained oleo-legs and what-not. The hangar itself was a shambles as aircraft were ranged, struck down, stowed, refuelled and re-armed at top speed and the hangar deck became more and more slippery with oil.'[5]

There were very real limits to what the carriers' fighters could achieve. The Sea Hurricane could tackle a Stuka, but the Ju.88 was faster and much more difficult. Vice-Admiral Syfret, in command of the operation, later wrote, 'The speed and the height of the Ju.88s made the fleet fighters' task a hopeless one. It will be a happy day when the fleet is equipped with modern fighter aircraft.'

The main covering force withdrew, according to plan, once this raid ended, but an hour later, twenty Luftwaffe aircraft from Sicily attacked the convoy at 20.00, sinking the cruiser *Cairo* and two merchant vessels, and damaging the cruiser *Nigeria* and three other ships, including the oil tanker, *Ohio*. The ships which were sunk by this force had already been badly damaged by earlier attacks.

Another five ships were sunk by MTBs, or E-boats, that night, while the cruiser *Manchester* was so badly damaged that she had to be sunk later.

At 08.00 on 13 August, twelve Luftwaffe aircraft from Sicily caused more damage, sinking another ship and inflicting further damage on the *Ohio*, which suffered still more damage when the Regia Aeronautica sent fifteen aircraft from Sicily at 11.25. After so much damage, the *Ohio*'s master decided to abandon ship as fires burnt out of control, but before they could be picked up they reboarded the ship, realizing that she was still afloat. Aided by one of the escorting warships, *Ohio* limped into Malta on 15 August, arriving behind the other four merchant vessels which had also survived the ordeal, and some of which had arrived on 13 August. *Ohio*'s crew were valiant, but they were also lucky. Another merchant vessel behind the main body of the convoy was quickly sunk by a U-boat, which pounced on stragglers without mercy.

The *Ohio*'s cargo of fuel proved invaluable in increasing offensive aerial activity out of Malta and attacks on Axis forces in North Africa.

The cost of the convoy was nine merchantmen sunk, the loss of the *Eagle*, two cruisers and a destroyer, damage to *Indomitable* and *Victorious*, and to two cruisers.

Strangely, after the battle to reach Malta, there were no attacks on the ships as they unloaded in Grand Harbour!

COMMENT

Operation Pedestal was costly, but the loss of Malta at a time when the tide of the war in North Africa was starting to turn would have been a major disaster, not simply a setback. The operation was a strategic success, bringing closer the day when the Allies could move to the offensive in the Mediterranean. Nevertheless, once again the Royal Navy was paying the price for neglecting naval aviation between the two wars.

ATTACKS ON CONVOY PQ18

RUSSIA TURNS TO THE WEST FOR SUPPORT

After Germany invaded the Soviet Union at the end of June 1941, Russia turned to the western allies for support. The Soviet Union had neither the manufacturing capability nor the technology to meet the German onslaught. Under pressure from Stalin and from Roosevelt, Britain's wartime leader, Winston Churchill, reluctantly agreed to a major convoy operation taking military equipment to the Soviet Union. The only practical route open for this was around the northern tip of German-occupied Norway to Murmansk and Archangel. In summer, the almost constant daylight left the convoys open to attack from the air, and from German U-boats and surface raiders, such as the giant battleship *Tirpitz*. In winter, many of these hazards remained, but there was also the almost continual bad weather, with just three hours of weak twilight in the middle of the day. One officer who had problems eating a meal as his cruiser rolled to angles of 30 degrees consoled himself with the thought that life must have been even more difficult on the corvettes and destroyers, which rolled as much as 50 degrees, and occasionally more!

The bad weather also hindered the defence of the convoy. Apart from the sheer misery of sea sickness and exhaustion, especially for wartime 'hostilities only' ratings, bad weather also made launching and recovering aircraft difficult, and often impossible. Gale force winds were enough to tear an aircraft off the flight deck, with winds exceeding the flying speed of a Swordfish. Problems with severe frost and ice meant that flying operations were simply impossible. The Swordfish by this time were being equipped with radar for anti-submarine patrols, but first they had to get airborne.

Shore-based protection for the convoys came from bases in the Shetland Islands, to the north-east of Scotland, Iceland, round which the summer convoy route passed so as to keep as far away as possible from Luftwaffe Focke-Wulf Fw.200 Condor anti-shipping aircraft, and from Royal Air Force units based in the Soviet Union. The lesson was clear: carrier-borne aircraft were a necessity, yet again.

This was a war in which the odds were incredibly high. Richard Woodman points out in his book, *Arctic Convoys*, 'the sinking of a single 10,000 ton freighter was the equivalent, in terms of material destroyed, of a land battle'. So often more than one such ship was lost. Worse still, survival in the cold seas could be measured in minutes for shipwrecked seamen and downed airmen. Sad to relate, on reaching their destinations, having fought the enemy and the weather, there was little in the way of a welcome from the Russians. Some of those involved were quite clear that it was a case not of allies, but of nations with a common foe. For this, the Russians received material which would have been invaluable on other fronts, including ships, naval and merchant, which could have made a difference elsewhere.

SHIPS AND AIRCRAFT

The aircraft consisted mainly of the Fairey Swordfish and the Hawker Sea Hurricane, both of which have been mentioned earlier.

Avenger at sea with six Sea Hurricanes ranged on her deck. Her merchant vessel origins can be seen clearly. (IWM FL1268)

The ship in this case was one of the then still new escort carriers, either converted from a merchantman or built from new on a merchant hull; the C.3 merchant vessel hull was the most popular. While most escort carriers, or CVEs, were American-built, a number were also built in British shipyards, as cargo ships under construction were taken over by the Admiralty and converted: some of these were converted to cargo vessels after the war. These ships were much smaller and slower than the fleet carriers, managing just 17 knots. An interim stage in the development of the escort carrier had been the MAC ships, which were merchant vessels with a wooden flight deck built over their holds, but this was not a very satisfactory compromise.

Although the first escort carrier *Audacity* had joined the fleet in December 1941, early operations had been confined to the North Atlantic. In 1942 the Royal Navy had still to acquire the skills of operating from a short flight deck, just 440 feet, in high latitudes, but it was to be the escort carrier which did so much to ensure the protection of convoys, with its first successes being on the North Atlantic. Later, the availability of so many inexpensive carriers was to ensure their participation at landings of Allied forces in the Mediterranean and the Pacific, for even though these ships were unable to keep up with the rest of the fleet, they could provide the air cover needed for troops ashore until airfields could be captured and secured.

ACTION

The most famous of the Russian convoys was the ill-fated PQ17, which sailed from Hvalfiordur, in Iceland, on 27 June 1942. This did not have a carrier among its escorts. Instead, we are concerned with PQ18, which left Loch Ewe in Scotland on 2 September 1942. The escort for this convoy included two destroyers, two anti-aircraft ships converted from merchant vessels, four corvettes, three minesweepers and two submarines. Four anti-submarine trawlers were also included, and there was a rescue ship, while three American motor minesweepers being delivered to the Soviet Navy were also to act as rescue ships. There was also the new cruiser, *Scylla*, and the equally new escort carrier, *Avenger*. *Avenger*'s aircraft were not the only ones available to the convoy. A CAM (Catapult Armed Merchant) ship, *Empire Morn*, had a single Sea Hurricane fighter, which could be catapulted off to intercept an enemy intruder, and afterwards her pilot would either bail out or ditch.

Avenger had three radar-equipped Swordfish for anti-submarine duties and twelve Sea Hurricanes of 883 Naval Air Squadron available for operations, although several aircraft were stored in a dismantled state in her holds, ready for assembly as replacements for the return voyage.

The rendezvous for *Avenger* to join the convoy and the other escorts was off Iceland. It was not an auspicious start. On her way north from her base at Scapa Flow on the mainland of Orkney, *Avenger*'s engines failed because her fuel was contaminated, and a Sea Hurricane was washed overboard in

Swordfish depth-charge a suspected U-boat in northern waters. (IWM A17567)

stormy seas. One of her crew recalled the passage north as being 'an absolute nightmare . . . in the hangar the aircraft were secured at wing tips and tail with steel ropes which were completely useless, in a matter of minutes they all broke loose and were smashing into one another and the sides of the hangar.'[1] Worse was to come. As they struggled with the aircraft and tried to keep their feet on the pitching and rolling hangar deck, there came the sound of rolling and banging from the lift well, where fused 500-lb bombs had broken loose. 'We finally secured the bombs by laying down duffle coats with rope ties and when a bomb rolled over the coats we secured them with the ties. God only knows how we did it, but we did!'[2]

While at Iceland attempting to remedy her engine problems, *Avenger* was discovered by a Focke-Wulf Fw.200 Condor. It dropped a stick of bombs which exploded close to the ship but failed to do any damage. The Luftwaffe mistook the ship for the elderly aircraft carrier *Argus*, which was a not unreasonable mistake to make, although the designer of *Argus* had been far better at concealing her merchant vessel origins!

On the way to Iceland, the convoy itself had been spotted by a German U-boat, which reported the sighting. On 8 September, after the convoy had departed the rendezvous, another Condor also discovered them, although *Avenger* was still at Iceland on this day and unable to offer the protection of her aircraft. After that, thick overcast cloud hid the ships from patrolling aircraft, until 12 September, when a Blohm und Voss Bv.138 flying-boat came out of the clouds. *Avenger* immediately launched a flight of four Sea Hurricanes, but these failed to catch the reconnaissance aircraft as it disappeared back into the clouds. A further attempt to intercept German aircraft was made at 04.00 the following day by the Sea Hurricanes, after these had come across some of the carrier's Swordfish on anti-

submarine patrol. Again, the Luftwaffe aircraft, a Bv.138 and a Junkers Ju.88 reconnaissance aircraft, disappeared into the clouds.

The role of the Swordfish was primarily that of anti-submarine work, but the aircraft also provided a constant lookout for other activity, and on this occasion noticed that Bv.138s were dropping mines ahead of the convoy. Attempts by the Swordfish to attack surfaced U-boats were foiled by attacks by the Bv.138s, as well as by the U-boats' own anti-aircraft armament.

As the day progressed, more Junkers Ju.88s arrived, making a high-level bombing attack on the convoy through gaps in the clouds. Once again, Sea Hurricanes were sent to intercept, but these early aircraft had only machine-guns, rather than cannon, and could not concentrate enough fire on the bombers to have any effect. The Sea Hurricanes landed on *Avenger* to refuel and re-arm. While this was in progress, the Luftwaffe launched its main attack against the convoy, with the first wave of aircraft being picked up on the long range radar of the escorts at 15.40.

Some twenty Luftwaffe Ju.88s from Kampfgeschwader 30 flew overhead to make a diversionary high-level attack, causing the ships below to take evasive action. As this was happening, twenty-eight Heinkel He.111 and eighteen Junkers Ju.88s of KG.26 made a torpedo-bombing attack, with another seventeen Ju.88s of KG.30 following, the aircraft being led to the convoy by shadowing Ju.88s and Bv.138s. The aircraft swept in at some 20 feet above the waves, ignoring the escorts and concentrating on the merchant vessels, which was the correct strategy. The Sea Hurricanes were still on the carrier's flight deck and could take not part in the operation. Her commanding officer, Commander A.P. Colthurst, later wrote, 'At the end of this unfortunate day, I realized that my operation of the ship and of her fighters had been very wrong'.[3]

[1-6] Richard Woodman. *Arctic Convoys*, John Murray, 1994.

A Sea Hurricane on *Avenger*'s lift. (IWM A10982)

Sea Hurricane takes off from *Avenger*'s cramped flight deck. (IWM A10978)

Below decks, *Avenger's* crew grab a hasty meal. (IWM A10968)

The convoy was signalled to make a mass 45 degree turn, the usual defensive measure against torpedo attack, but the large size of it, and the inexperience of many of those aboard, especially the American ships, meant that not all of the ships followed this manoeuvre. Wild anti-aircraft fire, often from ships not in danger of attack and unable to get anywhere near an enemy aircraft, also meant that exposed crew members on other ships were exposed to fire and to falling shells and bullets. The attack was pressed home with considerable courage and effectiveness. Ships were hit and one, the *Empire Stevenson*, with a cargo of explosives, disappeared in one huge explosion. The more fortunate were able to jump direct from their stricken ships onto the ice-encrusted decks of the escort and rescue vessels.

In just fifteen minutes, eight ships had been lost for just five Luftwaffe aircraft shot down.

A later attack by Heinkel He.115 floatplanes was beaten off. One of the aircraft was attacked by four Sea Hurricanes, but escaped after shooting one of them down.

Avenger now started to maintain constant patrols with the Sea Hurricanes, which spent no more than twenty-five minutes in the air before landing to refuel, so that there were always aircraft airborne. Their armament and relatively poor turn of speed meant that they could do no more than break up enemy bomber formations.

On 14 September, the first Swordfish of the day found a German submarine on the surface, but *U-589* dived, leaving the Swordfish to mark the spot with a smoke flare. After the Swordfish had departed, the submarine surfaced again to continue charging her batteries, a destroyer, *Onslow*, was promptly dispatched to attack her. On seeing the destroyer, *U-589* dived, but was eventually depth-charged and destroyed by *Onslow*.

A pattern emerged of the Swordfish being intimidated by the reconnaissance Bv.138s and Ju.88s, and then being forced back towards the convoy, where the anti-aircraft ships would fire at the Luftwaffe aircraft, which then moved away. The Swordfish would then venture out in front of the convoy again, only for the intimidation to resume, and the whole cycle to start again.

The next move was an attack on *Avenger*. Fortunately, this was spotted by the duty Swordfish as, at 12.37, the Ju.88 torpedo-bombers of KG.26 raced towards the carrier at wave-top height to evade her radar. *Avenger* took defensive measures with her two escorting destroyers, moving at full speed, a mere 17 knots, while her patrolling Sea Hurricanes attempted to intervene and break up the attack. This time, no ships were hit, but KG.26 lost eleven aircraft. Then KG.30 pressed home a dive-bombing attack at 12.45, diving from 2,000 feet. These attacks lasted until 14.10, and were constantly harried by the Sea Hurricanes, with a strong AA fire from the convoy. Just one aircraft was shot down, but none of the ships in the convoy was hit.

Meanwhile, another attack by twenty-two He.111s and eighteen Ju.88 torpedo-bombers flew in, attacking from ahead of the convoy, straight into the AA defences of the cruiser *Scylla* and four Sea Hurricanes. The Sea Hurricane fighters dived on to the dive-bombers as the Germans lined up on *Avenger*, flying straight into the convoy's AA fire so that three of the four Sea Hurricanes were shot down by 'friendly fire'. Fortunately, all three pilots were rescued. Commander Colthurst managed to manoeuvre *Avenger* to avoid the torpedoes, combing their tracks.

Only one ship, the *Mary Luckenbach*, was lost in this attack, but she was laden with explosives, and when she blew up she took one of the Luftwaffe aircraft with her. Horace Bell, Chief Radio Operator aboard the rescue

The munitions ship, *Mary Luckenbach*, blows up, taking her Luftwaffe attacker with her, as seen from *Avenger*. (IWM A12275)

Admiral Sir John Tovey, in command of the Home Fleet, visits *Avenger* and inspects the ship's company. (IWM A10963)

ship *Copeland*, recalled that the leading aircraft had come 'in to about 300 yards . . . before dropping his torpedoes and then swept on. . . . As he passed, the gunner raked him fore and aft and bright tongues of flame flickered from his starboard engine. He dipped, recovered, dipped again and seemed just about to crash, when his torpedoes reached their mark and the ship simply vanished into thin air. As for the plane, it broke up into small pieces.

'In the stupefying moments of silence that followed, we watched as an enormous column of smoke billowed upwards, slow, thick, black and ugly – no flame this time, just smoke, up and up until it reached the clouds. Gradually, from the over-hanging top, there drifted down dust, like a shower of rain, and that was all.'[4]

Altogether, five Luftwaffe aircraft were shot down, and another nine damaged so badly that they could not be repaired.

Avenger's aircraft claimed five certain and three probable kills during the day.

The following day, the remaining Sea Hurricanes and the Swordfish were in action again, with the fighters breaking up a number of high-level and dive-bombing attacks, although none of these compared with the massed attacks of the previous day.

Shortly after dawn on 16 September, the Swordfish were relieved of their patrolling by

Royal Air Force Consolidated Catalina flying-boats operating from their Russian base. Later that day, the convoy crossed with the homeward-bound convoy, QP14, with the survivors of PQ17, and *Avenger* and some of the other escort vessels transferred to this convoy.

Aboard *Avenger*, the ship's company struggled to replace the four Sea Hurricanes lost on the outward voyage, and managed to assemble five, more than replacing the losses.

As the convoy continued to Archangel, which it reached on 20 September, the *Empire Morn*'s Hurricane had to be launched as the convoy's sole remaining means of defence. Her pilot, Flying Officer Burr, was shot at by the ships in the convoy as soon as he was launched. Even so, he flew on to attack a flight of attacking torpedo-bombers, setting one on fire, so that none of the ships in the convoy was hit. Rather than waste his aircraft, Burr then sought a course to a shore base, and successfully landed at Keg Ostrov airfield, near Archangel, with fuel tanks almost empty.

THE WEATHER WAS A WORSE ENEMY

Conditions aboard the ships on the Russian convoys were grim, but worse still was the plight of those who had to take to the air.

The decks of the ships had to be cleared of snow and ice to save them from capsizing under the accumulated weight, and nowhere was this more essential than on the flat, exposed flight deck of an aircraft carrier. Each day, from early autumn through to the following spring, working parties would have to clear the decks so that flying could begin, and then keep the decks clear during the day using steam hoses, shovels and brooms.

Of the airmen, the crews of the Swordfish suffered most, and the telegraphist-air gunner, or TAG, and the observer, as the Royal Navy termed their navigators, in the exposed open cockpit behind the pilot, endured the worst of it. Pilots and other aircrew alike wore as much as they could, but as one pilot put it: 'We wore as much clothing as we could, but there is a limit to what you can get in a cockpit.'[5] The cold was so intense that it was not unusual for tailwheels to break off on landing, so brittle had the metal become when the Arctic cold was intensified by wind and by the slipstream even of the slow Swordfish.

In the Naval and Military Club in London, a barogram is displayed showing the weather conditions endured by Convoy RA64 during 17–27 February 1945. Leaving the Kola Inlet, near Murmansk, in a Force 8 gale, the convoy passed through Force 10, 11 and even 12 storms. That was in addition to the attacks by German submarines and aircraft.

It was important to make sure that the aircraft was completely clean of ice before take-off, but landing on presented a severe challenge, and it could be a cruel end to an exhausting flight in freezing conditions. As the ship pitched and rolled, catching the flight deck at exactly the right moment as it plunged down some twenty feet or so, and then reared up by the same amount, became an almost impossible task.

On 1 April 1944, a Grumman Avenger from the escort carrier *Tracker* attempted to land back on the carrier after making an abortive attack on a surfaced U-boat, when the aircraft's depth charges had failed to disengage from the fuselage. The pilot, Sub-Lieutenant Ballantyne, finally managed to drop his depth charges before attempting a landing. He approached the ship with his engine at full power, but rammed the 'round down' at the stern, embedding the aircraft's engine into the deck, and it promptly burst into flames. As fire swept around the aircraft, on the quarter deck below the ship's own depth charges were jettisoned, and fire-fighting parties started to hose the aircraft from both decks, despite the

Fighting fire aboard another escort carrier, *Tracker*, after one of her Avengers crashed during landing on 1 April 1944. (IWM A22863)

fact that they had been warned by the pilot that he believed that one of his depth charges was still 'hung up' on the aircraft and there was a real risk of explosion. With one wing of the blazing aircraft lying across one of the ship's Bofors gun, the ammunition in the ready-use locker started to explode, as did that in the aircraft itself. Ballantyne fell out of the aircraft, his clothing on fire, onto the deck below. The fire-fighters immediately started to hose him down, but before they could put the fire out the poor man, 'demented by pain . . . finally collapsed dead . . .'[6]

COMMENT

Sending an aircraft carrier to sea with just fifteen aircraft was an inadequate response to the threat from German air and naval forces. The irony of the situation was that large numbers of Hurricane fighters were shipped to the Soviet Union, and no doubt many were lost as the ships carrying them were sunk, yet the benefit of sending fewer aircraft to the Soviet Union and keeping more to protect the convoys, seemed to have been lost on the politicians. Worse still, the Russians often received better aircraft than those available for the convoys.

Commander Colthurst was very critical of his strategy for protecting the convoy, and took steps to change it, showing remarkable flexibility in his thinking as well as considerable integrity. However, maintaining constant air cover with such a small number of aircraft, was virtually impossible. The aircraft also required heavier armament, and ideally should have been the faster Seafire, or, even better, Grumman F4F Wildcat.

PART THREE

JAPAN ON THE OFFENSIVE

BACKGROUND

Of all the nations taking part in the Second World War, it could be argued that Japan was the most ready at the outset of the war. Nevertheless, before long, Japanese weaknesses in technology and industrial capacity, and in the planning and preparation necessary for a prolonged conflict, were to become apparent. By contrast, the United States may have been caught with its guard down at the outset, but had the technology and industrial capacity to fight the war, no matter how long it took. The more thoughtful Japanese knew that they needed to win time at the outset, but even these might not have been aware of just how overwhelming the American reaction, militarily and industrially, would be. Once the United States was in the war, its factories and shipyards, and, for naval aviators, training facilities, were enough not only for its own needs, but able to augment those of the United Kingdom and Soviet Union as well.

PEARL HARBOR

JAPAN'S PRE-EMPTIVE STRIKE

War between Japan and the United States had seemed inevitable to the Japanese, jealous of American influence in the Pacific. The Americans for their part were determined to curb Japan's advance into China. Japan's ambitions for Indo-China were also highlighted by the signing of a non-aggression pact between Japan and the Soviet Union. In December 1940 the United States imposed an embargo on the sale of scrap metal and war materials to Japan, following this with the freezing of Japan's American assets in July 1941, after Japan invaded Indo-China. The United Kingdom and the Netherlands followed the American lead, denying Japan the currency with which to purchase oil and other raw materials. This left Japan solely with a strategic reserve of 55 million barrels of oil, enough for eighteen months of war, unless she could find an alternative source by invading the Dutch East Indies.

The commander-in-chief of the Imperial Japanese Navy's First Fleet, Admiral Isoroku Yamamoto, was opposed to war with the United States. He knew that Japan could not match the United States militarily or in industrial output. With remarkable foresight, he felt that Japan could win a major victory in the first year of war, but that by the second year, the United States would have recovered and would move to the offensive. The Imperial Japanese Navy had superior strength to the Americans in the Pacific, but would be weaker than the United States Navy if it had to face the full strength of the combined Pacific and Atlantic fleets.

From 1940, Yamamoto and his staff began to consider ways of providing a major blow to the United States Navy, so that Japan would have at least six months, and ideally longer, in which to establish its planned empire, the Greater East Asia Co-Prosperity Sphere. Not least of the requirements was to establish a territorial base which would ensure access to supplies of oil and raw materials, vital for a country with few natural resources.

Admiral Isoroku Yamamoto, architect of the attack on Pearl Harbor, which he saw as buying time in the war against America. (IWM HU36485)

Akagi was Nagumo's flagship for the attack, and is seen here just before the outbreak of war in Europe. (IWM MH5933)

Yamamoto decided on a crippling blow to the US Pacific Fleet by attacking its main base at Pearl Harbor, on the Hawaiian island of Oahu. Without a base at Pearl Harbor, and with the loss of major units of the Pacific Fleet, it would take time for the United States to re-establish a significant naval presence in the area. The successful British raid on the Italian naval base at Taranto confirmed the feasibility of such an attack.

SHIPS AND AIRCRAFT

The Japanese carrier fleet for the attack on Pearl Harbor consisted of six ships: the First Carrier Division with the *Akagi*, converted from a battlecruiser, and the converted battleship *Kaga*; the Second Carrier Division had the smaller *Hiryu* and *Soryu*, and in the newly formed Fifth Carrier Division were the two new purpose-built carriers, the sister ships *Shokaku* and *Zuikaku*. These latter ships were in many ways the equivalent of the British Illustrious class, being large fast

carriers. In contrast to the British ships *Shokaku* and *Zuikaku* had relatively little deck armour, but they were faster with a maximum speed of 35 knots. Both ships had conventional starboard islands, albeit with the typical downward curving twin funnels so beloved by the Japanese. More than seventy aircraft could be accommodated on each of the new ships, which had three lifts and were probably among the first carriers to have bulbous bows to enhance speed and stability.

The six carriers were responsible for carrying the 423 aircraft of the First Air Fleet. These included fighters, torpedo-carrying aircraft, dive-bombers and level, or horizontal, bombers.

The most famous of the Japanese aircraft of the Second World War was the Mitsubishi A6M, known to the Japanese as the 'Zero', but known officially to the Allies as 'Zeke'. This was a single-engined, single-seat, carrier fighter of outstanding performance, carrying two 20-mm cannon and two machine guns, usually with a 925 h.p. Nakajima Sakae

Mitsubishi A6M Zero at the head of aircraft ranged for take-off for the raid. (US National Archives 80-G 71198)

12 radial, capable of speeds in excess of 300 m.p.h. Its weaknesses were the lack of armour protection for the pilot and the absence of self-sealing fuel tanks, but this produced an extremely light and agile aircraft. Of course, without a navigator, Zeros depended on the bombers which it was escorting for guidance on longer missions.

While advancing forces sometimes manage to capture enemy shore-based aircraft, by their very nature carrier-borne aircraft are less likely to fall into the hands of the opposing forces. Nevertheless, after the Aleutians campaign in 1942, the Americans did manage to obtain a Zero which was virtually intact. The aircraft had attempted a forced landing in the Aleutians, and was found upside down in a swamp, with the unfortunate pilot dead from a broken neck.

The aircraft was promptly retrieved and shipped to the test centre at Wright Field in the United States. After extensive examination of the aircraft, Colonel Heywood of the Wright Field Test Center reported it as being '. . . a light sports plane with a 1,300 h.p. engine'.[1] The Zero weighed just 3,920 lb unladen, against the L.2C Seafire's 6,200 lb, despite similarities in size. The Japanese had considered only speed and structural strength in designing the aircraft, but had no concern at all for the pilot, with the Zero providing no armour protection for the pilot, engine or fuel tanks. This information led to the advice to Allied fighter pilots that they should avoid

[1] Brian Johnson. *Fly Navy*, David & Charles, 1981.

dogfights with the much more agile Zero whenever possible, and instead attack from a dive or in a climb, so that one well-aimed burst of fire could destroy the Japanese aircraft.

Another aircraft, which has always been less famous, and was unknown at the time to many in the west, was one of the most advanced carrier-borne aircraft at the time of its first flight in early 1937. The Nakajima B5N was everything the Swordfish was not. Known to the Allies as 'Kate', this single-engined monoplane had all-metal stressed-skin construction, power-folding wings, retractable landing gear, integral wing tanks and a variable-pitch propeller. It was also powered by a Nakajima Sakae 12 radial, usually of 1,000 h.p., giving it a top speed of 230 m.p.h. Most of the damage to the US Pacific Fleet could be attributed to this aircraft, since there were 40 torpedo versions and 103 level bomber versions in the attack on Pearl Harbor.

The third aircraft to make its presence felt at Pearl Harbor was the Aichi D3A1, known to the Allies as 'Val'. Influenced by German work on dive-bombers, the Aichi D3A1 could carry a single 550-lb bomb. A low-wing monoplane, with a fixed spatted under-carriage, it was obviously slower than many of the other aircraft at Pearl Harbor, but it was manoeuvrable, powered by a single 1,075 h.p. Mitsubishi Kinsei 44 radial engine.

THE ACTION

The leader of the attack on Pearl Harbor was Commander Mitsuo Fuchida of the Imperial Japanese Navy, who had been volunteered for the task by his friend and fellow officer, Commander Minoru Genda. Fuchida had regarded the United States as the potential future enemy from his days as an officer cadet, opting to learn English. Fuchida was senior flight commander of the First Air Fleet.

Genda's preferred option was for an aerial torpedo attack. In fact he insisted upon it, despite Fuchida's objections to the shallow waters of Pearl Harbor, just 40 feet deep, and the likelihood that the American ships would be protected by torpedo nets, although Genda thought that this would be unlikely. What was indisputable was that torpedoes would be useless if ships were double berthed, as they would be if the main body of the Pacific

A captured Aichi D3A1 'Val' dive-bomber as used at Pearl Harbor. (FAAM For.Mil/90)

Fleet was in port. Dive bombs, on the other hand, while highly effective against aircraft carriers, and especially those without armoured decks, were likely to be of little use against the heavily armoured decks of battleships. Level, or horizontal bombing, was Fuchida's main strength. Although the Japanese Naval Air Force had shown itself to be poor at this, Genda allowed Fuchida to plan using this as one of his options.

Fuchida's commander, Vice-Admiral Nagumo, knew little about naval air power, and throughout the planning and the campaign itself, Nagumo seems to have been distinctly unenthusiastic about the enterprise. Meanwhile, Fuchida was given a free hand, selecting the best specialists to join his planning team, while attempting to maintain secrecy.

The JNAF had developed a nine-plane 'arrowhead' formation for bombing, but with fifty bombers available for training, Fuchida put the horizontal bombers onto five-plane formations – without doing any harm to their accuracy which reached 70 per cent in due course. This supposed Achilles heel was now a strong point, and it is strange to note that the great strength of the JNAF, dive-bombing, was by comparison only achieving 40 per cent hits.

The aircrew were ready and well prepared for their assignment by November. The decision was taken that the air strike should be in two waves, a decision largely dictated by the sheer impossibility of getting all of the aircraft away from the carriers in one wave.

During the afternoon of 17 November, Admiral Yamamoto visited the *Akagi* to wish the officers luck before the fleet sailed. Yamamoto's immediate concern was that the young airmen would seriously underestimate their opponent, so he warned them, 'Japan has faced many worthy opponents in her long history – Mongols, Chinese, Russians – but the United States is the most worthy of all. You must be prepared for great American resistance. Admiral Kimmel, commander-in-

chief of the Pacific Fleet, is known to be farsighted and aggressive, so you cannot count upon surprise. You may have to fight your way to the target.'[2]

Nagumo himself expected to lose between a third and half of his ships – his predictions of aircraft losses are not recorded, if he ever thought about these!

On their way to Hawaii, the fleet refuelled on 6 December, beginning at 08.30. They had already been advised that the war would begin on 8 December, the Japanese date which, due to the international date line, was a day ahead of the United States so that in fact war broke out on the morning of Sunday 7 December. Fuchida and his colleagues had no qualms about a surprise attack on the United States, since Japan had never declared war in advance of opening hostilities.

The Japanese aircrew for the first wave were awake at 05.00, breakfasting as their ships pitched and rolled in heavy seas – Fuchida afterwards recalled that had it been a training exercise, he would not have permitted flying in such weather. As it happened, the poor weather contributed to the element of surprise.

Fuchida's plane was being flown by Lieutenant Mutsuzaki, leaving Fuchida, although an accomplished pilot, free to concentrate on directing the operation. As Fuchida climbed in, the *Akagi*'s senior maintenance crewman handed him a white scarf. 'All of the maintenance crew would like to go along to Pearl Harbor,' he shouted above the roar of the engines. 'Since we can't, we want you to take this hachimaki as a symbol that we are with you in spirit.' Touched, Fuchida tied the scarf samurai-fashion around his flight helmet and scrambled into the aircraft.[3]

Despite the bad weather and heavy pitching of the ships, the aircraft took off in the dark with few accidents, and by 06.15 Fuchida was able to signal to the circling

[2-5] Gordon W. Prange with Donald M. Goldstein and Katherine V. Dillon. *God's Samurai*, Brassey's, US.

真珠湾 十二月七日午前八時

第一次真珠湾攻撃隊隊長

淵田中佐
（撮影者）

1945年 11月8日
横須賀海軍基地にて発見。

APPROX. 0800 DECEMBER 7, 1941
THE FIRST PLANE DROPS THE FIRST
BOMB ON PEARL HARBOR.

PHOTO TAKEN BY SQUADRON LEADER
LT. COMMANDER FUCHIDA, WHO LED
THE FIRST WAVE TO THE ATTACK.

PICTURE FOUND AT YOKOSUKA NAVY
BASE, SOUTH OF TOKYO NOVEMBER 8
1945.

This is what Mitsuo Fuchida saw during the attack – a photograph taken from his aircraft. (IWM HU55848)

aircraft to follow him as he turned southwards towards Pearl Harbor. Already, the hangar and deck crews were manhandling the aircraft of the second wave out of their hangars and into ranges on the carrier decks. Japanese figures indicate that 353 aircraft were launched on that day out of more than 423 aboard the ships. The first wave consisted of 183 aircraft; 170 were in the second wave.

Sunrise came while the aircraft were en route to their target. To Fuchida, the rising red disc of the sun looked like the Japanese naval ensign, a good omen. He pushed back the cockpit canopy of his aircraft and let his hachimaki stream out behind him. He waved with both arms to the following airmen before closing the canopy again. At this point, the thick storm clouds below were causing him concern, first of all that his pilot might overfly the target or, secondly, that the cloud might obscure the target. He needn't have worried – before long a radio station in Hawaii was broadcasting the weather details and promising good visibility. The attacking aircraft had a radio operator able to speak English, while the station's music programme also acted as a navigational aid.

At the height of the raid, shipping on fire and heavy anti-aircraft fire. (IWM MH6014)

The lead aircraft passed over the northernmost point of Oahu at 07.30, and shortly afterwards Fuchida called out the order for attack position: 'Tenkai'. With his confidence of the element of surprise, heightened by the absence of any fighter patrols, Fuchida fired a rocket to signal that the attacking aircraft should prepare. Murata, leader of the torpedo-bombers, immediately led his aircraft downwards to the target. Seeing that one of the fighter leaders was keeping his aircraft in the cruise, Fuchida assumed that he had missed the first rocket and fired a second, but the dive-bomber commander, Takashi, took this as a double signal, indicating that enemy fighters were about to strike, and immediately led his dive-bombers down towards their targets. Fuchida's initial reaction to this was one of annoyance, but he soon realized that it would make little difference to the outcome of the battle raging below.

As the attacking aircraft dived down towards Pearl Harbour, ready to attack, Fuchida's aircraft remained at an altitude of some 10,000 feet, and he watched the giant naval base through binoculars as his aircraft circled. He thought that he counted seven battleships rather than the nine expected, but did not realise that the *Pennsylvania* was in drydock, while the *Utah*, now a target ship, had also been counted among the active fleet. He had been led to believe that there would not be any aircraft carriers in port, and this was the case, although he had hoped that the intelligence report would have been wrong.

At 07.49, Fuchida gave the attack signal, 'To! To! To!', and almost immediately the attacking aircraft positioned themselves ready for their targets. The absence of fighter defence or, at this early stage, anti-aircraft fire, confirmed the element of surprise, causing Fuchida to cry out 'Tora! Tora! Tora!' (or Tiger! Tiger! Tiger!), the code for surprise.

Down on Oahu, the Zeros raced across the dockyard and the airfields shooting up anything in their sights. The dive-bombers swooped down on Ford Island, their bombs exploding and causing fires and debris, while smoke billowed upwards. On Battleship Row, the torpedo-bombers came in so low that it seemed that they would never clear the towering superstructures of the giant ships. Success depended on the torpedo attack inflicting severe losses on the American fleet.

Then it was the turn of Fuchida's own horizontal bombers, and they prepared for their bombing run over Battleship Row. Fuchida gave the signal for them to go into action, crying, 'Tsu! Tsu! Tsu!' By this time, the anti-aircraft gunners aboard the warships below had started to put up a heavy barrage of fire. Fuchida's own aircraft took a hit, and then was shaken by a near miss. His pilot, Mutsuzaki, assured him that all was well, but after they landed later on the *Akagi*, Fuchida was to see that the control wires leading to the tailplane of his aircraft had been almost severed.

Despite the anti-aircraft fire, Fuchida took three bombing runs over the battleship *California*, before dropping his bomb. It was during the second run that he saw an explosion.

'The flame and smoke erupted skyward together,' he recalled. 'It was a hateful, mean-looking red flame, the kind that powder produces, and I knew at once that a big magazine had exploded.' His plane shuddered in the suction of the after-blast, but Mutsuzaki, skilful as he was brave, kept the damaged aircraft on an even keel. [4]

Fuchida had witnessed the end of the battleship *Arizona*, which ironically had had additional anti-aircraft defences and radar added the previous year.

As commander of the units involved in the operation, Fuchida now had to stay behind and watch developments below, including the attack by the second wave. Successful strikes against the airfields kept all but a handful of American aircraft on the ground, and some of those which attempted to take-off were destroyed as they struggled to get airborne. Fuchida was safe as he remained out of range of the AA fire to assess the damage for his report to Nagumo. From his vantage point he could see the *Arizona* blazing 'like a forest fire' as he put it. The *Oklahoma* had capsized, as had the old target ship, *Utah*, while both the *California* and *West Virginia* were slowly settling. Some distance away from the battleships, the light cruiser *Helena* had been crippled. Genda had been right – the Americans had not used torpedo nets to protect their ships.

Some fifty minutes after the attack had started, the second wave arrived, on time. Fuchida had planned to take leadership of the second wave as well, but he saw that its commander, Shimazaki, had his force well in hand, and so he decided to continue to watch as events unfolded.

The second wave consisted entirely of bombers, both dive-bombers and horizontal bombers. This was because the torpedo planes were seen as being vulnerable once the element of surprise was lost. As it was, the American defences were ready for the second wave, which encountered far fiercer resistance than the first. There were even some American fighters in the sky, and most of the attackers' losses of twenty-nine planes were from the second wave. At this stage, the Japanese were also victims of their own success, as smoke from the many fires below obscured the target area.

The commanding officer of the battleship *Nevada*, realizing that she would be safer at sea than moored in Battleship Row, was attempting to get his ship out of Pearl Harbor. Japanese dive-bombers swarmed down onto the ship, hoping to sink her and block the harbour mouth. In the face of such a heavy attack, the crew did well to beach her where she would not cause an obstruction.

Other ships were damaged, including the *Pennsylvania* and two destroyers, which were in drydock.

After the attack, the aircraft had orders to fly to a rendezvous point before undertaking the return flight to the aircraft carriers. This was a matter of mutual benefit. The bombers and torpedo aircraft needed fighter protection for the homeward run, while the fighters were at risk of getting lost flying over the ocean and needed the services of the navigators carried aboard the other aircraft. As the last aircraft to leave Pearl Harbor, Fuchida's aircraft was able to round up some stragglers.

On Fuchida's return to the *Akagi*, Genda welcomed him with the news that twenty-nine aircraft had been lost during the attack, while another fifteen had to be pushed over the side to make room for the returning aircraft to land, and another forty or so were damaged but reparable, including Fuchida's own aircraft.

Fuchida had seen the damage, but he had also seen some opportunities for a third or even a fourth wave, which could destroy the fuel tanks and other shore installations, sink the many smaller ships which had been neglected in favour of capital ships and cruisers, and finish off any battleships and cruisers still afloat.

Fuchida delayed responding to Nagumo's call to report to the bridge of the *Akagi* while he confirmed his observations with his flight commanders. Nagumo was impatient for news and eventually demanded to see Fuchida. Fuchida found the Vice-Admiral with the *Akagi*'s commanding officer, Captain Kiichi Hasegawa. He was asked for his report.

'Four battleships sunk,' responded Fuchida. 'I am confident of this from my personal observation.'

'Four battleships sunk!' repeated Nagumo. He seemed to roll the figure around on his tongue, savouring it. 'Good! What about the other four?'

'There hasn't been time to check results precisely, but it looks like three were seriously damaged, the other somewhat damaged although not quite so badly.' He went on to list the other ships sunk, using the berthing chart.[5]

Once Fuchida had completed his report, Nagumo enquired whether or not the US Pacific Fleet would be able to operate out of Pearl Harbor for six months. While Fuchida was able to confirm that the main force, by which he meant the battleships, would not be able to come out within six months, he made the point that many smaller vessels were still operational, as indeed were the shore installations, and pressed strongly for a further attack. Meanwhile, the hangar and flight deck crews were re-arming and refuelling aircraft, putting torpedoes on the dive-bombers since these would be more effective against ships at sea, for the fear was that units of the US Pacific Fleet, and especially the three aircraft carriers, would attack.

The Japanese were by now also very concerned about an attack on the carrier force by land-based aircraft, although again Fuchida pressed for a further attack, explaining that aircraft parked on the apron had been destroyed, along with many in the hangars, but that a substantial number probably remained airworthy. No plans had been made for a post-attack reconnaissance.

While Fuchida had lunch, the decision was taken not to make a further attack, and the flagship signalled a withdrawal to the north-west. Fuchida did the unthinkable for a Japanese officer. He stormed off to the bridge and addressed Nagumo directly, asking why an attack was not being ordered, only to be told abruptly by Nagumo's chief-of-staff, Kusaka, that the objectives of the raid on Pearl Harbor had been met!

COMMENT

Given that the timing of the outbreak of war was largely in Japanese hands, it seems strange that they were in many ways so ill-prepared. The fleet which attacked Pearl Harbor consisted of the cream of the carrier

No attempt was made to follow up the raid with a second attack, to seek the American carrier fleet or raid the Panama Canal. In fact, it was not until October 1944 that a plan was hatched using these aircraft-carrying submarines to attack the Panama Canal, but it never took place. Here *I.400*, *I.401* and *I.14* are moored alongside the tender *Proteus* in Tokyo Bay. (IWM MH 6694)

force, and while it included some new ships, there were also many conversions of other warships into aircraft carriers. In some cases these were less than satisfactory. Japan also attacked the United States, provoking American entry to the Second World War, but without an intensive programme of pilot training already in place. This was to prove a crucial weakness before the first year of war was over.

The need to maintain the element of surprise meant that the Japanese lacked the advantages which aerial reconnaissance gave the British at Taranto. A post-attack reconnaissance would also have helped them decide on their next course of action. Even so, with timing so critical, it seems ridiculous that they failed to take advantage of Fuchida's highly comprehensive report. Yamamoto was disappointed that Nagumo had not authorized a further attack, and felt that the much needed major blow to the United States Navy had been bungled, whether by cowardice or incompetence. Certainly, for a commander who had expected to lose between a third and half of his fleet, but had in fact lost nothing, Nagumo's stance is difficult to understand. A third, and perhaps a fourth wave would have ensured that fuel tanks and dry docks could have been destroyed, making early use of the base impossible, and further damage could have been inflicted on ships still at Pearl Harbor.

Some of the Japanese carriers were short on range, and no doubt refuelling and replenishment of munitions would have been necessary after a third and fourth wave attack. Nevertheless, while they had the strategic advantage, the Japanese should have sought combat with the three aircraft carriers of the Pacific Fleet. A further significant target with a priority second only to that of Pearl Harbor itself should have been the Panama Canal, highly vulnerable to damage given its extensive system of locks. This would have made reinforcement of the Pacific Fleet still more difficult. It would not be until October 1944 that this option was acted upon, using aircraft-carrying submarines, but the operation was abandoned before it began!

Pearl Harbor was a tactical success, but a strategic blunder.

RABAUL

JAPAN KEEPS UP THE PRESSURE

Early in January 1942, Nagumo took the other four carriers of the First Air Fleet, the *Akagi*, *Kaga*, *Shokaku* and *Zuikaku*, with their supporting battleships, cruisers and destroyers, to cover assaults in Malaya, the Philippines, Dutch East Indies, New Guinea, and the islands off its eastern shore. *Soryu* and *Hiryu* were originally earmarked for this task, but were being replenished and their crews rested after Wake Island. This meant that Japan was committing its four best and largest aircraft carriers to the new operation.

Effective use was being made of carrier air power in the sense that carrier-borne aircraft were not expected to operate when land-based aircraft could mount operations. The invasion of the Philippines in late December had involved major fleet units but no aircraft carriers, since the area was within range of land-based aircraft.

The next target for the aircraft carriers and their aircraft was the Bismarck Archipelago, to the north-east of New Guinea, with particular attention being paid to the Royal Australian Air Force base at Rabaul.

THE ACTION

Mitsuo Fuchida felt 'like a hunter sent to stalk a mouse with an elephant gun'[1] when, on 22 January, he led ninety fighters and bombers against the Australian air base at Rabaul, at the northern end of New Britain Island. The advanced Australian bases had only token garrisons, and Fuchida's force found little opposition and not much more in the way of worthwhile targets, so that bombs had to be jettisoned over heavy jungle rather than retained for a hazardous landing aboard precious aircraft carriers.

Although Fuchida convinced Nagumo of the folly of such heavyweight attacks against lightweight enemy forces, Yamamoto compounded the mistakes by ordering the carrier force back westward to Palau, a small atoll at the south-western end of the Marianas chain.

Meanwhile, Yamaguchi's Second Carrier Division with *Soryu* and *Hiryu* were supporting the invasion of the Dutch East Indies, with air strikes against Ambon.

[1] Gordon W. Prange with Donald M. Goldstein and Katherine V. Dillon. *God's Samurai*, Brassey's, US.

DARWIN: AUSTRALIA'S PEARL HARBOR

STRIKING SOUTH

For all the euphoria following the raid on Pearl Harbor, the Imperial Japanese Navy's leadership showed no understanding at all of the potential of naval air power. In itself, this might have been understandable; the British and American navies contained many who still saw warfare in terms of set-piece actions between opposing battle fleets, and who often seemed to resent both the naval aviators and the submariners. What is beyond comprehension is the way in which any advantage gained at Pearl Harbor was frittered away. Between Pearl Harbor and the unnecessary raid on Rabaul, using fuel and munitions which would be much needed later, but not too much later, six weeks had elapsed.

Nagumo's four carriers were next ordered to join Vice-Admiral Nobutake Kondo's force of two battleships and three cruisers for an attack on the port of Darwin, in Australia's Northern Territory. Intelligence reports claimed that Allied forces in the area were being strengthened, and that there would be concentrations of shipping at Darwin. Fuchida protested again that the force was being sent to what he regarded as a side show, while the main objective, a decisive confrontation with the American Pacific Fleet's aircraft carriers, was being delayed. He and Genda knew that the Americans would be repairing the damage at Pearl Harbor and

rushing reinforcements to the Pacific. Already, aircraft from the *Enterprise* and *Yorktown* had attacked Japanese bases in the Marshall Islands, and although causing little damage, this strike back at the enemy helped to boost American morale.

SHIPS AND AIRCRAFT

The aircraft carriers *Akagi*, *Kaga*, *Hiryu* and *Soryu* were used for this operation, with the same combination of aircraft types as used at Pearl Harbor.

THE ACTION

The Japanese raid on Darwin on 19 February 1942 has been presented as 'Australia's Pearl Harbor'. This is true inasmuch as Darwin was as little prepared for the attack as Pearl Harbor was. Otherwise, the claim is an exaggeration. Darwin was indeed busy at the time of the attack, with two Australian transports, two American transports, a troop ship, a freighter, an American destroyer and aircraft tender, an Australian corvette and hospital ship, along with many smaller vessels, all in the harbour. However, there was nothing bigger than the destroyer – none of the battleships or cruisers which had made Pearl Harbor such a worthy target.

In excellent visibility, Fuchida led 180 aircraft on the attack, achieving complete surprise and destroying about a dozen vessels, including the destroyer and a ship carrying ammunition, before shooting up the town, damaging buildings, so that it was temporarily abandoned by its population. The nearby airfields received the same treatment, with some fifteen Australian and American aircraft destroyed on the ground.

Paradoxically, after the experience at Pearl Harbor, on his return to the flagship, the aircraft carrier *Akagi*, Fuchida found Nagumo anxious to send a second strike!

COMMENT

Fuchida and Genda were firm believers in a strategy which would have isolated Australia from the United States, taking Fiji, then Samoa and, finally, Hawaii, while also conducting major raids on Sydney and, perhaps, Canberra. To these officers, the raid on Darwin was yet another case of a sledgehammer being used to crack a nut. Both were impatient for an all-out attack on the United States Navy's Pacific Fleet, and most especially its aircraft carriers.

The raid on Darwin had little in the way of strategic implications, other than bringing the war home to the relatively sparse population of Australia's Northern Territory. Australia had been in the Second World War from the beginning, and was committed to fighting alongside the United Kingdom and, after Pearl Harbor, the United States.

The conclusion about the raid on Darwin has to be that it was an irrelevance, wasting precious time and resources for the Japanese. The resources committed to the attack were also far in excess of what should have been necessary.

STRIKING TO THE WEST AT CEYLON

THE ROYAL NAVY FALLS VICTIM TO JAPANESE ATTACKS

The First Air Fleet was reunited again after raids on Java, although damage to the *Kaga* which had scraped a reef meant that she had to return to Japan for repairs. With Nagumo still in command, the other five aircraft carriers were ordered by Yamamoto to support the imminent invasion of Burma, with the carrier force first charged with the destruction of all elements of the Royal Navy's Eastern Fleet operating in the Indian Ocean, and then to cut off supplies to Burma.

The force which sailed on 26 March for Ceylon also included four battleships, two heavy cruisers and one light, and nine destroyers. They faced a British force which at its peak included three aircraft carriers and five battleships, with supporting cruisers and destroyers.

SHIPS AND AIRCRAFT

The Japanese fleet included the aircraft carriers, *Akagi*, *Shokaku*, *Zuikaku*, *Hiryu* and *Soryu*, with the same mix of Mitsubishi Zero fighters and Nakajima bombers as before.

The British Eastern Fleet, under Vice-Admiral Somerville, included the aircraft carriers *Hermes*, *Indomitable* and *Formidable*, the last two being of the same class as *Illustrious*. By this time, *Hermes* was too small and too slow to be regarded as a fleet carrier, and indeed she would be a hindrance to any fleet including the other two

Illustrious class carriers, which would not be able to make full use of their high speed if accompanied by her. Her aircraft complement was now no more than a dozen Fairey Swordfish, effectively marking her down as an anti-submarine escort carrier.

THE ACTION

On 4 April, one of the RAF's Consolidated Catalina flying boats on reconnaissance discovered the approaching Japanese task force and managed to radio a warning to Ceylon, before being promptly despatched by Zero fighters.

The following day, Easter Day, 5 April 1942, at 08.00, Fuchida led an attack on Colombo, intending to repeat their triumph at Pearl Harbor. Instead, they found the British warships absent, although the harbour was congested with a large build-up of merchant shipping. The Royal Air Force was on the alert, committing its small force of fighters to the defence of the port, but almost all of the RAF Hawker Hurricanes were shot down by the faster and more agile Zeros, allowing the dive-bombers and horizontal bombers to inflict severe damage on the harbour and shore installations. An armed merchant cruiser and a destroyer were hit in the harbour. Despite the success of the raid for the Japanese, their losses on this occasion were heavier than in earlier actions.

On his return, Commander Mitsuo Fuchida reported to Vice-Admiral Nagumo, and recommended that they send reconnaissance aircraft to locate the British fleet. This time his recommendation was accepted. At noon, a flight of aircraft from the aircraft carrier *Soryu* found the two heavy cruisers, *Dorsetshire* and *Cornwall*. It took the attackers just twenty minutes to sink the two ships, which were completely without air cover. Fuchida was not present at this attack, although responsible for its direction, since he remained aboard the *Akagi* with aircraft ready in case a further strike on Colombo was ordered.

The British forces in Ceylon had not been not sure where the Japanese would strike. The main body of the fleet, including *Indomitable* and *Formidable*, had left the area to refuel at Addu Atoll, a hastily constructed refuelling anchorage unknown to the Japanese. The two heavy cruisers, *Dorsetshire* and *Cornwall*, had been sent to Colombo, while *Hermes* went to Trincomalee. The safest course was to order all warships in both harbours to sea. *Hermes* was still in Trincomalee on 4 April, and was immediately ordered to put to sea, heading north. The ship returned to Trincomalee on 6 April.

Donald Farquharson-Roberts was a young Royal Marines officer serving on *Hermes* at the time. He recalls the events of 8 and 9 April clearly: 'Shortly after noon (on Wednesday, 8 April), the recall went up and we had to get the crew back aboard sharpish. Intelligence had suggested that the next target for the Japanese was to be Trinco. We cleared the harbour about 8pm and this time went south. This was in fact an unfortunate decision as we were spotted early on Thursday, 9 April, and this fact was relayed to us and we were told to go about and head for the cover of the guns of Trinco with all despatch. I think Chiefie got the old girl up to 25 knots. No need to worry about funnel smoke, the Japs knew where we were!'[1]

The next target was Trincomalee, north of Colombo and Britain's other major base on the island. British reconnaissance located the Japanese and correctly assessed their intentions before the attack, so again the Japanese failed to find the British fleet, when Fuchida led 100 aircraft in the attack on 9 April shortly before 07.30. Nine out of the eleven RAF Hawker Hurricane fighters which faced the attackers were shot down. Fuchida's force attacked airfields, destroying parked aircraft with dive-bombers and using horizontal bombers against shore installations, but the first wave only managed to sink a single merchant vessel. Twenty of the Japanese aircraft were shot down. Leaving the remaining merchant vessels to Egusa's second wave of dive-bombers, Fuchida returned to the *Akagi*.

On his return flight, Fuchida was given the news that a British aircraft carrier and her escort had been sighted. Egusa's aircraft were ordered towards the aircraft carrier, by now known to be *Hermes* and her escort, the Australian destroyer, *Vampire*. While Fuchida's aircraft were hastily re-armed and refuelled, the horizontal bombers being armed with torpedoes in case they had to form a second wave to reinforce Egusa's attack, nine Bristol Blenheim bombers found and attacked the *Akagi*, without inflicting any damage.

Fuchida joined Itaya's Zeros as they headed towards *Hermes*, in case Egusa had had trouble with the aircraft carrier's fighters. They needn't have worried. *Hermes* was not carrying any aircraft that day, and indeed her small size meant that, as aircraft sizes had increased, her usual complement was no more than a dozen Fairey Swordfish, useful for torpedo attack or anti-submarine patrol, but not capable of air defence. The contest was uneven. Egusa had eighty aircraft, most of which seemed to strike either *Hermes* or *Vampire*. Fuchida arrived in time to find the aircraft carrier sinking, while the destroyer was crippled by explosions from her magazines.

[1–3] *I Could Have Killed Joe*, the private autobiography of Don Farquharson-Roberts.

After learning that Japanese reconnaissance had found them, those aboard *Hermes* did not have long to wait, with the first Japanese aircraft diving at *Hermes* at around 10.50, coming in on the ship's starboard side, as indeed did all of the aircraft which followed.

Farquharson-Roberts again: 'I was in charge of the 4-inch AA gun just abaft the island and I think we got off the first round set very much at short barrage. The planes seemed to have no fear. They came in at masthead height and at least one was reported as being below the fighting top! One of the detachment's .303 Vickers was mounted up there and Marine Youle, who had manned the same gun on the run in with Richelieu at Dakar told me he was firing downwards! My gun had fired about seven rounds when an accident happened and the new round of fixed ammunition got caught in front of the extractors and we could not free it nor close the breech and fire it. At this moment, I saw a plane coming straight for my gun. I saw the bomb swing clear and come straight for ME. I was standing about six feet behind the gun and it hit the deck a foot in front of me . . . and went straight through the deck! . . . By this time and 'tween decks must have been a shambles. The forrard lift had been blown up and back. This can be seen in the photograph of her sinking.

'I went after to try to free the two huge catamarans which were secured aft of the gun. They were used when in harbour to keep the ship's side away from the quay due to the overhang of the flight deck. Here I met the rating who was manning the .5-inch quad machine gun. He said the guns had jammed and that he was getting the hell out of it! I undid the clips holding down the cats and came back to my gun. The sergeant in charge, W.A. Crook, had a nasty wound on his leg and we put a first field dressing on it . . .

'I never heard the command to abandon ship, although I am told it was given. I took leave of the old girl by stepping into the water on the port side by P3 gun. There was then only a drop of about ten feet. I swam clear but the stern was swinging away from me as she had port helm on and the engines were still going full ahead. By this time there were a large number (of survivors) in a sort of tail from the ship so I must have been rather late in saying my goodbyes!'[2]

The first bomb struck *Hermes* at 10.55, and the ship had sunk by 11.15, within sight of the coast. On her way back to Trincomalee that day she had passed the *Vita*, an Australian hospital ship, which had left the port earlier. Fortunately, while both *Hermes* and *Vampire* were sunk, the Japanese either did not see the *Vita*, or abided by the convention of not attacking hospital ships. The former seems more likely!

Some of the survivors found their own way to the shore. Farquharson-Roberts recalls seeing the coast and the town of Batticola: '. . . before the ship actually went under, I saw one of the most incredible sights. A young boy seaman, South African RNVR, dived off the top of the fighting top over the flight deck and made a perfect swallow dive into the water! . . . he was one who reached the shore!'[3]

Farquharson-Roberts swam to a Carley raft, but as soon as he got there the Japanese returned and machine-gunned his raft, persuading him to return to the sea. A petty officer in the raft was less fortunate, being wounded in the attack, causing Farquharson-Roberts to return to the raft to provide what first aid he could – the petty officer survived to live to the ripe old age of ninety-two years!

The success only confirmed Fuchida's concerns that the mighty First Air Fleet was wasting its time on minor operations of secondary importance and neglecting its main opportunities. Worse still, the losses suffered during the raids on Ceylon could not be replaced in time for the next big battle, the Battle of the Coral Sea.

The First Air Fleet and its ships turned towards Japan for replenishment and

The loss of yet another British carrier, as *Hermes* succumbs to heavy Japanese aerial attack within sight of Ceylon. (FAAM Carrier H/11)

refuelling, calling at Singapore en route, where Vice-Admiral Jisaburo Ozawa had established his headquarters, with the two small carriers of the Fourth Carrier Division, *Shoho* and *Ryujo*.

COMMENT

The loss of several ships over a few days was a blow to British morale, although the Japanese did not venture as far west again. It is interesting to speculate on what might have happened had *Indomitable* and *Formidable* been present with their fighter aircraft, and whether a major set-piece battle might have developed if the two battle fleets had come within range of one another, since the Eastern Fleet had numerical superiority over the Japanese force in battleships, cruisers and destroyers at the outset. Nevertheless, apart from the pressing need to refuel, the Royal Navy had taken note of the use of air power, albeit land-based, against *Repulse* and *Prince of Wales*, and was more protective of its battleships.

The fact is that British forces in the area were inadequate, especially in terms of their equipment. Spitfires would have stood a better chance of success than Hurricanes against the Zero. *Hermes* had been engaged in raider patrols in the South Atlantic and Indian Ocean, not finding any German commerce raiders but on one occasion taking an Italian liner as a prize. No doubt she was ideal for this type of operation, and could have been more usefully employed during this stage of the war as a convoy escort.

Taking the War to the Enemy – Operation Shangri-La

An Attempt to Boost American Morale

The Japanese attack on Pearl Harbor had been a serious blow to American morale. The overwhelming force of the Japanese naval forces, and the distances involved, meant that striking back at the Japanese was a far from easy task. One United States Army Air Force officer, Colonel James Doolittle, advocated flying bombers from an aircraft carrier, not simply as an attempt at a tit for tat against the Japanese, but as a gesture of defiance, and one which would cause them to divert some of their energies to defensive measures. There was some initial resistance to the plan, but eventually it was overcome.

Ships and Aircraft

The aircraft carrier *Hornet* was selected for the task, and she was accompanied by the *Enterprise*, which provided fighter cover while *Hornet* had her flight deck packed with aircraft. Both of these aircraft carriers have been described already.

A twin-engined, high-wing, medium bomber, the North American B-25 Mitchell used two 1,700 h.p. Wright R-2600-29 radial engines for a top speed of 275 m.p.h., and for a range of 1,350 miles and a warload of 4,000 lb.

The Action

The idea of operating an aircraft the size of the Mitchell from an aircraft carrier appeared so preposterous to so many that when the *Hornet* left Pearl Harbor with the aircraft crammed onto her flight deck, everyone assumed that she was ferrying the aircraft. The Mitchell did not have folding wings, and even if it had, it would not have been able to strike down into the carrier's hangar. Since the aircraft could not land on the *Hornet*, the plan was that after bombing their targets in Japan, they should fly on to China, landing in an area not occupied by the Japanese. For this reason the operation was called Shangri-La, after the fictitious land beyond the clouds.

By 10 April, the radio intelligence unit of the Japanese Combined Fleet at Hagashishima was aware of the approach of an American task force with, it estimated, two or three carriers. The Americans had used the radio to ensure the rendezvous of *Enterprise* and *Hornet*. This was of little concern to the Japanese, since their network of picket ships was set at 700 miles from the home islands, and carrier-borne aircraft would have to move to within 300 miles in order to launch an attack. The assumption was that they would have fifteen hours warning of any attack.

Of course, the Japanese were in no position to deal with an American carrier force. Their main carrier strike force was just returning from the series of raids on Ceylon, while *Zuikaku*, *Shokaku* and *Shoho* were supporting the assault on Port Moresby. *Kaga* was in Japan, but not operational at the time.

The Americans maintained radio silence after 10 April, which left the Japanese guessing both their position and their intentions. The plan was to launch the Twenty-Sixth Air Flotilla's force of sixty-nine bombers when the American ships crossed the picket line. Nagumo's five carriers would be in place to strike back at the American task force on 19 April, but no earlier.

Early on the morning of 18 April the two carriers with their task forces crossed the picket line, by which time Halsey assumed that their position was known to the Japanese. He decided to launch the sixteen B-25s and withdraw. This was a wise decision. The Japanese had no idea that he had aircraft aboard which could be launched so far from the home islands: the B-25s were launched at a distance of 550 miles!

The bombers were spotted by a Japanese patrol aircraft, but its report was rejected, because intelligence knew that the Americans did not have twin-engined carrier-borne aircraft! The raid was successful inasmuch as none of the aircraft was shot down, and indeed they penetrated Japanese air defences with ease.

There were some Japanese fighters on patrol on 18 April, but these were cruising at 10,000 feet, and missed the bombers flying in at just 150 feet. The US planes bombed Tokyo, Yokosuka, Nagoya and other locations, causing relatively little damage, although the sudden appearance of the aircraft caused considerable alarm. In Tokyo they also strafed, accidentally machine-gunning two grammar school students. Their deaths formed the basis of the prosecution of the captured members of Doolittle's raiding party.

None of the aircraft had been shot down, but they were all destroyed in landing accidents on airfields ill-suited to such large aircraft. The crew of one which flew onto land in supposedly 'friendly' Russian territory was arrested. Still less fortunate were the crews of the two bombers which had crash-landed near Japanese-occupied Hankow. When the Japanese commander in Shanghai informed Tokyo of their capture, they were brought to Japan and prosecuted for the

deaths of the schoolchildren, and three of them suffered the death penalty. It was not until they heard of the two bombers which had crash-landed that the Japanese realized that the raid was a true one-way attack.

The presence of prisoners enabled the Japanese propaganda machine to claim that nine bombers had been shot down.

The immediate impact of the raid was that Japanese carriers were ordered to intercept the American warships, but they failed to find them.

COMMENT

Many Americans criticized the raid as meaningless bravado, and others were more vehement, judging it a waste of experienced aircrew and much-needed aircraft. Certainly, little damage had been done, not least because of the decision to split the small force between a number of targets; a concerted raid on one specific target, such as the Imperial Palace compound, could have had an even more marked effect on Japanese military thinking. As it was, concern for the well-being of the Emperor caused Admiral Yamamoto to adopt a less confident, more defensive strategy, and it was this which was to inhibit Japanese naval strategy for the rest of the war. No attack, and there might not have been a Japanese plan to take Midway, and no battle.

On the other hand, there can be no doubt that the raid was a disaster for America's Chinese Nationalist allies, whose leader Generalissimo Chiang Kai-shek, had objected, stressing that the Japanese would carry out reprisals against the Chinese. He was right. On 21 April the planned advance of the China Expeditionary Army was brought forward, and Operation Che-Kiang was launched against Chekiang and Kiangsi provinces. Chiang Kai-shek was later to report to the United States government that 'Japanese troops slaughtered every man, woman and child in those areas . . .'[1] In all, a quarter of a million Chinese were killed.

[1] Edwin P. Hoyt. *Japan's War*, Hutchinson, 1987.

THE FIRST CARRIER-TO-CARRIER COMBAT: BATTLE OF THE CORAL SEA

3–5 MAY 1942

THE FLEETS MEET

While the Japanese advance through Burma had been stalled, the Japanese were still able to advance across the Pacific. Instead of taking first Fiji, then Samoa and finally Hawaii, as favoured by some officers, including Fuchida, leader of the attack on Pearl Harbor, the leadership favoured a less adventurous course. Further landings on New Guinea were planned, starting with an invasion at Port Moresby in the south of the island, while also expanding northwards to the Aleutians. New bases were planned in the Solomon Islands and at Midway Island. While strengthening their hold on New Guinea would also have been a step towards one of their other objectives, isolating Australia from the United States, the strategy was now defensive, with the Aleutians and Midway seen as part of an outer defensive ring.

Homeward bound from their successes in Ceylon, Nagumo's First Air Fleet received orders to detach the Fifth Carrier Division, the *Zuikaku* and *Shokaku*, to sail towards Truk in support of the planned strike south towards Port Moresby.

In the attack against Port Moresby, the aircraft carrier *Shoho* was to cover the landings. Under the command of Rear Admiral Goto, the naval force also included four cruisers. *Shokaku* and *Zuikaku*, with 125 aircraft between them, under the command of Vice-Admiral Takagi and with two heavy cruisers and six destroyers for

support, were positioned off the Solomons.

Meanwhile, the American commander in the Pacific, Admiral Nimitz, in his headquarters at Pearl Harbor, sent Task Force 17 under Rear Admiral Fletcher to the Coral Sea. He had the aircraft carriers *Yorktown* and *Lexington*, with their 141 aircraft, as well as 5 cruisers and 9 destroyers of the United States Navy and, under Rear Admiral Crace of the Royal Navy, there were a further 3 cruisers and 2 destroyers.

SHIPS AND AIRCRAFT

Shokaku and *Zuikaku* have been described earlier. *Shoho* was a converted submarine depot ship, and could be regarded as a light fleet carrier, displacing some 13,000 tons. The new carrier had a maximum speed of 28 knots. In appearance, she had a hull which extended beyond the flight deck forward, although the flight deck at both ends was supported on struts and the hangar deck must have been relatively small as a result. As with many Japanese carriers, she did not have an island.

Aircraft available to the Japanese were much the same as those deployed at Pearl Harbor.

The mainstay of the United States Navy and Marine Corps strike aircraft by the time of Pearl Harbor was the Douglas SBD Dauntless series of dive-bombers and scout aircraft, which was fully operational from late 1940 until 1945. On the outbreak of war,

Shoho, shortly after the outbreak of war in the Pacific. (IWM MH5930)

the standard production machine was the SBD-3, with a 1,000 h.p. Wright R-1820 radial engine, which had two 0.5-in forward firing guns instead of the 0.3-in used on the SBD-1 for the USMC and the USN's original SBD-2s. A low-wing monoplane with a retractable undercarriage, the SBD-3 had self-sealing fuel tanks and armour protection. A 500-lb or a 1,000-lb bomb could be carried.

The philosophy of the day was to augment dive-bombing with torpedo-bombing, and this combination had already proved effective at Taranto and at Pearl Harbor. The standard USN torpedo-bomber at the outbreak of war was the Douglas TBD Devastator, which first saw service in 1937. Powered by an 850 h.p. Pratt & Whitney R-1830 radial engine, the three-seat monoplane could carry a 1,000-lb bomb or a torpedo. Although far more modern in appearance than the Fleet Air Arm's Swordfish, the Devastator too was obsolescent on the outbreak of war and has

been described as a 'good aircraft kept in service for too long'.

The other important aircraft was the Grumman F4F Wildcat, also known in the Royal Navy as the Martlet. On the outbreak of war, this was the only carrier-borne fighter in the USN. A single-seat monoplane, its wheels retracted into the fuselage, a hangover from the Grumman biplanes! The versions in service at this time had a 1,200 h.p. Wright R-1830 engine and a maximum speed in excess of 300 m.p.h. The aircraft had six 0.5-in guns and was noted for its sturdy construction. Although inferior in some ways to the Japanese Zero, throughout the war almost seven 'kills' were scored for every Wildcat lost, and although many of these would have been slower and less manoeuvrable bombers, the role of the fighter is to stop such aircraft pressing home their attack rather than simply seeking combat with other fighters.

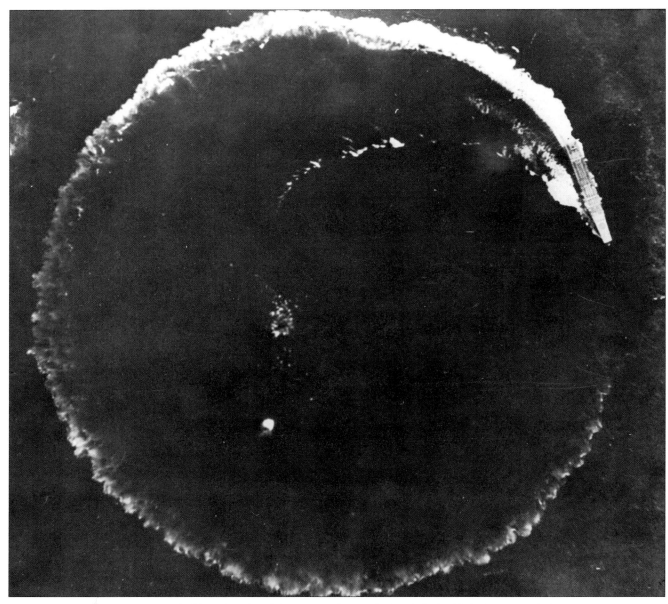

Both sides lost a carrier in the Battle of the Coral Sea, here *Shoho* circles to avoid American bombs at the height of the battle. (US National Archive 208-N-6509)

THE ACTION

The initial Japanese landings were on Tulagi and Gaudalcanal in the eastern Solomon Islands on 3 May, and they were unopposed. The following day, aircraft from the *Yorktown* surprised Japanese warships lying off Tulagi, and sank a destroyer and three minesweepers, as well as a number of seaplanes. Task Force 17 was then distracted by the Port Moresby assault force and the carrier *Shoho*, so while TF17 moved after this force, the main Japanese carrier force with the *Shokaku* and *Zuikaku* entered the Coral Sea from the east on 5 May.

On 6 May both the American and Japanese forces refuelled at sea, just seventy miles apart, and despite aerial reconnaissance by both sides, remained unaware of each other's presence. Later, USAAF reconnaissance aircraft were able to advise Fletcher of the location of the Port Moresby assault force.

On 7 May American aircraft from both carriers located the *Shoho* and the Port Moresby force, and concentrating their efforts on the *Shoho*, which circled desperately to avoid the bombing, they managed to sink her within minutes for the cost of three aircraft. This caused the Japanese to recall their troop convoy. Meanwhile, Japanese reconnaissance aircraft discovered an American destroyer escorting a tanker and mistook them for an aircraft carrier and a cruiser. As a result, Takagi sent sixty bombers to attack these two ships, and, faced with such overwhelming odds, both were destroyed within minutes.

That night, the four aircraft carriers were so close, that six Japanese aircraft attempted to land on the *Yorktown* in the dark.

The next day, reconnaissance aircraft from both fleets discovered each other almost simultaneously, with the two fleets some 200 miles apart. The ensuing air attacks were also virtually simultaneous, with the Japanese sending ninety aircraft against the Americans, who sent seventy-eight aircraft against the Japanese ships. While *Zuikaku* escaped from the onslaught into a rainstorm, three bombs struck *Shokaku*, forcing her to return to Truk. *Lexington*'s Devastators scored no hits at all. A Japanese officer later recalled derisively, when interrogated about US torpedoes, 'We could turn and run away from them'.[1]

The Japanese attack on the American carriers was anticipated, and reconnaissance aircraft had been put in the air. The first of the scouting pilots' reports was radioed to *Lexington*'s air control centre: 'Big force of enemy aircraft coming from right ahead: they are sixty miles away.' This was quickly followed by a more accurate message from Lieutenant-Commander Paul Ramsey: 'Enemy planes 17,000 feet, four groups of nine each. Two groups dive bombers . . . and Zero fighters in escort. I'm at 14,000 feet, 12 miles north-east of you and climbing hard. They are going awfully fast.' Then he added significantly, 'Doubt if I can catch them.' Another report gave warning of torpedo-bombers 'spilling out of clouds 8 miles out. They are 6,000 feet in a steep dive.'[2]

TF17 had the aircraft carrier *Lexington* steaming about two miles ahead and to starboard of *Yorktown*, with a cruiser and destroyer screen around the two carriers. The torpedo-bombers approached in three small groups each with six aircraft, two attacking the *Lexington* from both sides, and one attacking the *Yorktown*.

Lexington's commanding officer, Captain Sherman, took evasive action while his gunners put up an intense AA barrage, with one Nakajima B5N 'Kate' torpedo-bomber blowing up on its run towards the ship. It has been claimed that as many as eleven torpedoes were dropped at *Lexington* and missed, before two eventually hit their target;

[1] US Interrogation of Japanese Officials.
[2,3] Stanley Johnson. *Queen of the Flat Tops*, Dutton, 1942.

Badly damaged, *Lexington* burns fiercely after Japanese aerial torpedo attack. (IWM OEM1570)

an impressive piece of ship handling, especially since this was the first time that American carriers had closed with enemy aircraft. The first torpedo hit the ship on the port bow at 11.20, and a second also struck to port, amidships.

'I arrived on the main deck – two below the flight deck – to find dust and smoke drifting through the passageways coming from further aft. In the passageway amidships I found four men who were nearly naked . . . they were horribly burned. A Filipino cook . . . assisted me to get the men on to the cots in the passageway and take off the remainder of their clothes, give them a drink of water and a morphia injection. A hospital corpsman . . . treated their burns with tannic acid jelly and took over their care. Men kept coming in from the 5-inch gun galleries, sometimes alone, others with the help of comrades. We had about twelve men on the cots and during a brief lull I went to the gun galleries to see what had happened. There I saw several bodies: they seemed to have been frozen or charred into grotesque statues.'[3]

Commander Healey, the Damage Control Officer, reported by telephone to Captain Sherman: 'We've got the torpedo damage temporarily shored up, the fires are out and soon will have the ship back on an even keel. But I would suggest, sir, that if you have to take any more torpedoes, you take 'em on the starboard side.'[4]

No sooner had he finished this report than a tremendous blast ran through the ship, worse than any of the bomb hits or torpedo strikes suffered so far. The blast came from near the Central Control Station, killing Commander Healey and a large number of those nearby. Survivors described streams of

[4] Report by Stanley Johnson in the *Chicago Tribune*, 17 June 1942.

flame and sparks searing along passageways and through compartments, tearing off watertight doors, and opening up decks above and below. Twenty minutes later, another blast added still further to the damage and killed many more. The damage control parties were overwhelmed by the first blast, but the second shattered the water mains, making any attempt at fire control impossible. Then the electricity was cut, plunging the ship below decks into darkness. The first explosion had come from the aviation fuel tanks, damaged by the second torpedo hit, which in turn led to further explosions as other fuel tanks were damaged.

By this time, signals could only be sent from one part of the ship to another by messenger, and a chain of men over a distance of almost 500 feet had to transmit steering instructions from the bridge to the auxiliary steering position, four decks below.

Little of this had been apparent to the returning aviators, but at 13.45 smoke over the flight deck was so dense that all flying operations had to be suspended, leaving *Yorktown* to recover *Lexington*'s aircraft. At 14.30, the worst damaged areas were shut off after withdrawing the damage control parties, in the hope of containing the fires behind watertight doors. Fifteen minutes later, another major internal explosion wrecked the ventilation system into the engine room and boiler rooms, and as temperatures soared, these areas had to be evacuated and the ship lost further speed. Shortly after 15.00, assistance was requested in fighting the fires, and the destroyer *Morris* came alongside, but her fire-fighting capabilities were insufficient for the fuel-fed fires now raging out of control. The order was soon give to abandon ship and at 20.00, the destroyer *Phelps* torpedoed *Lexington*, by now nothing more than a floating, burning wreck.

Meanwhile, the *Yorktown* was also hit by a bomb, but this exploded close to the island, so that flying operations were not affected.

COMMENT

The Battle of the Coral Sea took place on 7–8 May, and was treated as a major Japanese victory. The Japanese sank the American aircraft carrier *Lexington* and severely damaged the *Yorktown*, but in return the Americans had sunk the light carrier *Shoho* and caused severe damage to the *Shokaku*, so that she would not be available for the forthcoming Battle of Midway. On this basis, the Japanese had won a tactical victory, having lost a light carrier for the loss of a significant American warship.

Nevertheless, the Japanese advance had been curbed and they had been forced to abandon their planned invasion of Port Moresby. Worse still, the Japanese had suffered heavy losses from the aircrew of the élite Fifth Carrier Division. The Japanese may have gained in the aircraft carrier stakes, since the US loss was a more important fleet unit than the *Shoho*, but they had lost twice as many men as the Americans, and had failed to gain their strategic objectives.

The Japanese failure to take Port Moresby effectively marked the end of their plans to isolate Australia from the United States. In foiling this ambition, the United States Navy had scored a vital strategic victory.

THE TIDE TURNS: THE BATTLE OF MIDWAY

THE JAPANESE PLAN TO INVADE MIDWAY ISLAND

The Japanese Imperial Headquarters in Tokyo was divided over whether or not to pursue the Midway option. Many preferred instead to isolate Australia from the United States. Nevertheless, planning for the Midway operation was accelerated after the Doolittle raid. The plan was to occupy Midway and in so doing lure the US Pacific Fleet beyond the atoll so that it could be destroyed by the Japanese forces. Nagumo's First Air Fleet was to support the landing, although the assault fleet had its own carrier, *Zuiho*. She was to cover the landings before acting as escort for the bulk of the Japanese fleet commanded by Admiral Yamamoto himself aboard the battleship *Yamato*. The battleships, cruisers and destroyers, with the light carrier, *Hosho*, were to remain 300 miles behind the carrier fleet, and then destroy the remnants of the American forces after Nagumo and his invincible carrier airmen had finished with them. To distract the Americans and also achieve another of Yamamoto's strategic objectives, a raiding force was also to attack American forces in the Aleutians.

Nagumo had no part in these plans other than their execution, his chief-of-staff, Kusaka, objected, explaining that the task force was not yet ready for another major operation. They needed to refit, not simply refuel and replenish ships. They needed to train new aircrew to combat readiness, not simply rest the existing veterans. This debate took place in March and April, before the Battle of the Coral Sea.

Genda also objected. He saw the potential of the plan, if postponed, but too many experienced aircrew had been withdrawn from the carriers after the Indian Ocean campaign, and taking into account the losses suffered in the battles off Ceylon, he felt that the pool of experienced pilots was too low. There were also concerns that the Aleutian raiding force divided the Combined Fleet, taking the aircraft carriers *Ryujo* and *Junyo*. Yamaguchi, with the Second Carrier Division, generally supported both Genda and Fuchida, and he did so again on this occasion.

It mattered little. These experienced officers, with their experience of naval aerial warfare, were overruled. Fuchida even attempted to reach Yamamoto through an officer on his staff, Commander Akira Susaki, but to no avail. Even his argument that the base on Midway was no good and suggestions that the plan was flawed because the large guns of the battleships would be too far away to be of any use were overruled by senior officers who believed that the US Pacific Fleet was already a broken reed.

One final opportunity at least to modify the plan came with a big planning conference aboard the *Yamato* on 28 and 29 April 1942. The senior officers were full of praise for the exploits of the naval airmen, and reviewed the record of Nagumo's force to see if any lessons could be learned. Fuchida once again argued for a single force, with the First Fleet, or main body, fighting as a single unit under

Soryu was one of the Japanese carriers taking part in the Battle of Midway. (IWM MH6490)

Yamamoto, with six aircraft carriers and the substantial battleship and cruiser force operating together.

Meanwhile, the Americans had broken the Japanese codes and were aware of their intentions.

SHIPS AND AIRCRAFT

The main striking force comprised the *Akagi*, flagship for Vice-Admiral Chuichi Nagumo, with *Kaga*, *Hiryu* and *Soryu*. The *Hosho* was Japan's first aircraft carrier and has been described already. The sixth carrier, the *Zuiho*, was a converted submarine tender displacing 11,262 tons after conversion. She had a narrow beam, but despite this her speed was just 28 knots. Instead of an island, a navigating bridge was provided forward under the flight deck.

The American forces comprised Task Force 16, under Rear Admiral Spruance, with the *Enterprise* and *Hornet*, and Task Force 17, under Rear Admiral Fletcher, with the *Yorktown*.

Aircraft on both sides remained unchanged from the types present at the Battle of the Coral Sea. The Imperial Japanese Navy's Carrier Fleet had 270 aircraft available, while there were additional aircraft on the *Zuiho* and *Hosho* – the Aleutian Assault Group's carrier aircraft were, of course, too far away to be relevant to this action.

THE ACTION

Realizing that the invasion of Midway Island by the Japanese was set for early June, the commander-in-chief of the United States Navy's Pacific Fleet, Admiral Nimitz, concentrated the available naval forces to defend the island. The Japanese in turn expected a strong defence and amassed all of their available naval forces, hoping for a decisive battle with the American forces. The Americans were not distracted from the main objective when, on 3 June, aircraft from the *Ryujo* and *Junyo* attacked Dutch Harbour in the Aleutians, close to Alaska. Instead, the main Japanese fleet was located and, during the afternoon of 3 June, USAAF Boeing B-17 Flying Fortresses were sent from the base on Midway to bomb the Japanese landing fleet, but without success.

Mitsuo Fuchida was originally marked to lead the attacks on Midway, but as the *Akagi* sailed, he succumbed to appendicitis. He refused the offer of a destroyer to take him to a naval hospital in favour of an operation by the ship's chief surgeon, so that at least he would be available for consultation should his superiors require his advice. On 4 June, the day chosen for the first attack, he was still recovering from his operation. Fuchida was determined not to remain in the sick bay while his pilots flew off on their mission, but

he was still very weak from his operation, having only had his stitches removed the previous day. He decided to go to the flight deck. This was no small undertaking. The ship was closed up for action stations, and all the watertight bulkheads had been closed. Each had a manhole which had to be unlocked using a wheel, and then locked again after he had passed through; there were ten of these between the sick bay, which was below the waterline, and his cabin. On reaching his cabin, he rested briefly to regain his strength, then shaved and changed into his uniform. Thanks to his persistence, we have an eye-witness account of events aboard the Japanese carriers that day.

Fuchida arrived in the control centre before the dive-bomber squadrons were ready to take off, to find that Lieutenant Tomonaga was to take his place leading the attack. Reconnaissance aircraft were being flown off first, and he was shown the search patterns which these were to fly. He was disappointed to find that their search patterns would leave large areas of sea uncovered. Despite their hopes for a confrontation with the American

Hiryu was designed to operate with *Soryu*, and had a port-side island so that aircraft could use a different take-off and approach pattern. (IWM MH 5928)

fleet, and especially the aircraft carriers, the Japanese had left major gaps in their reconnaissance effort, and it seems that they were unaware of the presence of the American carriers at this early stage.

The first wave of the Japanese attack left their aircraft carriers at dawn, when Nagumo sent more than a hundred aircraft to Midway to destroy the island's defences. As this was happening, a mixed force of USAAF and USN shore-based aircraft from Midway located and attacked the Japanese carriers, disrupting the formation of the fleet and strafing and killing a number of crewmen working on the decks. However, they lost seventeen aircraft to anti-aircraft fire and Zero fighters scrambled from the carriers.

One USAAF Martin B-26 Marauder missed the *Akagi*'s bridge by some thirty feet, and headed towards the *Hiryu*, before finally plunging into the sea. Many of those watching jumped for joy. 'This is fun!' exclaimed Fuchida.[1] A few of those around him, as he sat on the flight deck, propped up against the island, watching, and taking notes, were not so sure. The difficulties of the Battle of the Coral Sea had been noted by some at least, even if the Imperial Japanese Navy's leadership had refused to change its plans or assumptions.

While this was happening, the Japanese were inflicting heavy damage on Midway's shore installations, but the airfield and the anti-aircraft defences were still fully operational. Tomonaga radioed the striking force, and Nagumo decided to send the second wave to maintain the pressure on the defending forces. The aircraft still aboard the aircraft carriers were armed with torpedoes, intended for an attack on American warships, and these now had to be changed to bombs for a second wave attack against Midway. While this was being done, the reconnaissance aircraft radioed that it had seen ten American warships. Nagumo changed his mind. Midway

could wait, they would attack the American warships first, so the order was reversed, and bombs being loaded onto the aircraft were now to be taken off and the torpedoes put back on again. In consultation with his staff officers, it was agreed that the second wave should not leave until the aircraft from the first wave, who were now returning and short of fuel, had been recovered.

While waiting for the first wave to return, at 09.00, a reconnaissance aircraft reported that it had sighted an American aircraft carrier, probably the *Yorktown*. The Japanese had assumed that the Americans did not have an aircraft carrier nearby, because of the lack of fighter cover for the earlier attacks.

None of the Japanese ships had radar of any kind. The first wave had landed on, and the second wave with their torpedoes were ranged on the flight decks ready for take-off when the first wave of American aircraft attacked. Spruance had put his entire force into the air from *Enterprise* and *Hornet*, while Fletcher had put up half of *Yorktown*'s aircraft. A total of 156 American carrier-borne aircraft were sent to intercept the Japanese carrier fleet.

The first wave consisted of forty-one Douglas Devastator torpedo-bombers, of which thirty-five were shot down by anti-aircraft fire from the Japanese fleet and by fighters which managed to get into the air. Whole squadrons virtually disappeared, with all but one aircraft from *Yorktown*'s VT-3 Devastator squadron shot down: many of their crews had neither the time or the altitude to escape from their low-flying aircraft before they crashed into the sea. Those aboard the Japanese carriers were jubilant. They felt that they were on the brink of yet another great victory, with their confidence restored after the set-backs during the Battle of the Coral Sea. Taking into account the aircraft sent from Midway as well as those from what they thought was a

[1-3] Gordon W. Prange with Donald M. Goldstein and Katherine V. Dillon. *God's Samurai*, Brassey's, US

The Douglas Dauntless dive-bomber was the great success of the Battle of Midway.

single American carrier, almost sixty aircraft had been shot down, and yet the ships of the striking force remained unscathed.

Low-flying Devastators with their torpedoes might have escaped radar detection, but had radar been available, the second wave of American aircraft would not have been missed. The striking force was still preoccupied with the torpedo-bombers and its fighters were still at sea level, as the Dauntless dive-bombers, high above at 19,000 feet, approached unobserved.

At 10.22, the first of the Douglas SBD Dauntless dive-bombers, each armed with a 1,000-lb bomb, started their nearly vertical dives on the unsuspecting carriers.

Kaga was first, taking four direct hits from 1,000-lb bombs from the twelve aimed at her. These four were enough, penetrating her flight deck and exploding in her hangars among the parked, fuelled and armed aircraft. The ship was almost immediately abandoned.

Akagi, the flagship, had a near miss, but was then hit by two 1,000-lb bombs.

Fuchida, sitting taking notes on *Akagi*'s deck had seen the first American aircraft diving, and yelled a warning to the command post, and the carrier's anti-aircraft guns burst into life. He could see that the first bomb was going to be off-target, but guessed, correctly, that the following aircraft would see this and adjust its aim. He was right. The first bomb missed the carrier by some thirty feet, but it created a huge geyser of black water which washed over the carrier's bridge, blackening the faces of everyone there.

Fuchida spreadeagled himself on the deck close to the island's superstructure as the second bomb fell, hitting the amidships hangar lift, and smashing through it into the hangar. The third bomb hit the flight deck to port and smashed through this into the hangar. These hits were serious enough in themselves, but their impact was to be far worse than it should have been. In their haste

to re-arm the aircraft of the second strike with torpedoes, the hangar crew had left the bombs, each weighing around 1,750 lbs, in the hangar rather than having these removed to the ship's magazine. The American bombs hit stacks of bombs, setting these off in a chain reaction. On the flight deck, fully armed aircraft, each full of fuel, exploded in flames from the fire and explosions below, and again, a chain reaction occurred as each plane set its neighbour alight. Soon flames were sweeping across the flight deck, while the hangar had become a blazing inferno.

Fuchida went to the briefing room, where he found sailors bringing in the wounded, but confusion reigned and there seemed to be no attempt to move the casualties to the sick bay.

Fuchida stopped one rescue worker to ask, 'Why aren't you taking the wounded down to the sick bay?'

'The entire ship is on fire and no one can get through,' he replied. Horror-struck, Fuchida recalled the thirty-one men still in the sick bay, now hopelessly trapped. He reeled out of the briefing room with the idea of reaching his cabin to salvage what he could, but fire and smoke turned him back.[2]

Fuchida now looked to see what was happening to the rest of the fleet. What he saw stopped him dead. Both the *Kaga* and the *Soryu* were huge balls of smoke and flame, although *Hiryu*, some distance ahead of the other carriers, seemed to be untouched. Although he had objected to this operation, he had never doubted that it would be yet another Japanese victory, but he now realized that they had lost. *Soryu* had received three direct hits from Dauntlesses of *Yorktown*'s dive-bomber squadron, with 1,000-lb bombs exploding in a line straight along her crowded flight deck, and a bomb exploding in the hangar, turning this into an inferno.

Soon after this, the order was given to abandon the *Akagi*. Nagumo wanted to go down with his flagship, but was persuaded

With much of her flight deck blown away, *Hiryu* burns during the Battle of Midway, her port-side island can be seen clearly. (IWM MH 6492)

that his duty lay in continuing the battle, transferring his flag to the *Nagara*, a light cruiser. Fuchida broke both his legs in leaving the *Akagi*, but was rescued and put aboard in the sick bay of the *Nagara*.

The entire action had a witness with a most unusual, and doubtless uncomfortable vantage point. Ensign George Gray was the only survivor of *Hornet*'s torpedo-bombing squadron, VT-8. He had crashed within the fighter screen and was hiding behind a seat cushion which had floated up from his sinking Devastator. He was picked up by a Consolidated Catalina thirty hours later and described the Japanese carriers as burning 'like blow torches'.[4]

The speed and coordination of the attack had been impressive, with the first dive-

bomber striking at 10.22, and the raid completed just four minutes later.

In a desperate bid to salvage something from the defeat, Rear Admiral Yamaguchi ordered a strike against *Yorktown*. The aircraft took off at 11.00 from *Hiryu*. Just eight Aichi D3A 'Val' bombers got through the ship's anti-aircraft fire and fighter screen, but they managed to drop three 500-lb bombs onto the carrier. The first bomb struck the deck among parked aircraft, setting them alight, a second hit the funnel and blew out the fires for five of the six boilers, while the third penetrated three decks and ignited her aviation fuel tanks. Prompt damage control saw the aviation fuel fire smothered with carbon dioxide, while the magazines were flooded as a precaution against the intense heat of the fire.

Early in the afternoon, Hiryu sent a further wave of aircraft to attack the *Yorktown*. This was another much reduced force, with just ten Nakajima B5N Kates and six Mitsubishi A6M Zeros. As soon as the aircraft were sighted, *Yorktown* stopped refuelling her aircraft and, as a further safety measure, drained her aviation fuel system. This left her six Grumman F4F Wildcats on standby to take off with whatever fuel remained in their tanks.

One of the F4F pilots was Lieutenant (later Captain) J.P. Adams, who remembers:

'We only had forty gallons of gas apiece, but nonetheless they wanted to get us off to try to oppose the torpedo attack. Lieutenant Thach (later Admiral) and myself and four others manned the planes. By the time we had got off the deck, all the ships in the Fleet were firing. I vividly remember taking off, trying to crank up my wheels and charge the guns, which we had to do manually and then trying to catch the torpedo planes. I did catch one and possibly another.'[5]

Yorktown's six fighters managed to shoot down five of the torpedo planes, but four got within dropping range. The crippled ship

---

[4] Brian Johnson. *Fly Navy*, David & Charles, 1981.

[5, 6] Interview with Captain J.P. Adams, USN (Rtd) for BBC TV programme, *Pilots at Sea*, 1975.

Despite effective anti-aircraft fire, *Yorktown* was hit and eventually sank. (IWM OEM3672)

The scene aboard *Yorktown* as she lists heavily to port. (IWM OEM3673)

could not manoeuvre easily, but she avoided two torpedoes before being hit by another two on the port side. The ship was also hit by three bombs. Adams again, still in the air:

'I saw the torpedoes hit her and there was no way of course to land back aboard and so I ended up landing on the *Enterprise* which was about forty miles away. And very happy to get aboard with a few gallons of gasolene left.'[6]

Soon after, the order to abandon ship was given aboard *Yorktown*.

The Kates attacking *Yorktown* had been led by Lieutenant Tomonaga, one of the few to return to *Hiryu*. He reported the hits on the US carrier. Strangely, Yamaguchi was by this time under the impression that the Vals and the Kates had attacked two different carriers and, since he believed there were only two US carriers in the South Pacific, the Americans must now be without a strike capability. *Hiryu*, which had picked up the surviving aircraft from the other carriers, prepared a final all-out attack on the American fleet, but as the aircraft were ranged ready to take off, Dauntless dive-bombers from *Enterprise* and *Hornet* attacked, with at least four bombs hitting the desperately manoeuvring carrier, plus four near misses, so that aviation fuel fires soon started in her hangar.

That afternoon, the abandoned *Soryu*, still burning, blew up late, about 190 miles north-west of Midway, to be followed just fifteen minutes later by *Kaga*, 40 miles away, as fires reached her magazines. This left *Akagi* to be sunk in a torpedo attack by Japanese destroyers at dawn. The *Hiryu* was also attacked by destroyer torpedoes, but survived this and a Boeing B-17 Fortress attack from Midway. At 09.00, she finally sank, taking Admiral Yamaguchi and her captain with her.

The Japanese had lost 2,280 men and 258 aircraft. The Aleutian raiding force was too far away to help.

Yamamoto was still some distance away, to the north-west of Midway Island, and on learning of the loss of all four carriers, he abandoned the operation, withdrawing westwards. Spruance then took the *Enterprise* and *Hornet* in hot pursuit of the seven Japanese battleships.

The following day, two heavy cruisers, the *Mikuma* and *Mogami*, from the assault group collided at sea, and as they fell behind the rest of the retreating Japanese fleet, USAAF and USN aircraft attacked, causing little damage. On 6 June, aircraft from the *Enterprise* and *Hornet* attacked the two cruisers, sinking *Mikuma* and severely damaging *Mogami* and two destroyers.

Efforts continued to save the *Yorktown* throughout the rest of the action, but on 7 June the Japanese submarine *I-168* found the carrier and her escorting destroyer, and torpedoed and sank both ships.

COMMENT

It is hard to believe that, almost exactly six months after the raid on Pearl Harbor, the Japanese had lost their advantage in the Pacific War. Indeed, the advantage now rested with the United States Navy, which had destroyed Japan's naval air arm within a morning and part of an afternoon. The admirals and politicians were so confident that they failed to take the advice of experienced naval airmen. They also made the mistake of underestimating their enemy and of believing their own propaganda. They believed that they were almost invincible and that they would prevail. Intelligence was poor, and reconnaissance little better. The Battle of Midway Island showed that the whole basis on which the war in the Pacific was planned and executed by the Japanese Imperial Headquarters was seriously flawed. The only objective after Pearl Harbor was to seize territory, and as much of it as possible. After the Doolittle raid on Tokyo, the emphasis switched to defence, but this raid should have warned them that they had a worthy opponent.

The presence of Yamamoto's battle fleet some 300 miles away was pointless. A combined carrier and battleship force off Midway would have posed a far more serious threat to the American forces. Anti-aircraft fire would have been more dense around such a fleet, and the presence of a strong battle group advancing towards the American carriers would have meant the Americans having to divide their efforts. Yamamoto's flagship, *Yamato*, survived many direct hits during the war, and would have been difficult to stop. The Americans risked either withdrawing their carriers so as not to come within range of her 18-inch guns, or concentrating on trying to sink her while having to abandon their attacks against the Japanese striking force's carriers.

Had the planning been right, and had an intensive programme of aircraft and shipbuilding, and of pilot training, all been in place before the outbreak of war, they might still have been able to salvage something. Since such plans had not been implemented, from now on the Japanese were to face one defeat after another. By contrast, it was not until the end of 1943 that defeat became inevitable for the Germans.

There were, of course, other major differences between these two Axis allies. One of the most significant was the absence of worthwhile technical and scientific developments in Japan's war effort, while the Germans made vast strides during wartime, and had many more developments at an early stage when the war ended.

It might be an exaggeration to suggest that the United States won the war at Midway, but Japan certainly lost all chance of winning.

As for the men who survived the great defeat at Midway, on their return to Japan they were confined to naval barracks until posted to new ships or the ships in which they served sailed again, so that no news of the disaster could leak out. Fuchida, with two broken legs, was confined in a naval hospital, although when his condition improved, he eventually managed to slip away with another officer from the JNAF.

PART FOUR

THE ALLIES SEIZE THE INITIATIVE IN EUROPE

BACKGROUND

The accepted wisdom is that it was not until the end of 1943 that German defeat was inevitable, but the real changes started to come during 1942, as the Allies regained the initiative in the Mediterranean, and as the German invasion of the Soviet Union proved to be a mistake of catastrophic proportions.

By this time, the Fleet Air Arm had better ships and the aircraft to go with them. The fast armoured carriers were also supplemented by the new escort carriers, being mass produced in American shipyards, sometimes little more than six weeks in construction. Many of these were regarded as far less safe than the purpose-designed aircraft carriers in the Royal and United States navies, but the lives saved in the convoys as these ships overcame the menace of the U-boats and anti-shipping air strikes more than outweighed those lost as a result of poor design.

OPERATION TORCH – ALLIED LANDINGS IN NORTH AFRICA

8 NOVEMBER 1942

STARTING A SECOND FRONT IN NORTH AFRICA

After the fall of France and of Norway, British and Commonwealth forces, mainly Australian, were fighting first the Italians and then the Germans in North Africa, where the British Eighth Army, or 'Desert Rats', under Lieutenant-General (later Field Marshal) Bernard Montgomery faced the German 'Afrika Korps' under Field Marshal Irwin Rommel. Montgomery had already started

the advance across North Africa, pushing the Germans towards Tunisia after the Battle of El Alamein, which started on 23 October 1942 and ended on 5 November.

The landings in French Morocco and Algeria were designed to open a second front in North Africa, squeezing the Germans between the advancing British forces and American forces, with almost 100,000 men landed in Vichy territory, behind the Germans.

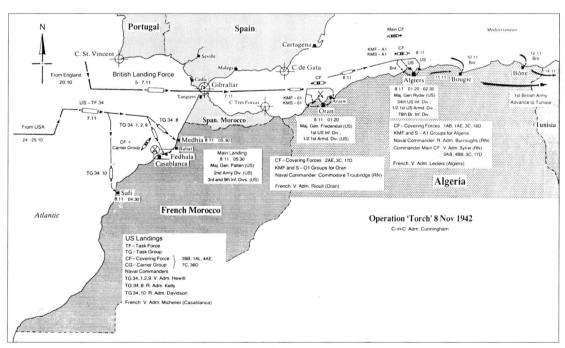

Operation Torch required good coordination, with the Allies landing on a long front interrupted by neutral territory.

SHIPS AND AIRCRAFT

The aircraft carriers covering the invasion forces were the now familiar American light aircraft carrier *Ranger*, displaced from the Pacific because of her small size, with four escort carriers, and the *Argus* and *Furious*, as well as two British escort carriers, with the invasion fleets. Force H under Vice-Admiral Syfret had responsibility for protecting the eastern flanks of the invasion force against the Italian fleet and German submarines, and was deployed in the western Mediterranean, with three battleships, including the new *Duke of York*, and the aircraft carriers *Victorious* and *Formidable*, three cruisers and seventeen destroyers, having detached *Furious* to support the landings.

Aircraft included the Fairey Albacore, supposedly a Swordfish replacement, and the Grumman Martlet or Wildcat, Fairey Fulmar and Supermarine Seafire.

The Seafire was a naval version of the Spitfire fighter, offering a much higher performance than other British carrier fighters, and considerable agility. In some ways it was also very strong, offering good armour protection for its pilot and capable of taking much punishment from enemy fire. Its weakness was that its undercarriage was not robust enough for carrier landings, and its long nose meant that, when arrested, it tended to topple forward onto the propeller. Another problem which it shared with other adapted RAF fighters was its lack of range, which was insufficient for carrier warfare.

THE ACTION

Responsibility for the invasion was divided between the UK and the USA, with Admiral Andrew Cunningham as Allied Naval Commander, under the Supreme Commander General Dwight Eisenhower. The invasion forces were divided into three.

The Western Task Force, TF 34, came from the United States with twenty-three transports to land Major-General Patton's 34,000 troops to the north and south of Casablanca in French Morocco. Support for the invading troops was provided by three USN battleships, the *Ranger* and four escort carriers, seven cruisers and thirty-eight destroyers.

Since Morocco was divided between France and neutral Spain at this time, with Spanish Morocco consisting of the area to the east and south of Tangier, the Centre Task Force landed at Oran in Algeria. Centre Task Force came from England, led by Commodore Troubridge, RN, with two escort carriers, three cruisers and thirteen destroyers escorting, then supporting, twenty-eight transports and nineteen landing craft. The ground forces were commanded by Major-General Frendall, and were 39,000 strong.

The Eastern Task Force arrived under the command of Rear Admiral Sir Harrold Burrough. The aircraft carriers *Argus* and *Furious*, as well as three cruisers and sixteen destroyers, covered sixteen transports and seventeen landing craft which landed 33,000 British and American troops, commanded by Major-General Ryder, near Algiers.

Coordinating such a large force spread over a lengthy section of coastline which was broken by Spanish Moroccan territory relied upon good communications. Commodore Troubridge had his signals team in the ex-armed merchant cruiser *Large*, headed by Robert Phillimore, who later reached the rank of captain. The team used a dozen wave bands and more than a hundred signals specialists. The preparations for Operation Torch had been hasty, 'The bunk house for staff officers at the back of the bridge was so unfinished,' recalled Phillimore, 'that we had to protect ourselves from the weather with umbrellas.'[1]

[1] *Daily Telegraph*, 3 March 1997.

Grumman Wildcats on the flight deck of *Ranger* during exercises with the British Home Fleet in September 1943. (IWM A19330)

The landings started on 8 November, an hour or so after midnight at Oran, and shortly afterwards at Algiers, while those on the west coast started at 04.30. There was almost complete surprise. Aboard the American ships, many of the naval aircrew were very inexperienced – so much so that while crossing the Atlantic there was concern about accidents and damage to the *Ranger*. One of the escort carriers, *Santee*, had just five experienced pilots aboard, and during the operation she lost twenty-one out of her thirty-one aircraft, with only one of these 'just possibly'[2] to enemy action.

A confused diplomatic and political situation arose at the outset. Admiral Darlan, commander of the French forces, agreed to a ceasefire, provided that Marshal Henri Petain, the Vichy French dictator agreed, but this was complicated by the Vichy attempts to prevent German forces from entering unoccupied France. In the event, Darlan sided with the Allies and ordered his forces to do so, but a number of French commanders disagreed, and allowed German forces to enter Tunisia.

The British naval forces pounded the French fleet with heavy gunfire from the battleships and cruisers. The aircraft were to attack Vichy French airfields. One of the pilots tasked with this duty was George Baldwin, later a captain but then the senior pilot, or second in command, of a Supermarine Seafire L.2 squadron, No. 807 embarked in *Furious*. Waiting in his cockpit for the signal to take off, he could hear the thunder of the distant gunfire and a glow on the horizon which suggested that the efforts of the battleships and cruisers were bearing fruit.

Twelve Seafires from *Furious* took off well before dawn, and for most of the pilots it was their first night take-off from an aircraft carrier. George Baldwin remembers the raid well.

'We thought that we had taken the French Air Force by surprise as we caught their bombers on the ground, and this was just before the sun came up over the horizon. It was just light enough to see targets for strafing and we went in among those French bombers rather over-confidently. I certainly made at least three strafing runs, which was later a forbidden . . . tactic . . . it became doctrine that you only ever made one run on a strafing attack because the danger rose so rapidly after the first run. I was sure that I had done very heavy damage to three bombers.

'After pulling out of the . . . attack, I was horrified to see a French Dewoitine fighter coming straight at me head on at about a thousand feet. I managed to evade him and turn in behind him, and give two bursts of machine-gun fire, because all my cannon ammunition had been used in the strafing. Saw hits and his undercarriage fell down.

'I then decided it was time to get home as quickly as possible . . . but just as I was making my way back to the coast, I saw a second Dewoitine at right angles to me on my port side. And as I saw him, I saw machine-gun fire coming underneath me, and this was followed instantly . . . by a huge explosion in the fuselage behind my seat, and I expected the aircraft to go out of control, but curiously nothing seemed to happen at all . . .'[3]

Baldwin, at about twenty-one years old, was already an accomplished naval test pilot having previously flown with the Naval Air Fighting Development Unit at Yeovilton. He carefully tested the controls of his aircraft, but everything seemed fine. It was not until he came within radio hailing distance of *Furious* that he realized that his radio wasn't working, and then that his aircraft's pneumatic system had also been damaged. He flew past the ship, signalling that he would

[2] Norman Gelb. *Desperate Venture*, Hodder & Stoughton, 1992.

[3, 4] Imperial War Museum Sound Archive.

have to land without using flaps. Fortunately, his undercarriage worked, and he made the hazardous landing without flaps, involving a faster than usual approach, and succeeded in putting the aircraft down on the flight deck.

'As soon as I was down, a large crowd of sailors and other pilots surrounded the aircraft, and as I climbed out I could see why. There was a huge hole about two feet in diameter on the port side of the fuselage directly behind my seat, and the whole of the rear fuselage was full of acid where the accumulator had been blown apart, and the radio was in pieces. The control wires to the rudder had been completely severed except for one wire, so I had been very lucky indeed.'[4]

Extremely lucky! The armour plating behind his seat had been peppered with shrapnel, yet he was unhurt. The Seafire had taken good care of its pilot. Later, Baldwin calculated that, since the shot had been at right angles to his aircraft, which was flying at well over 300 m.p.h., the Dewoitine's machine-gun burst had probably missed him in the cockpit by a 400th of a second!

Baldwin's squadron commanding officer, Lieutenant Fraser Harris, had been the only person shot down, and in his case by anti-aircraft fire over the target, which Baldwin and many of the other pilots claim not to have noticed. Baling out safely, he was taken prisoner by the Vichy French, and spent some time in the French general's office while they agonized over what to do with him. They eventually surrendered and he was back aboard *Furious* and with his squadron two days later. He must have enjoyed one of the shortest spells on record as a prisoner of war!

French naval forces in Casablanca, commanded by Rear Admiral de Lafond, also attempted to disrupt the landing forces using a light cruiser and six destroyers, but failed, and in a lengthy battle with the escorting forces, all of the French ships were either sunk or driven ashore. Air attack from the *Ranger*, followed up by heavy fire from an American battleship, badly damaged the battleship *Jean Bart*, which was lying in the harbour. An attempt at a break-out by French destroyers at Oran was also defeated by British naval forces. In the face of the superior Allied forces, resistance by the Vichy French ended on 8 November in Algiers, and in Oran the following day.

The Vichy French surrender in North Africa convinced the Germans that they should invade Vichy France and they occupied Toulon on 27 November. Italian forces invaded and occupied Corsica.

COMMENT

The action was well timed and well coordinated, persuading the enemy forces that resistance would be pointless after their initial attempts to attack the invasion fleet and the use of coastal artillery near Algiers. Morale among the Vichy French must have been poor, and many were inclined to side with the Allies against the Germans and Italians. The weakness of the defences also vindicated the earlier attacks by the Royal Navy on Vichy French naval vessels at Oran and Dakar. Although Force H was there to protect the invasion forces from Italian intervention – and it would have been foolhardy not to have done so – the Italian Navy was reluctant to fight by this time, and short of fuel.

An end to the North African campaign was a necessary prerequisite for the invasion of Sicily, leaving the Allied rear well protected. Nevertheless, a fiercely fought campaign lay ahead, with German reinforcements landing in Tunisia. It was to take until May 1943 before resupply of Axis forces in North Africa finally became impossible, leading to their surrender.

OPERATION HUSKY – ALLIED LANDINGS IN SICILY

THE FIRST STEP INTO AXIS TERRITORY

Having secured North Africa, the next stage was to carry the war directly into enemy territory. Up to this time that had been the sole preserve of the bomber in the European theatre. The United States would have preferred to leave the Mediterranean for the time being and plan for a major invasion of France, but at the Casablanca Conference in January 1943, the British argued that an invasion of France was premature, and that Sicily would provide a stepping-stone for an invasion of Italy, which would in turn free the shipping lanes through the Mediterranean. The British case was based not simply on a need to relieve the pressure on Malta, but a desire to route convoys to India through the Mediterranean and the Suez Canal once again, having had to route these via the Cape of Good Hope since 1940. Cutting the lengthy voyage around the Cape by using the much shorter Suez Canal route not only saved time and fuel, but would also provide a massive one-off boost in both merchant shipping tonnage and naval vessels. Fewer of both would be needed, and the spare ones could be used to alleviate pressure elsewhere.

On 11 and 12 June 1943 the garrisons on two small Italian islands, Pantelleria and Lampedusa, to the west of Malta, surrendered after being bombarded by the Royal Navy and subjected to shore-based air raids from Malta by the RAF and the Fleet Air Arm.

Designated Operation Husky, the Allied invasion of Sicily was set for 10 July.

SHIPS AND AIRCRAFT

Once again, the Royal Navy's Force H was present, but now under Vice-Admiral Willis, with six battleships and two aircraft carriers, *Indomitable* and *Formidable*, as well as six cruisers and twenty-four destroyers. There was no escort carrier on this occasion.

Indomitable, in common with other carriers of the Illustrious class, had an upper and a lower hangar. Before the operation she had been equipped with a new system for handling aircraft in the upper hangar. The aircraft were mounted on trolleys and the deck was fitted with rails, the intention being both to increase the capacity of the upper hangar so that it could take three squadrons of Seafires, about 36–40 aircraft, and at the same time reduce handling damage to the aircraft, which was a constant danger, especially if aircraft were packed closely together during rough weather. After the ship sailed for the Mediterranean, the trolley system was abandoned after a few days at sea because it proved to be too cumbersome and was likely to be a hindrance under intensive combat conditions.

The Allies had 3,700 aircraft available to them, mainly operating from land bases on Malta and in North Africa, against 1,400 Axis aircraft. The force of almost 3,000 ships for the invasion included 2,000 landing craft, among which were the new Landing Ship Tank, or LST. In terms of manpower, the Allies landed 180,000 men under the supreme command of General Dwight Eisenhower, but they had to face more than 275,000 men in General Guzzoni's Italian Sixth Army.

The aircraft for the operation included the now familiar Martlets and Seafires.

THE ACTION

The plan was for an American Western Naval Task Force, under Vice-Admiral Hewitt, to land the US Seventh Army under Lieutenant-General Patton on the south coast of Sicily, while the British Eastern Naval Task Force, under Admiral Ramsay, landed the British Eighth Army under Lieutenant-General Montgomery, on the south-east point of the island. Priority was to be given to the Americans taking the port of Licata and the British the port of Syracuse. Then the airfields around Catania were to be secured before the troops advanced to the Straits of Messina.

The attack was mounted from North Africa. Bad weather the night before the invasion nearly caused the landings to be postponed, but had the advantage of lulling the defending forces into a false sense of security. Some of the Axis commanders had in any event expected the initial landing to be on Sardinia. The element of surprise meant that the initial landings from the sea were a great success. Unfortunately, the airborne assault was less so, with many paratroopers landing in the sea, and gliders slipping their tow lines early and landing in the sea.

Force H's aircraft were committed to provided fighter cover for the landings. George Baldwin, by this time flying his Seafire fighters from *Indomitable*, recalls not seeing a single enemy aircraft for the first four days. Two Seafires did find a single Junkers Ju.88 bomber, nevertheless, which

shot down one of the British aircraft.

The following day, 11 July, the Axis forces mounted a massive counter-attack spearheaded by German Panzer divisions. This was successfully driven off by a combination of the invasion forces, air power and a heavy bombardment by the guns of Force H.

The apparent lack of aerial activity, nevertheless, must have lulled Force H into a false sense of security. One night, an Italian torpedo-bomber managed to spring a surprise attack on *Indomitable*, which, according to Baldwin, should not have happened and was an event 'to be ashamed of'.[1]

It was a brilliant moonlit night and many of the ship's company were on the flight-deck taking the air. One of the chief petty officers in Baldwin's squadron saw an approaching aircraft set against the moon, which was low on the horizon. Baldwin recalls, 'He shouted up to the bridge "Enemy aircraft on the port beam", and somebody learnt over and said, "Don't worry, it's only one of the Swordfish returning." Not a shot was fired at it and it dropped its torpedo so close . . . that it almost hit the mast as it flew over the ship.'[2]

Baldwin maintains that the circumstances were in favour of the defence. Visibility was good and *Indomitable* was supposed to be under the protection of a battleship acting as radar guardship, while the fleet had a massive anti-aircraft capability. As it was, the torpedo struck the ship and blew a 30-foot gash in the side, forcing her to divert to Malta, where she was patched up amidst intensive Axis air attack, and then had to leave the Mediterranean for repairs in the United States. Meanwhile, her squadrons were disembarked and the officers and men suffered in poor tented accommodation in the baking heat of summer and endured bombing by German and Italian aircraft.

Despite the success of the campaign over the next month, by 17 August the Axis forces had successfully evacuated Sicily, with more

[1,2] Imperial War Museum Sound Archive.

than 100,000 troops escaping across the Straits of Messina over successive nights using ferries and other vessels.

COMMENT

Sicily had to be the obvious toehold in Italy, although the enemy believed that Sardinia might have been a more likely location for an Allied landing, which explains the initial weakness of the defences until a counter-attack could be mounted. There is little doubt that the operation was a success, despite the heavy losses suffered by the airborne troops, but as many critics have pointed out since, it was a failure to allow so many Axis troops to escape across the Straits of Messina.

Operation Avalanche – Allied Landings At Salerno

Capitalizing on an Italian Armistice

Montgomery's Eighth Army crossed the Straits of Messina into Calabria on 3 September 1943, the same day as an armistice was signed secretly at Syracuse between the Allies and a new Italian government under Marshal Badoglio. Badoglio had taken over from Mussolini who had been deposed in late July. The armistice was announced on 8 September, the eve of the Allied landings at Salerno. The Germans moved quickly to seize Italian airfields, while the Italians moved equally quickly to save their fleet from falling into German hands. The landing at Salerno was coordinated with a British airborne landing at Taranto, to seize the port and allow the warships there to escape to Malta.

The armistice had been some time in negotiation because of Allied suspicions over Italian intentions, but this was probably a blessing in disguise. The Germans, after all, could not have been expected to leave quietly, and the only choice was for Allied landings at Salerno and Taranto, which needed time for the necessary organization.

Despite the fact that Salerno was chosen because it was within range of aircraft flying from Allied airfields in Sicily, it was only just within range for fighter aircraft, so that a Spitfire could only spend twenty minutes on station over the beachheads. Given the number of aircraft available and flying time to and from the operational area, this also meant that no more than nine aircraft could be over the invasion area at any one time.

This was clearly an operation for aircraft carriers, and the fleet carriers were augmented by the light fleet carrier *Unicorn* and four auxiliary carriers, the five of them comprising what was named Force V.

German ingenuity was to be displayed at Salerno, with radio-controlled glider bombs used against the fleet.

The other advantage of attacking Salerno, the choice of the American Fifth Army, which included some British units, was that it offered the prospect of cutting off a substantial number of German troops. A landing further north would have been still better in that sense, but the difficulties of air support would have been even greater than at Salerno, despite the presence of aircraft carriers.

The aircraft carrier did play an important role in the landings. Vice-Admiral Hewitt landed Lieutenant-General Clark's US Fifth Army in a landing fleet which included an Independence class light aircraft carrier and four escort carriers. Force H again, with Vice-Admiral Willis, provided protection for the landings from *Illustrious* and *Formidable*, plus the escort carriers in Force V, *Attacker*, *Battler*, *Hunter* and *Stalker*, and the light fleet carrier, *Unicorn*.

Ships and Aircraft

Illustrious and *Formidable* were sister ships. We have already come across the CVEs. *Unicorn* was a simplified version of the Illustrious class carriers, with two screws instead of three, and a heightened hangar deck, intended to act as a maintenance carrier.

Aircraft aboard the escort carriers and *Unicorn* were Supermarine Seafires, the role of which was to be air defence of the landings, and then fighter-bomber support against opposition forces. Each escort carrier had a single large Seafire squadron of thirty aircraft, with another sixty aboard *Unicorn*. These were different aircraft from the Seafires used in Operation Torch. The new Seafire L.2C's Merlin engines were tuned to provide maximum power below 5,000 feet rather than the 15,000 feet of the original aircraft. This was much better for naval operations.

Not content with this, while working up the new squadrons in Northern Ireland, George Baldwin, one of the fighter pilots, had visited the RAF to find out about the latest tactics and technical developments. The news

was bad, with the latest mark of the Messerschmitt Bf.109 and the new Focke-Wulf Fw.190 being formidable opponents, so that increasingly the skill of the individual pilot was the deciding factor. On his return to his unit, Baldwin and the engineers started to make 'local modifications' to enhance the performance of their Seafires. They removed the exhaust manifolds and replaced them with exhaust stubs to cut drag and increase the thrust from the exhaust. Good quality furniture polish was obtained and everyone spent hours polishing the leading edges of the wings. Knobs designed to enable the aircraft to operate from catapults were removed, again to reduce drag, since the Seafire rarely needed a catapult take-off. These changes were made during May and June 1943, and they gave the aircraft an extra 15 knots top speed.

The Supermarine Seafire was one of a number of naval fighters which tended to bounce when landing on a carrier. (IWM A25020)

THE ACTION

The British carrier fleet left Grand Harbour in Malta as if to attack Taranto, although in the event the British airborne landings at Taranto were covered by the guns of four of Force H's six battleships, and by aircraft from Malta, now becoming increasingly useful as an RAF base.

After the armistice, the Italian fleet fled from the Germans, leaving its naval bases at La Spezia, Castellamare, Genoa and Taranto, to sail to Malta. The battleships which had covered the landings at Taranto now escorted the Italian warships to Malta, while the other two accompanied *Illustrious* and *Formidable* to Salerno. The escaping Italian warships came under heavy German air attack, which sank the new battleship *Roma*, and damaged the *Italia*.

On 9 September, the day of the landings, the aircrew aboard *Unicorn* were awakened at 04.30 after a night of little sleep for many of them. Few of the pilots had any great appetite for the bacon and eggs on offer at breakfast. Before dawn the carrier flew off eight Seafires from 809 and 887 Naval Air Squadrons, with four of them for high cover and the other four for low to medium cover. These aircraft were carrying extra fuel in drop tanks, which they had to use first so that the tanks could be dropped as soon as the Luftwaffe appeared. That first day there was little sign of the Luftwaffe at the landings, although the troops ashore encountered fierce resistance.

In the days which followed the invasion forces came under heavy Luftwaffe aerial attack, and ashore a strong counter-attack was mounted. The operation soon appeared to be running into trouble.

The escort carriers and *Unicorn* had been given a 'box' in which to operate, flying off and recovering their aircraft. The problem was that this box was too small, which gave the commanders of the carriers great difficulties, but these were as nothing compared to those of the pilots. With large numbers of aircraft circling there was a very real danger of mid-air collision while they were preparing to land on ships steaming in close proximity to one another.

All of these problems were intensified by the dead calm conditions, and by the short flight decks of the escort carriers, which meant that the arrester wires had to be especially tight, as did the wire barrier two-thirds of the way along the flight deck. The Seafire needed a wind of 25 knots over the deck for a safe take-off or landing on, but the escort carriers could only manage 17 knots. Landing on was difficult. The fragile Seafire tended to pitch forward during landing, seriously damaging the propellors, a fault made worse by the tautness of the escort carriers' wires. Throughout the naval air operations, there was seldom more than 3 knots of wind. A haze also contributed to the poor conditions for flying, making landing on especially difficult. George Baldwin was by now the Naval Air Wing Commander, as an acting lieutenant-commander, responsible for the four squadrons embarked aboard the four escort carriers.

'Judgment of speed over the water, and height above the water, on the approach to land was extremely difficult,' Baldwin recalls.[1]

Eventually, Captain Henry McWilliams, commanding officer of *Hunter*, signalled the commanding officer of the British fleet, Rear Admiral Sir Philip Vian, asking for permission to saw 9 inches off the wooden propeller blades of the Seafires. Vian decided that it would be best to trust to McWilliams' superior expertise, and permission was given. Fortunately, the modification seemed to do the trick, without affecting the performance of the aircraft. It was also relatively easy for the ships' carpenters to carry out the modification, and Baldwin recalls that the carriers' store of spare propellers was also given the treatment before fitting to aircraft.

[1] Imperial War Museum Sound Archive.

During the operation, the casualty rate among pilots flying the Seafires was high; too few seemed to be able to bale out quickly enough. Eventually it was discovered that the RAF-recommended method of baling out was unsuitable for the aircraft. The RAF Spitfire pilots had been recommended to invert their aircraft and after opening the canopy and undoing their seat belts, eject from the stricken plane. For some reason, possibly the extra weight of the aircraft, this didn't work with the Seafire. Eventually, the pilots were told to jump over the side of the aircraft, resulting in a much higher survival rate.

The intense Luftwaffe attacks against the aircraft carriers on Saturday 11 September saw the ships using a considerable quantity of fuel as they raced up and down the 'box' assigned to them for air operations. That evening, Vian signalled Vice-Admiral Henry Kent Hewitt, the American officer in command of the invasion armada, who had just been visited by the ground forces' commander, Lieutenant-General Mark Clark: 'My bolt will be shot this evening, probably earlier.'

Hewitt guessed that the carriers were low on fuel, although he was unaware that the escort carriers were on emergency supplies. He guessed, correctly, that more major air attacks were imminent. He signalled back, 'Air conditions here critical. Can your carrier force remain on station to provide earlier morning coverage tomorrow?'

Vian sent him an affirmative: "Will stay here if we have to row back to Sicily.'[2]

The problem was that the planners thought that the Fleet Air Arm would be needed for two days, or three days at the most in an emergency. The original plan, not taking fierce German resistance into account, assumed that within that period airfields would have been taken and secured to allow the RAF to bring forward aircraft from Sicily.

A.O. 'Cappy' Masters was a Sub-Lieutenant pilot in the Royal New Zealand Navy Volunteer Reserve, RNZNVR, flying Seafire L.2Cs for 809 Squadron from *Unicorn* at Salerno. He recalls flying one dusk patrol.

'As before we reported to HMS *Euryalus* [Vian's flagship and task force fighter direction ship] for instructions. We were to patrol at 18,000 feet and be alert for possible bogeys. We were no sooner on patrol than we received an urgent call, "Bogey angels 28 vector 030 buster buster!" In laymen terms this meant that the fighter direction officers had picked up an aircraft on radar at 28,000 feet which was not displaying IFF (Identification Friend or Foe). "Buster buster" was the instruction to push the throttle to maximum boost and highest revolutions to climb to the required height as quickly as possible, steering 30 degrees from our present position. The sun was behind us so we were in a good position for surprise. As we closed on the bogey, *Euryalus* gave us slight adjustments in course, until finally we spotted him from behind. The target was flying alone, so obviously Willie would have the privilege of attacking first. If he missed, I would be next. It was a tense moment until suddenly Willie screamed out: "It's a bloody Lightning – an American P-38 fighter."'[3]

The Lightning pilot seemed unconcerned. The Seafire pilots waved to him, and he waved back at them. Masters decided to switch his guns to 'safe', and to his horror found that he had forgotten to switch them to 'on' in the excitement of the chase. The Seafire pilots did notice that the Lightning pilot was not wearing goggles, and on reporting this fact at their debriefing, were surprised to hear the intelligence officer suggest that perhaps they had come across a captured aircraft flown by a German! True or not, they had correctly recognized the aircraft, and its USAAF markings, and in the circumstances, there was little else they could have done.

[2] Des Hickey and Gus Smith. *Operation Avalanche: Salerno Landings* Heinemann, 1943.

[3] A.O. 'Cappy' Masters, *Memoirs of a Reluctant, Batsman*, Janus.

In addition to providing fighter cover against Luftwaffe attack, the carrier aircraft had to help the guns of the fleet in breaking the German Army's counter-attack between 12 and 14 September.

Damage in deck landing accidents accounted for a higher loss rate than did the Luftwaffe, with the support force's 180 aircraft eventually reduced to just 30 aircraft by the last day, 14 September. Baldwin again: 'Looking back on it, the operation, in terms of what had been expected of the Fleet Air Arm . . . support, was tremendously successful. More than the planned number of sorties was carried out, in spite of the accident rate.'[4]

Even so, afterwards many senior naval officers were reluctant to use the Seafire, ignoring the advice of their pilots, even when the aircraft could be used to good effect.

COMMENT

The speed and intensity of the German reaction to the Allied invasion and Italian capitulation surprised the Allies, but no less impressive was the coordination of future German responses. In January 1944 the Allied landings at Anzio, an attempt to by-pass the strong German resistance further south, did not have carrier air support, and it took four months for the invading forces to break out of their bridgehead.

[4] Imperial War Museum Sound Archive.

NOW SINK THE *TIRPITZ*!

THE MENACE WAITING TO POUNCE ON CONVOYS TO RUSSIA

Having successfully disposed of the *Bismarck*, the Royal Navy wanted to ensure the same fate for her sister ship, the *Tirpitz*. Like the *Bismarck*, *Tirpitz* was intended as a commerce-raider, and the German Navy was sufficiently weak in major surface units so that a major fleet action with the Royal Navy was seen as something to be avoided. Unfortunately for the British, the *Tirpitz* rarely put to sea. On one occasion, when the ship ventured forth in March 1942, looking for the convoy to Russia, PQ12, the battleship missed her prey in bad weather and was forced to return to her base. A torpedo attack by aircraft from the carrier *Victorious* was beaten off. The ship remained a threat, and indeed it was the mistaken belief that the *Tirpitz* was at sea which caused the British Admiralty to order the convoy PQ17, on passage to Russia, to scatter, with disastrous consequences as the ships were picked off by U-boats. On 22 September 1943 an attack by British midget submarines while the *Tirpitz* was in the Altenfjord damaged the huge warship sufficiently to put her out of action for six months.

Inevitably, attack from the air was attempted. This was far easier said than done. The large ship had extensive AA defences and was close to Luftwaffe fighter bases, but no less important, the terrain favoured her defence by hindering attack. The steep-sided fjords meant that often in the poor northern weather, the ship would be missed completely, while a precision bombing attack was fraught with difficulty and danger.

Nevertheless, on 3 April 1944, a determined bombing attack was launched by the Fleet Air Arm.

SHIPS AND AIRCRAFT

The aircraft carriers were the *Victorious*, sister ship of *Illustrious*, and *Furious*, plus three escort carriers or CVEs, sometimes referred to as auxiliary carriers by the British, which were *Emperor*, *Pursuer* and *Searcher*.

The attacks were carried out by Fairey Barracuda torpedo and dive-bombers from the large carriers. It is difficult to be complimentary about the Fairey Barracuda, which was an ugly aeroplane, of ungainly appearance. A high-winged monoplane with a crew of three, the Mk II typically had a 1,650 h.p. Rolls-Royce Merlin engine, two machine-guns in the rear cockpit, and it could carry either a 1,620-lb torpedo, a bomb load of 1,500 lbs, or four 450-lb depth charges. The maximum speed was 230 m.p.h. Despite its appearance the aircraft was highly effective and 2,600 were built.

Fighter cover for the raid came from the escort carriers, which had a mixture of Corsairs, Wildcats and Hellcats aboard. By this time, British and American designations for aircraft had been standardized.

THE ACTION

For the dawn raid, the aircrew were woken at 01.30 for a bacon and egg breakfast. Few had slept well and few now found an appetite for breakfast.

Although ungainly, the Fairey Barracuda was nevertheless a highly effective aircraft. (FAAM Barr/122)

Barracudas on their way to Norway, and *Tirpitz*! (FAAM Barr/37)

Barracudas over hostile territory. (FAAM Camp/266)

The role of the batsman required keen judgement, physical stamina, strong nerves and, if things didn't work out, extremely quick reactions. (IWM A22693)

One of those on the operation recalled, 'We were told it was going to be a very dangerous attack, and that we must expect heavy casualties.'[1]

The first strike aircraft took off at 04.30, with the aircraft flying at sea level to avoid detection on enemy radar, and then climbing to 8,000 feet to cross the mountains. The weather was excellent. They reached the ship at 05.30.

Sub-Lieutenant John Herrald was a New Zealander serving with the Fleet Air Arm and flying a Fairey Barracuda. He recalls that the attacking aircraft 'reached the coast of Norway when the sun had reached the edge of the horizon . . . snow was so brilliant, it was a light blue colour . . .

'Then ahead of us we could see the hill which sheltered the fjord and the *Tirpitz*. As I looked at this hill, it fell below us slowly, and then with a sudden surge we were over the top. There below us lay the *Tirpitz* in the exact place we had been told to look for her.

Suddenly the leader shouted over the intercom: "Attention fighters! Anti-flak! Over, Over!" and as he said that he was slowly doing a half-roll and going down to the target. We peeled off and dived down behind him. While we were going down on our attack, the fighter squadron were strafing the anti-aircraft positions and ships. They supported us with everything they had got, no risk seemed too great for them to take.

'I had the nose of my aircraft pointing just below the funnel of the *Tirpitz*. I could see the fighters raking her decks, and for a few seconds I lived in a world which just contained my aircraft and the *Tirpitz*. I kept her nose glued to that point of the ship. I gazed at my altimeter and saw that I had a thousand feet to go until I got to my bombing height. In the few seconds that followed I could see the details of the ship; the swastika painted on her funnel, the faces of the ack-ack crews glaring up at us, and, a great sight, the leader's bombs bursting on the turrets.'[2]

[1] Ludovic Kennedy. *Menace: Life and Death of the Tirpitz*, Sidgwick & Jackson, 1979.

[2–4] Imperial War Museum Sound Archive (2508).

A Barracuda and a Seafire aboard *Furious* off Norway. (IWM A22695)

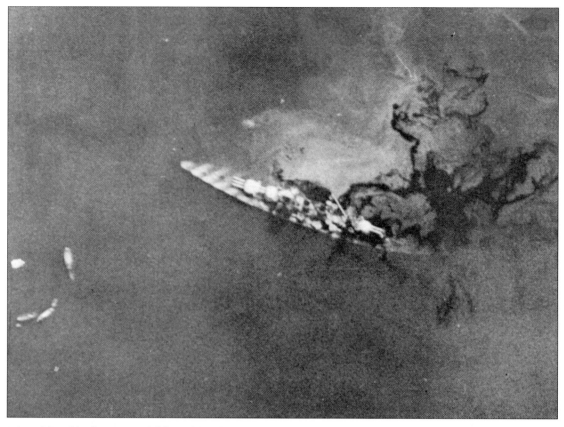

Leaking oil showed that despite terrain which favoured the defence and heavy AA fire, the Fleet Air Arm had succeeded in inflicting serious damage to *Tirpitz*. (FAAM Camp/568)

He dropped his bombs as he pulled out of his dive and 'started weaving to avoid the flak. There was enemy tracer about, but the fighters beat the hell out of them.'[3]

The aircraft returned to the ship and was struck down into the hangars. 'The ground crew gathered around. "How did it go? How did the aircraft perform?"'[4]

The attack had enjoyed complete surprise, so that the fighter leader had called 'Out lights', meaning that there were no enemy fighters and the fighter aircraft were to dive down and strafe the battleship's anti-aircraft positions.

'Some of my ammunition was red tracer,' said Sub-Lieutenant Laurie Brander, 'and I well remember seeing it strike the *Tirpitz*'s armour plating, then bouncing up into the sky and disappearing.'[5]

An hour later the second strike appeared, expecting to be savaged by the AA fire of an alert enemy. The Germans had put up a smoke screen from canisters based around the fjord hoping to make a second attack difficult, but the attacking aircraft could see the *Tirpitz* while the smoke made it difficult for her AA gunners to see the incoming aircraft.

The attack resulted in damage to the warship, putting her out of action for a further three months.

[5] Ludovic Kennedy. *Menace: Life and Death of the Tirpitz*, Sidgwick & Jackson, 1979.

A substantial proportion of Fleet Air Arm wartime aircrew were volunteer reservists, hence the 'wavy navy' rings, many of them New Zealanders. Here four RNZNVR pilots relax by their Seafire after escorting a raid on *Tirpitz*. (IWM A24774)

One of the fighter pilots, another New Zealander, was Lieutenant-Commander Ron Richardson, flying a Grumman Hellcat and in command of 1840 Squadron, most of whose pilots were members of the Royal Netherlands Navy. After strafing *Tirpitz*, he started the return flight. Ahead of him, he saw a radar station on a hill top. Having used all of his ammunition, he dropped his arrester hook to catch the wire between the two masts, and as he did so he was shot down by German anti-aircraft fire and killed.

COMMENT

This was one of seven attacks by the RAF and nine by the Fleet Air Arm on the *Tirpitz*.

On 15 September 1944 a force of Avro Lancaster bombers from the elite 617 'Dam Busters' Squadron used 12,000-lb 'Tallboy' bombs, but again only damage was caused, although sufficiently serious for the ship to have to be moved further south to Tromso for repairs. There she was a far easier target and also closer to the RAF's bases, so that on 12 November more 617 Squadron Lancasters found her without defending fighters and, in perfect visibility, scored three hits with the 'Tallboys', causing her to capsize.

One senior British naval officer, with amazingly bad grace, tried to suggest that the *Tirpitz* had still not been sunk since her hull was out of the water!

Lieutenant-Commander George Baldwin is in the back row, second from right, in this photograph taken after Operation Dragoon, when *Hunter* sailed for the Far East via the Suez Canal. King Farouk of Egypt (front centre) and senior Egyptian naval officers visited the ship. (IWM A28114)

OPERATION DRAGOON – ALLIED LANDINGS IN THE SOUTH OF FRANCE

15–24 AUGUST 1944

TACKLING THE SOFT UNDERBELLY OF GERMAN RESISTANCE

By August 1944 the situation had changed considerably. The bottlenecks in the Allied advance northward through Italy had been broken, and Rome liberated. American and French forces in Italy had been reduced considerably for the planned invasion of the south of France, two months behind the invasion in Normandy. Now that the pressure on the shipping routes through the Mediterranean had gone, the Italian campaign was fulfilling another objective, forcing the Germans to divert air and ground forces from other more important fronts.

In August of the previous year the Combined Chiefs of Staff had considered an invasion of the south of France, but the British had objected on the grounds that this would divert resources from the advance through Italy, which they hoped would result in an invasion of Germany through Austria. Eventually, it was agreed that the invasion of the south of France should follow that of Normandy, and that the Normandy invasion would lead to the liberation of the Low Countries and invasion of Germany. Although aircraft carriers had not been involved in the Normandy landings, Fleet Air Arm Seafires from shore-bases had flown reconnaissance missions over enemy-held territory, acting as 'spotters' for the heavy guns of the invasion fleet's covering battleships and cruisers.

Originally, the invasion of the south of France was code-named Operation Anvil, but as it slipped down the list of Allied priorities, the revised code-name Operation Dragoon was adopted.

The south of France was viewed as being the soft underbelly of German resistance, with resources and attention being concentrated on Normandy and, to a lesser extent, Italy. It is possible that the Germans did not take the risk of invasion too seriously, possibly expecting to fight to hold the Allies in Italy, and assuming that, if that failed, the Allies would enter France from Italy. Of course, the Germans had only taken the south of France in late 1942, by which time the resources to build massive coastal defences would have been in increasingly short supply compared to the situation in the north of France in 1940.

SHIPS AND AIRCRAFT

The risk of interference by strong enemy surface forces had disappeared by this time, and the forces required were those needed in support of the landing, and suppression of the defences. This meant nine escort carriers to provide fighter and ground attack cover, while the fast, armoured carriers of the Royal Navy were released to fight elsewhere.

For this operation, the Seafire was still much in evidence, and again the L.2C version, with 'local modifications' in many cases.

The American escort carriers carried the new Grumman Hellcat.

THE ACTION

The American Vice-Admiral Hewitt commanded a fleet which included 500 landing and 200 escort vessels to land Lieutenant-General Patch's US Seventh Army between Cannes and Toulon on 15 August 1945. The covering fleet included three US battleships plus one each from the Free French and the British, as well as nine escort carriers, twenty-five cruisers and forty-five destroyers. Nevertheless, the landings met little resistance, so that within a few days both the naval base at Toulon and the major port at Marseilles were in Allied hands.

The aircraft aboard the carriers found that there was little Luftwaffe resistance, and ended up in close support of the ground forces. Fortunately, this had been expected, and Lieutenant-Commander Baldwin had sought, and been given, permission already to undertake ground attack sorties with the RAF ashore in Italy. Indeed, he only arrived back aboard his ship, which on this occasion was the escort carrier *Attacker*, just in time for the start of the operation.

For many of the American pilots, it was their first time in a war zone.

'We were very worried about the Americans, they were . . . unblooded,' Baldwin recalls. 'They had come straight from the United States and had never seen any kind of action before. So they had been given a very considerable briefing by some of our air staff on the sort of things they needed to know about the German opposition . . . type of anti-aircraft fire and what not to do . . .'[1]

The intention was to minimize American losses on their first few sorties. The briefing was that aircraft should never fly in formation or in a straight line, but be well spaced to allow weaving, and never fly between 9,000 and 11,000 feet unless ascending or descending, since German 88-mm anti-aircraft artillery was very accurate between these heights. Baldwin maintains that the advice was either not taken or did not pass down through to the squadrons.

'The poor chaps, they flew a flight of four aircraft over Marseilles the first morning in formation in a straight line and the first salvo from the 88-mm guns knocked two of the four aircraft out of the sky. Sad loss . . .'[2]

The lessons of the Salerno landings had been learnt. Not only were there more aircraft carriers, but adequate manoeuvring space was allowed. No less important, flying conditions were ideal, with a breeze and a gentle swell at sea.

Much of the naval air operation comprised reconnaissance for the ground forces. 'We had a very good deal with the American Army commanders . . . who were able to use our information most effectively,' said Baldwin.[3]

After forty hours it was clear to the pilots that the Germans were pulling out, mainly to the north. One group retreated west before moving north, and this force was attacked by the Seafire squadrons after 19 August while the Germans were around Avignon.

The USN and RN pilots harried the retreating Germans until they were out of effective fighting range of the carriers. This took until 24 August, after which the USAAF took over.

During the operation the escort carriers were able to return to Corsica for replenishment and replacement aircraft, without any of the fuel shortages of the Salerno débâcle.

COMMENT

This was too good an opportunity to miss, putting additional pressure on German forces in France and Italy. It was to be followed up in September and October by British naval forces, with nothing heavier than cruisers and escort carriers, cutting the German evacuation routes out of Greece across the Aegean, and destroying all remaining German naval units in the Aegean.

[1–3] Imperial War Museum Sound Archive.

PART FIVE

TAKING THE WAR TO JAPAN

BACKGROUND

The United States Navy's overwhelming success in the Battle of Midway changed the balance of power in the Pacific. Nevertheless, the Japanese still had a substantial fleet, including an untried surface fleet of battleships and battlecruisers, and the capability of building aircraft carriers or converting other ships to this role. The rapid growth of the Japanese empire across the Pacific and South-East Asia also meant that Japan's supplies of fuel and raw materials had been secured.

This was a carrier war. Initially in the war against Japan, operations were often conducted over distances beyond the range of land-based planes, and even when long-range bombers were able to tackle these ranges, fighter protection lagged behind. The terrain of many of the islands which had to be recovered from Japanese occupation favoured defending forces, and it could take time before these were secure enough for airfields to be used. By comparison, the carriers offered greater security for aircraft and airman alike.

For the soldiers and marines fighting in the jungle, carrier aircraft were also a blessing. Not only did the large carriers operate to suppress the defences before a landing, the escort carriers proved invaluable in carrying aircraft to support forces ashore.

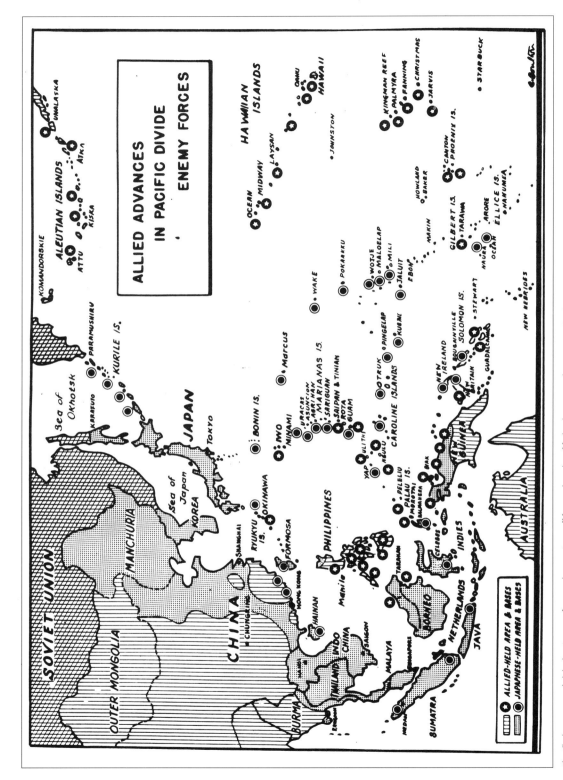

The Allied strategy entailed dividing Japanese forces and cutting Japan off from vital supplies of fuel and raw materials. (IWM NYF73462)

THE AMERICANS TAKE THE INITIATIVE – GUADALCANAL

7–20 AUGUST 1942

REMOVING THE JAPANESE THREAT

Having crippled Japanese naval air power in the decisive victory at Midway, the Americans took the initiative in the Pacific. The immediate priority was to secure essential strategic communications across the Pacific, and the construction of Japanese naval and air bases on Guadalcanal, in the Solomon Islands, was viewed as posing a threat to the sea lanes between the United States and Australia.

The landings which took place on Guadalcanal and Tulagi on 7 August 1942, marked the start of the advance across the Pacific towards Japan. It was also the first occasion when British and American forces fought alongside each other in the Pacific theatre.

SHIPS AND AIRCRAFT

Support for the operation was provided by the three American aircraft carriers, *Enterprise*, *Saratoga* and *Wasp*, who have been described already, while the aircraft were the same as those involved at Midway, with the exception of the ill-named Douglas Devastator torpedo-bomber, which was withdrawn after its poor performance during that battle.

THE ACTION

Named Operation Watchtower and under the overall command of Vice-Admiral Ghormley, the operation was also known to many of those involved as Operation Shoestring, because of the haste and short cuts in preparation. Many commentators also draw attention to the poor morale resulting from quarrels between the United States Army and Navy over who should take the lead in the war. The assault force consisted of nineteen transports under Rear Admiral Turner, which carried the 19,000 men of Major-General Vandegrift's 1st Marine Division.

Covering fire for the landings was provided by eight cruisers and fifteen destroyers commanded by Rear Admiral Crutchley, RN. Air support was provided by the three aircraft carriers, *Enterprise*, *Saratoga* and *Wasp*, with a battleship, six cruisers and sixteen destroyers under Vice-Admiral Fletcher.

The bombardment of Guadalcanal started at 09.00 on 7 August, and the 11,000 men allocated to Guadalcanal were all ashore by the evening. Resistance on Guadalcanal was light; most of the Japanese there were construction workers who, in one description, 'ran into the jungle when the first bomb dropped'. The airfield being built by the Japanese was just completed, and it was taken on 8 August. Renamed Henderson Field, it acted as the focal point for the Japanese counter-attack, and some months of fighting around the airfield ensued.

For the 6,000 men landed on Savo, the situation was completely different, as they encountered fierce resistance and were later to be cut off from supplies until the first

American aircraft started operating out of Henderson Field on 20 August.

Japanese forces appear to have been taken by surprise, and it was not until the night of 8/9 August that any naval action resulted. At midnight the Japanese attacked the covering cruisers and destroyers in a night action off Savo Island, but failed to break through to attack the invasion fleet. The Japanese force of seven cruisers and a destroyer had the element of surprise and suffered little damage. Only the flagship *Chokai* received a number of hits, but the attack managed to inflict severe damage on the Allied cruisers, to the extent that the following morning two cruisers sank and another two capsized.

COMMENT

The action at Guadalcanal has been criticized for hasty preparation, but one could argue that the Americans had little choice but to act quickly. Had Guadalcanal become an operational Japanese base, it would have been far more difficult to take. Worse, it would have been an offensive base, threatening links between the United States and Australia. It was also the first invasion of enemy-held territory of the Second World War, and if mistakes were made, it would not have been surprising. Indeed, during the First World War, United States forces had not been involved in an invasion of enemy-held territory.

The real question was, of course, how did such a large force of Japanese cruisers manage to come within striking distance of the fleet, and with such an element of surprise? The only answer can be that the range of the carrier aircraft was not enough to find the Japanese force, and that such a fast moving force was able to cover the distance after darkness fell.

BATTLE OF THE SOLOMON ISLANDS

23–25 AUGUST 1942

STOPPING THE 'TOKYO EXPRESS'

After the American invasion of Guadalcanal, the Japanese had sent reinforcements, seriously underestimating the American strength at first, so that the first batch of combat troops was wiped out by the Americans. The Japanese managed to land reinforcements on Guadalcanal, often doing this under cover of darkness in an operation known to the Americans as the 'Tokyo Express'. Nevertheless, more was needed, and four transports were sent by the Japanese to reinforce their troops on Guadalcanal.

SHIPS AND AIRCRAFT

Vice-Admiral Fletcher with Task Force 61 still had the two carriers *Enterprise* and *Saratoga* with 176 aircraft, while *Wasp* was away refuelling. Vice-Admiral Nagumo, still in command after the disaster of Midway, had 131 aircraft aboard the *Zuikaku* and *Shokaku*, while the light carrier *Ryujo* had 37 aircraft, and with a cruiser and 2 destroyers was detailed to act as a diversionary force.

The Japanese had a far stronger force of surface ships than the Americans. Fletcher had a battleship, four cruisers and eleven destroyers, while Nagumo had three battleships, ten cruisers and twenty-one destroyers, as well as the ships with the diversionary force. The Japanese 'transports', however, were simply old destroyers and were carrying a total of just 1,500 men.

THE ACTION

Expecting a Japanese attack after spotting the *Ryujo*, the Americans then lost track of the Japanese by 21 August, although Fletcher had his forces in position. American reconnaissance aircraft searching for Japanese ships on 23 August, found the troop transports, but a strike from the American carriers failed to find them. The next day, aircraft from *Saratoga* found the *Ryujo* at 10.00, some 300 miles north of the American fleet. A strike was launched which sank the *Ryujo*, using bombs and torpedoes, while at the same time Japanese aircraft from *Shokaku* and *Zuikaku* found and attacked *Enterprise*. Fighters from *Enterprise* and the ship's AA defences managed to fight off the first wave of torpedo-bombers, but the second wave of dive-bombers scored three hits on the ship, causing fires. The fires were soon extinguished, leaving the ship capable of limited operations.

The following day, shore-based United States Marine Corps bombers operating from Guadalcanal and Esperitu Sanctu attacked the Japanese troop transports, sinking the largest one and one of the escorting destroyers, while severely damaging a cruiser. This persuaded the Japanese to abandon the entire operation, having lost ninety aircraft in addition to the ships. The Americans had lost just twenty aircraft, although *Enterprise* was badly damaged.

COMMENT

The Americans won mastery of the sea around Guadalcanal as a result of this battle, although it did not stop the Japanese sending supplies and reinforcements under cover of darkness, using destroyers so that the Japanese force on the island soon built up to 6,000 from virtually nothing after the invasion. The destroyers used on the 'Tokyo Express' also took the opportunity to shell Henderson Field, although they never managed to inflict serious damage. Airborne radar, had it been available operationally at the time, would have curbed the night-time resupply operation. As it was, using improved shipborne radar, the Japanese were to suffer a further defeat in a surface vessel action with American cruisers and destroyers during the night of 11/12 October.

The *Wasp* was soon to be sunk by the Japanese submarine *I–19*, off Guadalcanal.

BATTLE OF THE SANTA CRUZ ISLANDS

THE ODDS SEEM TILTED IN JAPAN'S FAVOUR

In the continuing struggle for Guadalcanal in October, the Japanese Navy received a report claiming that Henderson Field had been recaptured, ending American aerial superiority in the eastern Solomons. The report was premature, but unaware of this, Admiral Yamamoto sent the Japanese Combined Fleet to cover the reconquest of the island. In one sense only the timing was opportune for the Japanese, since Admiral Halsey, in overall command, had just two aircraft carriers available to him.

SHIPS AND AIRCRAFT

The Americans had the recently-repaired *Enterprise* in Task Force 16 under Vice-Admiral Kinkaid, with eighty-four aircraft, and the *Hornet* in Task Force 17 under Vice-Admiral Murray, with eighty-seven aircraft. They also had another sixty aircraft, mainly USMC, at Henderson Field. Overall, the American fleet was inferior to the Japanese, with just one battleship, six cruisers and fourteen destroyers, and many of these ships were being used to block the 'Tokyo Express' resupply operation.

By contrast, the Japanese could muster four aircraft carriers. The van of the fleet under Vice-Admiral Kondo had the *Junyo* with fifty-five aircraft, as well as two battleships, five cruisers and fourteen destroyers. Vice-Admiral Nagumo had the aircraft carriers *Shokaku*, *Zuikaku* and *Zuiho*, with 157 aircraft, another 2 battleships, 5 cruisers and 15 destroyers.

THE ACTION

After a strike on 25 October had failed to find two Japanese carriers, early on 26 October 1942 American reconnaissance aircraft found the *Zuiho*. At 07.30, *Hornet* sent a strike of torpedo-planes and dive-bombers, escorted by Grumman Wildcat fighters, which managed to inflict serious damage with one bomb. Expecting the American attack, at 07.10 Nagumo sent his first wave to attack the *Hornet*, reaching the warship shortly after 09.00. Fifteen dive-bombers and twelve torpedo-bombers struck at the ship, with a bomb hitting the flight deck and then a bomber struck the island, although it is not clear whether this was a suicide operation or a case of the aircraft being out of control. Two torpedoes hit the *Hornet* on her starboard side, before three more 500-lb bombs crashed through the wooden flight deck and into the hangar. The ship was ablaze within ten minutes and listing to starboard.

At 09.30, the *Shokaku* was hit by five bombs, which did not sink her, but put her out of action for nine months. A second wave of Japanese aircraft then concentrated on *Enterprise*, hitting her with three bombs but failing to put the carrier out of action. While the Americans had fighter aircraft providing air cover, most of the heavy Japanese losses were due to highly effective AA fire, with the battleship *South Dakota* alone accounting for twenty-six Japanese aircraft.

A further attack by aircraft from *Junyo* and *Zuikaku* that afternoon again concentrated on the *Hornet*, and with a further torpedo hit and two bombs as well, the carrier had to be abandoned. American destroyers then tried to sink the carrier, but most of the torpedoes failed to run straight, and those that did hit seemed to do very little damage, since nine hits failed to sink her – a sad reflection on the quality of USN torpedoes at this stage of the war. She was later sunk with more torpedoes from a Japanese destroyer.

By this time, the true situation at Henderson Field had become apparent to the Japanese, and they ordered a withdrawal, realizing that they did not have sufficient aircraft left to assist their ground forces in recapturing the airfield.

COMMENT

While the loss of the *Hornet* was a serious blow to the United States Navy, of greater importance was the fact that they had lost 70 aircraft compared to the 100 lost by the Japanese, who were to have greater difficulty in replacing aircraft and, even more importantly, pilots. Victory in this battle belonged to the Japanese, but it was a costly victory and one which they could not afford, with so many aircraft lost and two aircraft carriers seriously damaged. In having just two carriers available, the Americans had let their guard drop to some extent. With Henderson Field besieged by the Japanese, it would have been difficult, and even unwise, to have had more aircraft ashore.

During November there were two night battles off Guadalcanal, the first on the night of 12/13 November, and the second on the night of 14/15 November. These were surface actions, provoked by Japanese bombardment of Henderson Field, although the second battle followed the sinking by aircraft from Henderson Field of seven out of eleven Japanese transports. Aircraft carriers were not involved in the actions themselves, but, on the morning of 13 November aircraft from the *Enterprise* and shore-based aircraft finished off the battleship *Hiei*, which was drifting after receiving serious damage during the night battle with American cruisers and destroyers.

Again, on the morning of 14 November, after Japanese bombardment had destroyed twenty aircraft at Henderson Field, a strike from *Enterprise* sank the cruiser *Kinugasa* as she tried to leave the area; two other Japanese ships were also damaged in this attack.

US Landings on the Gilbert Islands

The Push Towards Japan

Having secured the Solomon Islands, the Americans were ready to push across the Pacific towards Japan, with their next objective being the Gilbert Islands, more than a thousand miles to the north-east. There had been few opportunities for carrier forces during most of 1943, until 5 November, when the *Saratoga* and *Princeton* struck at Rabaul in the Admiralty Islands in a surprise attack, damaging six Japanese cruisers for the loss of ten aircraft. A repeat attack on 11 November saw 185 aircraft from the new carriers, *Essex*, *Bunker Hill* and *Independence*, damage another cruiser and sink a destroyer, while a Japanese air attack on the fleet was repulsed with a heavy loss of Japanese aircraft and without one hit on the American warships. After capturing Rabaul in 1942, the Japanese had built strong defences, and it had been American policy to isolate the island and weaken these defences before any invasion.

As the war progressed, American AA defences became highly effective, and sights like this became commonplace as Japanese aircraft such as this torpedo-bomber, disintegrated before reaching their target. (IWM NYP 11545)

Meanwhile, with only three aircraft carriers fully operational and a heavy loss in aircraft and aircrew, the Japanese had attempted to spend 1943 on training and rebuilding the First Air Fleet. In a sense, the Americans had been doing the same thing, building up their fleet of wartime aircraft carriers with the arrival of the first of the new Essex class carriers and the light carriers of the Independence class, converted from Cleveland class cruisers, although, for the most part, the conversions were started while the cruisers were still under construction. New aircraft were also entering USN service, and a massive expansion in aircrew training had been implemented. The extent of the American training programme was considerable, training aircrew for the Royal Navy as well as for the USN and USMC.

For the landings on the Gilbert Islands in the latter half of November 1943, the newly formed United States Fifth Fleet under Vice-Admiral Spruance, with its carrier force commanded by Rear Admiral Pownall, was able to field six large aircraft carriers and five of the light carriers of the Independence class, as well as five battleships, six cruisers and twenty-one destroyers. No less important, aboard the American carriers were 700 aircraft, including up-dated versions of earlier types, and one significant new type, the Grumman F6F Hellcat fighter.

In addition to the Fifth Fleet, the landing fleet, commanded by Rear Admiral Turner, included 8 escort carriers with a combined total of 216 aircraft. This was a significant force in its own right, with two of the new dock landing ships, twenty troop and supply carriers, seven battleships, six heavy and two light cruisers, and thirty-eight destroyers.

SHIPS AND AIRCRAFT

The American fleet had undergone many changes, of which the most significant was the introduction of the Essex class aircraft carriers, displacing 27,000 tons. Ten had been ordered in 1940, while another fourteen were ordered the week after Pearl Harbor, although these were longer and displaced 28,000 tons. Essentially an improved Yorktown class carrier, the first ten ships had the high speed of 33 knots combined with a capacity for up to eighty aircraft. Apart from the *Enterprise* and the *Saratoga*, the latter returning to service after surviving her second submarine torpedo attack, the large carriers of the US Fifth Fleet were all of the new Essex class, including a new *Yorktown* and *Lexington*, as well as *Essex* and *Bunker Hill*.

A good indication of the pace at which the United States could develop its naval forces comes from the fact that the *Essex* joined the fleet on 31 January 1943, and within a year another six vessels had followed!

Nevertheless, the United States Navy needed more aircraft carriers, and it needed them urgently, to augment the purpose-designed Essex class vessels. The solution was to convert a cruiser class, taking the Cleveland class light cruisers to create the Independence class light carriers, or CVLs. Once converted, these ships displaced 14,000 tons, and could accommodate a theoretical forty-five aircraft, although this was generally reduced to thirty for operations. An unusual design, four small funnels were aft of the small starboard island, although these and the island were clear of the flight deck. Maximum speed was 31 knots, and two catapults were fitted to assist take-off, although generally the USN preferred to operate fighters and fighter-bombers from these ships rather than the heavier dive-bombers. At the Gilbert Islands, the light carriers of the Independence class included *Independence*, *Belleau Wood*, *Cowpens*, *Monterey* and *Princeton*.

Finally, there were the escort carriers, or CVEs. These had evolved from the need to provide ships for convoy escort duties, especially in the North Atlantic where such

The United States fleet off the Marshall Islands, February 1944. In the foreground is one of the new Independence-class light carriers, while in the background the familiar 'pyramid' superstructures of Essex-class ships can be seen. (IWM NYF 22732)

ships overcame the U-boat menace. Converted from merchant ships, or on hulls designed for merchant ships, these ships were quick and cheap to build, so they became known as the 'Woolworth Carriers' or, to the Americans, as 'Jeep Carriers'. The more cynical described them as 'Combust-able-Vulnerable-Expendable', since poor standards of construction and the lack of any armour meant that these ships were of little use in battle. An interim stage had been the merchant aircraft carrier, which was a cargo ship manned by the merchant navy, but with a wooden flight deck over the holds so that a small number of naval aircraft could be operated. The escort carriers were much slower than the purpose-built ships, with a maximum speed of about 17 knots and accommodation for just 18 aircraft.

By this stage of the conflict, the convoy war in the North Atlantic was all but won, and two new roles had emerged for the escort carrier. The first was to act as an aircraft tender, bringing spare aircraft for the battle carriers, while the second was to carry fighter-bombers for close support of ground forces during and after an invasion, before airfields ashore could be secured and made ready for use. This was the role of the force of eight CVEs in the Gilbert Islands.

The American aircraft included the latest versions of the Douglas Dauntless, the SBD-4 and SBD-5, the latter having up-rated 1,200 h.p. engines compared with the 1,000 h.p. of earlier versions.

The new *Yorktown* had the distinction of having the first operational Grumman F6F Hellcat fighters. This aircraft was soon to become the mainstay of the USN's carrier

The USN and USAAF worked hard at softening up targets before sending in the Marines or US Army. This is a 'before', 'during' and 'after' sequence of Dublon Island, part of the Truk Atoll. (IWM NYF45286-8)

fighter squadrons, capable of gaining and maintaining aerial superiority wherever it appeared. There were several variants of this popular aeroplane, but generally a 2,000 h.p. Pratt & Whitney R-2800 radial engine gave the single-engined fighter a maximum speed approaching 400 m.p.h. It usually mounted six 0.5-in machine-guns in each wing, although later versions had four 20-mm cannon. Rockets under the wings, or 2,000 lb of bombs under the fuselage, were also options with later versions, with a night fighter variant having a radar pod under a wing.

THE ACTION

Starting on 19 November 1943, the Fifth Fleet's 700 aircraft began a series of attacks on all Japanese airfields within range of Makin and Tarawa, the two islands selected for the initial landings. Within three days most of the shore-based aircraft, mainly of the Japanese Navy Air Force, on both the Gilbert Islands and the nearby eastern Marshall Islands, were out of action. On 20 November, the landing fleet put ashore the US 2nd Marine Division and part of the Army's 27th Infantry Division. Some 7,000 men were landed on Makin, and 18,000 on

Tarawa, which had the main Japanese garrison of some 5,000 troops, prepared to fight to the last. Despite softening up the defences, a third of the Marines on the initial assault were hit by intensive enemy fire. Makin, with a garrison of just 800, was taken that same day following heavy fighting, but Tarawa took another three days, culminating in Japanese infantry suicide attacks on the night of 22/23 November.

Despite the intensive strikes against Japanese airfields, on the first day of the landings the light carrier *Independence* was struck by a torpedo dropped by a Japanese aircraft. On 24 November, the CVE *Liscombe Bay* was torpedoed by the Japanese submarine *I-175*, and sank shortly afterwards

Despite the fierce resistance, by 26 November the Americans had occupied the Gilbert Islands.

COMMENT

The overwhelming force necessary to capture these islands showed just how stiff a resistance Japanese ground forces were to offer, often with the assault forces fighting over difficult terrain. Even at this stage, however, American superiority in the air and at sea had become apparent.

THE GREAT MARIANAS TURKEY SHOOT

19–20 JUNE 1944

THE SITUATION IN THE PACIFIC IN 1944

By the beginning of 1944, the American advance across the Pacific was gaining momentum. An established pattern was emerging, as the carrier aircraft suppressed Japanese air power and then tackled shore defences, softening up the enemy's defences before marines and soldiers were finally put ashore. The step-by-step progress was not simply logical. It meant that as each piece of territory was taken, its airfields could be pressed into use, and the aircraft operated from them augmented the work of the carrier aircraft.

After the Gilbert Islands were occupied, the American Fifth Fleet under Vice-Admiral Spruance jumped to Kwajalein Atoll in the Marshall Islands, something which Spruance himself felt was a step too far, but which the commander-in-chief in the Pacific, Admiral Chester Nimitz, saw as an essential step, by-passing the many small islands and atolls spread over some 400,000 square miles of ocean. Under Spruance, Vice-Admiral Marc Mitscher commanded Task Force 58, the main carrier force. Kwajalein was invaded on 31 January.

Expecting a strong Japanese counter-attack with major surface vessels, the next major

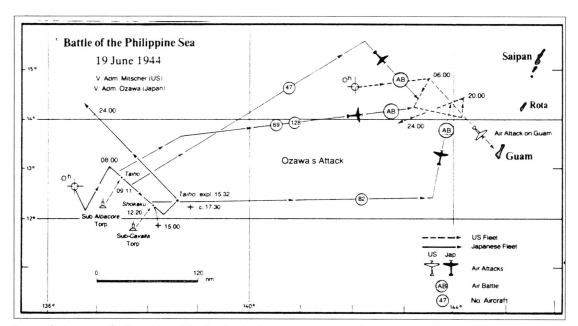

Known to the Americans as the 'Great Marianas Turkey Shoot', and to the Japanese as the 'First Battle of the Philippine Sea'.

advance was Truk Atoll, in the Caroline Islands, which the Japanese had converted into a major naval base used by major units of the Imperial Japanese Navy. Truk was neutralized in the same way that Rabaul and then Kwajalein had been earlier. For the two days of the assault, 17 and 18 February 1944, the aircraft carriers operated in an area some 50 miles wide and 100 miles deep, with its western boundary just over a hundred miles east of Truk Atoll.

Unfortunately, the large Japanese warships which the Fifth Fleet was hoping to catch at Truk were simply not there. Carrier aircraft sank a cruiser and a destroyer, as well as twenty-six merchantmen, a total of 130,000 tons of merchant shipping. Nevertheless, the real victory was in the air, where the Americans shot down 300 out of a total of 365 aircraft based on Truk, for the loss of just 25 of their own aircraft. In a hastily scrambled counter-attack, a force of seven Japanese torpedo-bombers managed a single hit on *Intrepid*.

THE MARIANAS

By June 1944 the Americans were continuing their long advance across the Pacific, with Task Force 58 under Vice-Admiral Marc Mitscher attacking both the Marianas and the Bonin Islands (between the Marianas and Japan). The raids on the Bonin Islands were particularly successful, with 300 Japanese aircraft destroyed for the loss of just 22 USN aircraft.

The Japanese had been having great difficulty in keeping up with the loss of their experienced aircrew. In April, the Japanese had had fewer than a hundred pilots available for duty in the area because losses and sickness from malaria had reduced their numbers. Even when 500 new pilots and 500 radio operators emerged from the training school at Kasumigaura, their training was incomplete. They were sent to Admiral

Ozawa for further training, but he lacked airfields and his carriers, now at Tawi Tawi in the Sulu Islands, rarely ventured to sea for fear of attack by American submarines. Japan still had nine aircraft carriers left, with the new *Taiho* completed on 7 March 1944, but the *Shokaku* and *Zuikaku* were badly battered and in need of an extensive refit, even though the worst of their earlier damage had been repaired. The others were at best what might be described as light fleet carriers, and at worst were no better than escort carriers.

The initial United States landings in the Marianas took place on the island of Saipan on 15 June, with air cover provided by Task Force 52 under Vice-Admiral Turner, whose assault fleet of 550 ships included just 8 escort carriers with 170 aircraft. These ships also held some reserve aircraft for TF58. The Japanese planned a robust counter-attack using land- and carrier-based aircraft.

SHIPS AND AIRCRAFT

The *Essex* herself was one of the seven large aircraft carriers in Mitscher's force in the Marianas, along with a new *Lexington*, *Yorktown*, *Hornet* and *Wasp*, and the *Bunker Hill*. The seventh carrier was the veteran, *Enterprise*. Mitscher also had all but one of the Independence class carriers available at that time, the *Bataan*, *Belleau Wood*, *Cabot*, *Cowpens*, *Langley*, *Monterey*, *Princeton* and *San Jacinte*. There were also the escort carriers covering the landings at Saipan.

Two new aircraft which entered service with the United States Navy, following the highly successful Grumman F6F Hellcat fighter, were the Curtiss SB2C Helldiver dive-bomber, and the Grumman TBF Avenger, a torpedo-bomber which was also a highly effective bomber.

A scout and carrier-borne dive-bomber, the typical Helldiver was powered by a single 1,900 h.p. Wright R-2600-20 radial engine

Vice-Admiral Marc Mitscher, commander of TF58. (IWM NYP31440)

for a maximum speed of 295 m.p.h., and a maximum warload of 2,000 lbs, although this fell to 1,000 lbs if the range of 1,165 miles was to be exploited. The two-seat aircraft had two wing-mounted 20-mm cannon, plus a pair of 0.3-in machine-guns for the observer to use.

One of the most flexible aircraft to be operated from wartime aircraft carriers, the Grumman TBF Avenger, was powered by a single 1,700 h.p. Wright R-2600 radial engine. The torpedo, or up to 2,000 lbs of bombs, could be carried internally. A three-seat aeroplane, the rugged Avenger included a rear-gun turret on the long cockpit. Before the war ended, some Avengers were equipped with radar, cameras or searchlights, and could be used on a variety of tasks, including anti-submarine patrols or close support for ground forces.

The Japanese aircraft carrier force included the new *Taiho*, completed in March 1944 and one of the most conventional aircraft carriers ever operated by the Imperial Japanese Navy. *Taiho* had been the last aircraft carrier to be laid down before the attack on Pearl Harbor. A large fast carrier, she displaced 29,000 tons and had accommodation for up to 60 aircraft, with a good maximum speed of 33 knots. The starboard island incorporated a funnel, although this was still angled outwards in typical Japanese fashion. The hull was plated up to flight deck level, British-style. The original idea was that she should be the lead ship of a new class which would incorporate all that the Japanese had learnt about carrier construction and operation, but the severe shortage of shipyard capacity meant that no sister ships were ever constructed.

As the war progressed, the USN received new and improved aircraft types, in marked contrast to the JNAF. This is a Curtiss Helldiver dive-bomber. (FAAM US MIL/199)

The other Japanese aircraft carriers in the Marianas were, in addition to the *Taiho*, the *Shokaku*, *Zuikaku*, *Hiyo*, *Junyo* and *Ryuho*, while *Chitose*, *Chiyoda* and *Zuiho* operated with Admiral Kurita's Van Force of battleships.

The Japanese introduced relatively few new aircraft types as the war progressed, but one of these was an improved torpedo-bomber, the Nakajima B6N, known to the Allies as 'Jill'. This three-seat aircraft could have been a formidable opponent if there had been sufficient numbers of them, and the aircraft carriers and pilots to fly them. The single Mitsubishi Kasei 25 radial engine produced 1,850 h.p., sufficient for the aircraft to carry a 1,750-lb torpedo. The maximum speed of the aircraft once the torpedo was dropped was around 295 m.p.h.

The American carriers had more than 900 aircraft, including 450 fighters of which 300 were the new Grumman F6F Hellcats, while Mitscher's opponent, Vice-Admiral Ozawa, had just 430 aircraft, although there were additional aircraft in both JNAF and JAAF units ashore.

THE ACTION

Mitscher's TF58 became part of the US Fifth Fleet, under the command of Vice-Admiral Raymond Spruance, with a total of fifteen fast aircraft carriers.

Vice-Admiral Jisaburo Ozawa's carriers were to operate as a Mobile Force, which in turn was divided into two, Force A under Ozawa himself consisted of the *Taiho*, *Shokaku* and *Zuikaku*, with 207 aircraft, and Force B had the *Junyo*, *Hiyo* and *Ryuho*, carrying 135 aircraft. Kurita's Van Force had the *Chitose*, *Chiyoda and Zuiho*.

The engagement started on 19 June. The Japanese Fleet assembled east of Saipan, and both fleets sent submarines into the Philippine Sea. Kurita's battle plan was to get the Fifth Fleet between his aircraft carriers and the Marianas, so that his aircraft could attack the Americans and then fly on to bases on Guam and Rota to refuel and re-arm before making a second attack on the Americans on their way back to the carriers. His reconnaissance aircraft had spotted the Americans the previous day, but Mitscher was still not certain of the Japanese positions. Anticipating an attack, Mitscher ensured that all of his fighters were on standby or flying combat air patrols, CAP, over the Fifth Fleet.

The first Japanese attacks started at 10.00 with shore-based aircraft from Guam. Additional aircraft were launched from the American carriers, and in the dog fights which ensued only 24 out of 69 Japanese aircraft in the first wave survived. The next wave saw 98 Japanese aircraft out of 130 shot down. These strikes continued for five hours, but each successive wave was repulsed by the fleet's fighters before it could reach the warships.

An attack in four waves by the Japanese carrier-borne aircraft followed, but Mitscher had sent his fighters fifty miles ahead of the American fleet and inflicted heavy losses on the Japanese, with many of those who evaded the fighters falling prey to the intense anti-aircraft fire put up by the American ships. The twenty or so aircraft which managed to reach the American ships scored hits on the *Wasp* and *Bunker Hill*, but the ships suffered only minor damage. Only a hundred Japanese aircraft survived to return to the carriers.

During the attack 300 F6F fighters operated in rotation to provide round the clock fleet air cover – on one raid picked up by the battleship *Alabama*'s radar, sufficient warning was given for the carriers to get 200 F6F fighters airborne.

The USN also pressed home attacks on the Japanese bases on Guam, which the Japanese had convinced themselves could be regarded as 'unsinkable aircraft carriers'. Unsinkable,

Shokaku was present at many of the major battles in the Pacific. (IWM MH5931)

Ryuho in her original form, but after the 'Great Marianas Turkey Shoot', her flight deck was extended over the bows. (IWM MH6495)

perhaps, but these fixed bases lacked the manoeuvrability of an aircraft carrier and were far easier targets to hit. Butch Voris flew an escorting F6F Hellcat on one of the raids he recalls, 'So, we got word that a great number of Japanese planes were being staged into Guam, and we immediately launched half of our ready strike force, for Guam, to intercept them and try to destroy them there before they could get to our fleet. So we sent the first wave out . . . that first wave caught the aeroplanes both landing and on the ground re-arming and refuelling. I happened to be in what . . . would be the second strike to go on out and the first strike . . . was sending back battle reports . . . the Admiral launched the second strike . . . I guess that we were about 225 miles from Guam at that time. I remember taking off . . . in anticipation that this was going to be a great day.'[1]

Butch's aircraft climbed to 20,000 feet, and suddenly his wave had an emergency recall,

which could only mean one thing, the fleet was about to come under attack.

He continues, 'It was a major wave and I would think that it would be somewhere around two to three hundred Japanese fighters and dive-bombers and torpedo planes. A major strike against our carrier force. And they were at high altitude . . . they were at somewhere between 25 and 30 thousand feet. Now that's way above our normal operating altitude in those days, and so as we climbed up to intercept them . . . we saw them coming . . . they had already started their run in . . . and were heading downhill picking up speed. And I remember the fighters criss-crossing over the dive-bombers, and the attack, and the torpedo planes, and we just went full throttle and came right on top of 'em . . . right on down . . . we were able to work the attack force for a period of about a hundred miles and we just started as you will, one at a time, dibbling them away and by the time they had

[1–7] Imperial War Museum Sound Archive.

traversed that last hundred miles I don't think more than a dozen . . . ever reached our task force.'[2]

He remembers that the Japanese tactics were similar to those of the USN, with torpedo aircraft diving down to about 200 feet for their run towards their target, while the dive-bombers remained higher, at medium height, ready to make their diving run on a carrier, while the Japanese fighters remained above the other aircraft: '. . . naturally the first thing you contact are the fighters, yet we had to kill the dive-bombers and torpedo planes. So we had . . . to get a fighter on the way through and then keep going after the . . . main body of the striking force . . . I couldn't get through the fighters . . . I got tied up with a fighter immediately and I couldn't disengage . . . in fact we got right into anti-aircraft range of our own forces before we got the last ones.'[3]

While the aircraft were making their abortive attack on the Fifth Fleet, the American submarines found the Japanese aircraft carriers. The *Albacore* torpedoed the *Taiho* just before 10.00, and while there was little obvious damage at first, gas vapours from the ruptured fuel lines spread throughout the ship. Ozawa moved to the cruiser *Naguro*, just two hours before a huge explosion shattered the *Taiho*, killing half her crew. She sank at 16.40. Meanwhile, the submarine *Cavalla* had put four torpedoes into the *Shokaku* at 12.20, and within three hours she also blew up as aviation fuel fumes ignited.

With the loss of three-quarters of his aircraft and two of the largest Japanese carriers, Ozawa had little option but to withdraw. Mitscher sent three of the Fifth Fleet carriers after the Japanese, leaving the rest of the fleet to cover the landings on Guam. American submarines had radioed sightings of the Japanese fleet, and to confirm the strength and location of the enemy, at 05.30 the following morning, 20 June, the Americans launched their search aircraft. Butch Voris was on the first search, flying out 350 miles, then flying 50 miles on a cross leg, before returning to his carrier, the *Hornet*. Having been on duty since 02.30 that morning, Butch was feeling tired, and by 15.00 felt that the Japanese were out of reach and steaming at full speed for home: 'and I guess I was sort of half asleep in my bunk and all of a sudden emergency flight point was sounded . . . that's a very special call aboard a carrier which means everybody man your flight quarter stations on the double . . . I looked up on our teletype and it said contact report Japanese fleet . . . I think it was a bearing of about 330 degrees and I think that they had it at a distance of 225 . . . we could get there and get home and that it should be a fairly good operation . . . we didn't suspect that the force was as far away as it actually was . . . 225 miles would have gotten everybody back.'[4]

Late in the afternoon of 20 June more than 200 aircraft were sent at extreme range to attack the Japanese ships, which had just 35 fighters left to defend them.

Butch was in his Hellcat, engine roaring as his aircraft readied to start its take-off run, when he happened to see the 'talker' with the blackboard 'about three foot square standing there in the wind, and I remember in chalk – new enemy position 350 miles away. Then the next thing I knew I was at full power and going down the flight deck but thinking "350 miles away, how can we do this" . . . we knew this was our great opportunity.'[5]

The pilots flew on as lean a mixture as possible, taking two hours to cover the distance to the Japanese fleet as they struggled to conserve fuel. This was a long time for the aircrew to think about what lay ahead, and the question of whether or not they would make it back, or have to suffer a night-time ditching, loomed larger in their minds than any reception they might receive from the Japanese. Butch recalls that the torpedo-plane pilots and navigators reckoned that they could not make it back to their carriers, while the dive-bomber crews thought that it would be touch and go. The fighters thought that they might make it, if they didn't get into a dogfight, or have to use full power for any length of time. All of this, of course, was on the assumption that they would find the Japanese fleet exactly where they expected to find it!

The attackers were flying at 18,000 feet in late afternoon sunshine, although they believed that down on the surface it should be sunset. Ahead, Butch saw a huge cumulus cloud, and below it he could make out the wake of large ships, which seemed to be turning. His immediate reaction was that they were getting ready to launch aircraft. Realizing that they had been detected, the commander of the strike broke radio silence and gave his instructions.

'The fighters were loaded with bombs,' recalls Butch. 'Everybody was going to get a shot at those carriers, even fighter pilots who were not real bombing experts . . . we held our altitude in case we ran into Japanese Zeros . . . got out ahead . . . and then just rolled over and just came straight down because that increases your accuracy . . . don't have to compute for slant range and angle of attack . . . I remember just saying "boy, that's an awful small target when you're that altitude" . . . you see that flight deck get larger . . . I could see an anti-aircraft screen . . . it was magnificent . . . their bursts were purple, and green and lavender . . . and I remember being taken in this and then coming back real quickly to realize that if I end up in one of those it's all over . . .'[6]

Apart from being distracted by the use of coloured powder in Japanese ammunition, the other factor which many pilots found fascinating as they dived towards a carrier's deck was the different markings.

In a bombing run like this, the pilot would not have seen whether or not his bombs had inflicted any damage, because after releasing the bombs he had to head straight out over the sea to pick up the torpedo aircraft and dive-bombers. There were very few fighters in the air, Butch noted, and those that were showed little organization. A Zero nearly caught Butch, and he turned on it, but before he could shoot it down his flight commander was ordering him to get back into formation for the long flight home.

The carrier *Hiyo* was badly damaged and within two hours was also to sink, again victim of a fuel fume explosion. Two of the fleet's oilers were also sunk. The *Zuikaku*, *Junyo*, *Ryuho* and *Chiyoda* were badly damaged.

Darkness fell as the force started the long run home, and according to Butch it was the blackest night he had ever seen. They flew at 7,000 feet, the best altitude for conserving fuel, hearing nothing but the call from pilots that they were 'going to have to land in the water . . . out of fuel.' This became a constant refrain until all of the torpedo aircraft which had survived the raid were in the water, and then the dive-bombers started to run out of fuel as they got to within a hundred miles of the task force. They got back to the task force using a homing beacon, but because the ships were blacked out, they could see nothing. Fortunately, Admiral Clark, in command of the three carriers, turned searchlights onto the water so that the returning pilots could see.

Butch again: 'I saw the three lights of the landing signal platform. I made my left turn and started in towards the 180 degree turn to the . . . stern of the ship and as I got right in and the landing signal officers used two great wands, that's all you could see about three foot long and at first I remember a high and then an okay and then a frantic wave off, the ship wasn't into the wind yet, it was still 40 degrees turning . . . had I gone straight on I'd have run right into the island so I made an emergency turn away . . . the next time . . . I landed and I stopped right behind a number of four five-inch turrets and had I missed a wire I'd have been killed.'[7]

Butch's wingman followed, missing all of the wires and then hitting all of the barriers, destroying five of them and wrecking his aircraft, which was promptly pushed over the side by fifty men of the flight deck crew so that nothing would delay the landing on of the remaining aircraft. The problem was that now there were no barriers to stop an aircraft which missed the wires from hitting the aircraft parked on the flight deck waiting to be struck down into the hangar. Another aircraft missed the wires and hit the AA guns on the port side of the flight deck.

The attack itself cost the Americans just twenty aircraft, but on the return flight, another eighty ran out of fuel and crashed on carrier decks or ditched in the sea, with the loss of fifty airmen. Given the scale of these losses, Spruance forbade Mitscher's request to continue the pursuit. It would have been pointless anyway – most of the force's strike aircraft had been lost.

The events of the 19 and 20 June were known to the Americans as the 'Marianas Turkey Shoot', although officially the title was the Battle of the Philippine Sea.

Nagumo finally committed hari kiri on Saipan on receiving news of the defeat. Kakuta also seems to have committed suicide with members of his staff, although in his case there is some doubt and his death may well have been an accident.

COMMENT

This was the last occasion when the Imperial Japanese Navy and the United States Navy met on any kind of parity, and even taking into account the shore-based aircraft, it was clear that the Japanese had inferior numbers of aircraft and carriers, and they had lost so many of their experienced pilots. The new American aircraft were more than a match for the Japanese aircraft, which lacked the more dramatic advances in performance of Allied aircraft.

The desire to catch the Japanese is understandable, but sending off aircraft at the limits of their range was foolhardy. The strike should have been recalled as soon as the true range became known. The Japanese carriers could have waited for another day since, after all, they had few aircraft left and little striking capability. The loss of the *Hiyo* hardly justified the loss of so many aircraft and airmen.

ATTACK ON SABANG

THE ROYAL NAVY MOVES BACK INTO THE EAST

With the invasion of France imminent, Italy out of the war and the pressure on Malta lifted, the British were able, by early 1944, to start sending ships back into the Pacific. Their presence was not always welcomed by the Americans, who felt, with some justification, that they could finish the job without any help. The British, on the other hand, had political reasons for not wishing to leave it to the Americans. Apart from not wanting to be seen leaving an ally on its own, there was the question of supporting the efforts of two important members of what was still called the British Empire, Australia and New Zealand. In addition, attacking Japanese forces in the Pacific also reduced the

pressure which the Japanese could afford to bring to bear on British and Indian forces in Burma. Finally, much of the territory which the Japanese had overrun was British, including Malaya, Singapore and Hong Kong.

No one should be under any doubt about the difficulties of coordinating activity between two forces. In the Battle of Leyte Gulf, we will see how different elements of the United States Navy were not where they were expected to be. The Japanese experienced even worse problems, with people in effect doing as they pleased, sometimes for what appeared to them at the time to be good reasons. These problems are compounded when another navy becomes involved, especially at task force or fleet level.

Throughout the war in the Far East, Trincomalee, or 'Trinco', in Ceylon was a major British base, especially after the fall of Singapore. Here are *Illustrious* and *Saratoga* in early April 1944, before their joint operations against targets in Sumatra. (IWM A23475)

The cramped hangar of *Illustrious* with Vought Corsair fighter-bombers only just fitting in. (FAAM Cors/109)

It is only since the end of the Second World War that international cooperation and integrated command structures have been honed to a fine art, largely thanks to the work of the North Atlantic Treaty Organisation, NATO.

There was another reason for American hesitation over a combined operation with the British Eastern Fleet, and for the strong reservations felt by many American admirals, including both Chester Nimitz and Ernest King. The Americans felt that the British had neither the experience of mounting mass air attacks from carrier aircraft, nor the means of effectively supporting a fleet some distance from its nearest bases. The American fleet was operating at full stretch at considerable distance from Pearl Harbor and even further from San Diego, its two main bases in the Pacific, and had nothing to spare in terms of fleet support for a British operation. This was not the only problem. The Royal Navy had seldom put a balanced fleet to sea of adequate strength. Had they done so, they might not have lost *Glorious* for lack of aerial reconnaissance and battleship or battlecruiser support, or *Prince of Wales* and *Repulse* for the absence of good air cover, or *Cornwall* and *Dorsetshire*, or *Hermes* for that matter.

For a start, the decision was taken to allow the British Eastern Fleet to operate in one area, while the US Fifth Fleet operated elsewhere. This did not mean that there was no cross-over, and British, Australian and New Zealand ships did sometimes operate with the Americans and under American command. An American aircraft carrier,

Saratoga, was also attached to the British Eastern Fleet during spring 1944 for the first raids on Sabang.

Sabang was on a small island off the northern end of Sumatra, and the harbour and airfields were of vital strategic importance to Japan's war effort, supplying their forces in Burma. It was to prove to be an ideal target for the Royal Navy to hone its techniques on massed aerial attack. It was well away from the American ships, so problems of command and coordination could be shelved for the time being, but it was also undoubtedly a useful operation.

SHIPS AND AIRCRAFT

The British aircraft carrier involved was *Illustrious*, of Taranto fame, and the American carrier was *Saratoga*. The great benefit of having this warship with the British forces was that she brought some excellent aircraft with her, including the new Grumman Avenger, Douglas Dauntless and the Grumman F6F Hellcat. Nevertheless, *Illustrious* also had a good carrier fighter, the Vought F4U Corsair, as well as the Fairey Barracuda torpedo and dive-bomber, which we have already come across on the Fleet Air Arm's raid on the *Tirpitz*.

The American Vought Corsair has been described as 'Arguably the best US fighter of World War II', or by others as 'the bent wing bastard from Connecticut'. As a fighter, it had strong competition for the claim of 'best', and even if nominations were limited to carrier-borne fighters, the Grumman F6F Hellcat and the Fairey Firefly would offer stiff competition.

Nevertheless, when the first Corsairs arrived, they were something of a revelation to British Fleet Air Arm pilots, who had at last got a single-seat carrier-borne fighter with the range for naval operations and the strength to cope with carrier life.

A prototype Corsair had been the first American aircraft to exceed 400 m.p.h. in level flight. During its development the design was altered as experience in Europe suggested a change in the aircraft's armament, which meant moving the cockpit back 3 feet. This meant that the pilot's view forward was restricted, especially in the critical final phase of landing on a carrier flight deck. The United States Navy was at first reluctant to use the aircraft from its carriers, and initially the Corsair was used by shore-based USMC units and by carrier-based Fleet Air Arm units. Raising the cockpit canopy helped to mitigate the position of the cockpit on later versions, including those embarked aboard *Illustrious*.

A low-wing, crank-wing monoplane, the Corsair had first entered service in 1941. Depending on the version, engine power varied between 2,000 h.p. and 2,200 h.p. from a Pratt & Whitney R-2800-18W piston engine. The crank wing was necessary because of the size of the propeller, supposed to have been the largest fitted to a single-engined fighter at the time. Later versions could accommodate a warload of 3,000 lbs, but when used as a fighter-bomber from *Illustrious*, two 500-lb bombs were usually carried, one under each wing. Armament was six wing-mounted 0.5-in machine-guns. The aircraft had armour protection for the pilot and self-sealing fuel tanks. A maximum speed of around 400 m.p.h. was possible on wartime versions, and later versions took this to around 440 m.p.h.

Norman Hanson flew Corsairs off *Illustrious*. He had had experience of both the earlier version and those embarked aboard the ship later for the operations in the Far East. He recalled the aircraft as being difficult to handle, especially for the relatively inexperienced wartime intake of pilots. 'For one thing, they were damnably big fighters for their day. They had a vast length of fuselage between the cockpit and the propeller which,

The sign of success, as a large cloud of smoke gathers over the oil refinery at Palembang. (FAAM Camp/66)

Briefing aircrew before a raid on Palembang – Norman Hanson, by this time a Lieutenant-Commander, RNVR, is probably second row, fifth from right, hand under chin! (IWM A28006)

together with a rather low sitting position and a not too clever hood [both of which were modified and greatly improved in the Mark II version], made for very poor visibility when taxiing and landing. . . . Fuel was supplied to the engine through a Stromberg injection carburettor, which precluded "cutting-out" on the top of a loop – a disconcerting feature to which aircraft fitted with the normal carburettor were prone.'[1]

Nevertheless, Hanson appreciated the strength of the aircraft and believed that 'everything about it was high-class and great attention to detail proclaimed itself wherever one looked'.[2] Not the least of the aircraft's features was the cockpit, with controls conveniently to hand without the need to search or grope, and with all of the dials easily visible. By contrast, he felt that the cockpits of the Corsair's British contemporaries must have been designed by the office cleaner!

For the harassed fighter pilot bringing a damaged aircraft back to the carrier, the Corsair had further advantages. The undercarriage and arrester hook were hydraulically activated and the hook would fall automatically if pressure was lost. In an emergency the undercarriage could be put down using a CO_2 bottle.

THE ACTION

As usual, the first attack was made early in the day, with the aircraft flying off *Illustrious* at 06.50 on 19 April. *Illustrious* had

[1-3] Norman Hanson. *Carrier Pilot*, Patrick Stephens, 1979.

Loading bombs into an Avenger aboard *Illustrious*. (IWM A24250)

Saratoga seen from *Illustrious* with an Avenger in the foreground. (IWM A24265)

seventeen Fairey Barracudas and thirteen Vought Corsairs, which acted as fighter escorts for the Barracudas.

Norman Hanson recalls, 'My first sight of enemy territory was of a luscious green island, basking in the early morning sunshine. It was all so very beautiful that when red flashes burst from the deep, verdant green, I felt considerably put out. Good God! It's enemy fire! . . . I was appalled that some vandal should set fire to Paradise. We dived down ahead of the Barracudas, firing enthusiastically at warehouses and quays and suddenly found ourselves at the far end of the harbour, unscathed. We were still green and hadn't yet learned about targets of opportunity. So we milled around like a lot of schoolgirls and left it to the Barracudas, who made a splendid attack on the harbour and oil installations. The Corsair boys returned

. . . with a feeling of anticlimax. We had been to the enemy and had found no opportunity to cover ourselves with glory.'[3]

COMMENT

The target was important to the Japanese, and obviously deserved the attention of the Allies who had managed to halt the Japanese advance through Burma, which in turn had threatened India. Nevertheless, Sabang only seemed to receive occasional attention, almost hit and run, which always meant that the Japanese could repair the damage. Obviously, resources did not permit a prolonged campaign, but a single day's outing for two aircraft carriers was probably not enough. It was not until additional ships arrived that the Royal Navy was able to pull its weight in the Far East.

BATTLE OF FORMOSA

'BULL' HALSEY TAKES COMMAND

In September 1944, Admiral William 'Bull' Halsey took command of the main American naval force in the Pacific, now known as the US Third Fleet, while Vice-Admiral Marc Mitscher remained in command of the carrier force, now designated Task Force 38. The number of aircraft carriers available to the United States in the Pacific had increased still further to a new total of nine large carriers and eight light carriers, while invasion forces now routinely had escort carriers accompany them. The aim of the carrier force by now was to weaken the JNAF and JAAF still further in preparation for the next invasion. At the beginning of September, one of TF38's carrier groups attacked the Ogasawara-shoto Islands (known to the Americans as the Bonin Islands), to the south of Japan, for three days, before rejoining the rest of the Task Force for a sustained series of raids against airfields and naval installations in the southern Philippines during 7–10 September. They met only light resistance.

The warships were operating at considerable distances from their main bases, and so one priority as significant progress was made was to ensure that good harbours or anchorages were selected and developed as naval bases. Therefore, while landing on the Paulau Islands from 15 September onwards, the atoll of Ulithi, virtually undefended, was occupied and became a forward naval base for the fleet.

During late September, TF38 was busy again, first of all in attacking Manila harbour, where carrier aircraft sank three destroyers and twenty merchant vessels, as well as causing severe damage to the harbour installations. Then the emphasis changed, with air attacks against airfields and shipping, which resulted in an incredible 1,200 Japanese aircraft being destroyed, and another 13 ships sunk, for the loss of just 72 American aircraft. The weakness of the islands' air defences encouraged General Douglas McArthur, in overall command of the advance across the Pacific, to bring forward the invasion of the Philippines from December to October. While Admiral Nimitz and his naval forces were put under McArthur's command, Halsey's Third Fleet was allowed to operate independently.

The priority once again was to protect the invasion fleet from air or naval attack. As most Japanese air power in the Philippines had been suppressed, the real threat now lay in aerial attack from Formosa or Okinawa. This led to the Battle of Formosa, which lasted from 10 to 16 October, and prepared the way for the first US landings on Leyte in the Philippines on 20 October. That in turn led to the Battle of Leyte Gulf, the biggest naval battle ever!

SHIPS AND AIRCRAFT

The aircraft carriers and aircraft types are by now familiar, with TF38 broken up into four Task Groups. TG38.1, under Vice-Admiral McCain, had *Wasp* and *Hornet*, and the light carriers *Monterey*, *Cabot* and *Cowpens*; TG38.2 under Rear Admiral Bogan, had *Bunker Hill*, *Hancock* and *Intrepid*, as well as the light carrier *Independence*; TG38.3

under Rear Admiral Sherman had *Essex* and *Lexington*, which was also Mitscher's flagship, as well as the light carriers *Langley* and *Princeton*; while TG38.4 under Rear Admiral Davison had *Enterprise* and *Franklin*, and the light carriers *Belleau Wood* and *San Jacinte*. Each of the groups had battleships, cruisers and destroyers.

THE ACTION

On 10 October, Halsey sent 340 aircraft to attack Okinawa. Two days later, the main thrust of the attack was directed towards Formosa, home of Vice-Admiral Fukudoma's Second Air Fleet. Early on 12 October, aircraft from all seventeen aircraft carriers attacked Formosa, where a major air battle developed, which the Americans eventually won, shooting down 160 Japanese aircraft for the loss of 43 of their own. The following day, the aircraft from the carriers again attacked Formosa, seeking to destroy airfields and port facilities, and on this occasion the Japanese launched a counter-attack against TF38, scoring a torpedo hit on the cruiser *Canberra* (the only American warship to be named after a foreign city).

Further air attacks against Formosa followed on 14 October, while air attacks were also made against northern Luzon in the Philippines. Again, the Japanese counter-attacked, and on this occasion they scored a torpedo hit against another cruiser, *Houston*.

As the Third Fleet prepared to withdraw on 15 October, heavy air battles developed over northern Luzon, base for the Imperial Japanese Navy's First Air Fleet under Vice-Admiral Terouka. A further torpedo hit on *Houston* from Japanese aircraft still failed to sink the cruiser. Throughout the period from 10 October, the Japanese lost 600 aircraft in Luzon, Formosa and Okinawa, while the USN lost 90.

This was not what the Imperial Japanese General Headquarters had wanted. A series of war games had been conducted to assess the best strategy for such an attack as the threat both to the home islands and to the supply lines for fuel and raw materials began to be fully appreciated. According to the war games, all available aircraft were to be evacuated to Kyushu for use later in defence of the home islands. Fukudoma ignored his orders and gave battle. The Japanese estimates of their losses were lower than those of the Americans, at 312 aircraft – although other sources vary between 143 and 500!

Undeterred by facts, the Japanese press proclaimed another great victory. On 19 October the *Asahi* newspaper published its list of alleged enemy losses: 'sunk, eleven carriers, two battleships, three cruisers and one destroyer; damaged, eight carriers, two battleships, four cruisers and thirteen unidentified ships. . . .'[1]

COMMENT

The series of attacks on northern Luzon, Formosa and Okinawa followed a pattern which the Americans had found to be successful, softening up enemy defences in advance of any landings to reduce the risk to the troop transports and the troops themselves during the vulnerable transfer from ship to shore. That the Japanese could not prevent their own commanders from giving battle, contrary to orders to preserve aircraft and aircrew for the defence of the home islands, shows certain weaknesses in their staff training. It also shows an inability of many Japanese commanders to appreciate wider strategic considerations.

[1] Gordon W. Prange with Donald M. Goldstein and Katherine V. Dillon. *God's Samurai*, Brassey's, US.

LEYTE GULF – THE BIGGEST NAVAL BATTLE IN HISTORY

23–26 OCTOBER 1944

A DESPERATE BID TO USE THE BATTLE FLEET

By summer 1944, the situation for the Japanese was recognized as increasingly desperate. Their response was Operation Sho-Go, meaning 'to conquer', although the more realistic officers such as Fuchida recognized that the intention was to inflict unacceptable casualties in order to force a compromise between Japan and the United States. All pretence at seeking ship-to-ship or air-to-air combat was to be abandoned, and the objective was to strike at American troop transports while they were still at sea, exacting a heavy toll in American lives.

The Japanese still had an incredible capacity for self-deception. Not only did newspapers accept propaganda at face value, so that the mass of the population felt that Japan was still winning the war, but survivors from the worst defeats were detained in barracks until their next posting abroad, or their next ship, so that the bad news would not leak out. What is less easy to comprehend is that this self-delusion extended to the ruling classes and the higher echelons of the armed forces, who knew the truth. In their hands, after seeking the support of the Emperor, Sho-Go became a plan to defeat the Americans, and give Japan ultimate victory. To be fair, the Imperial Japanese Navy knew better, but as before, it was the Army faction that dominated political life, and which effectively took the decisions.

The press were willing agents in this game. Typical of their involvement was their reaction to the Battle of Formosa earlier in October, which was proclaimed as a great victory. The newspaper list of the American losses was pure fiction, and far-fetched at that!

The decision to mount a major effort in defence of the Philippines was forced upon the Japanese because the loss of the island group would cut off their oil supplies from Sumatra, as well as their other sources of scarce raw materials. The Japanese expected the American forces to invade the Philippines through Leyte.

Meanwhile, the Navy staff played war games to prepare for the battle to come, while the carrier fleet, *Zuikaku*, *Zuiho*, the two converted submarine tenders *Chitose* and *Chiyoda*, and in due course the new sisters, *Unryu* and *Amagi*, was hidden camouflaged in the Inland Sea. It did not matter that much – there were few aircraft and even fewer trained and experienced pilots. Ashore, by this time, many operations were being directed from caves!

The action which resulted was known to the Japanese as the Second Battle of the Philippine Sea, and to the Americans as the Battle of Leyte Gulf.

In fact, the Americans had been divided over whether to invade the Philippines first, or instead invade Formosa. The argument had been won by General Douglas MacArthur, who had promised on leaving the Philippines after the Japanese invasion that 'I shall return'.

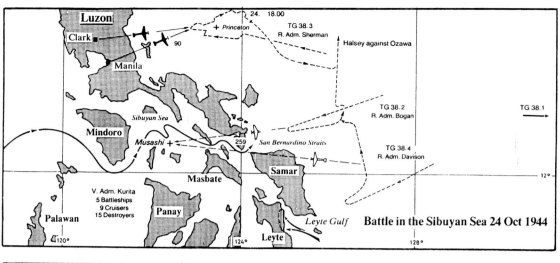

Battle in the Sibuyan Sea 24 Oct 1944

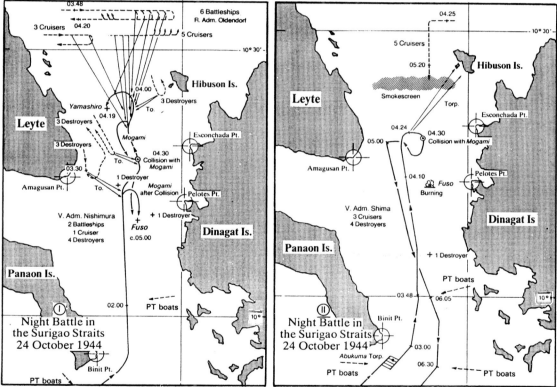

Night Battle in the Surigao Straits 24 October 1944

Not all of the Battle of Leyte Gulf centred around the aircraft carrier, but the Battle in the Sibuyan Sea was the main carrier element.

SHIPS AND AIRCRAFT

The American forces consisted of the Third Fleet and Seventh Fleet.

The Third Fleet, under Admiral Halsey, with the carrier fleet commanded by Vice-Admiral Marc Mitscher, included the aircraft carriers *Wasp, Hornet, Lexington, Hancock, Intrepid, Essex, Franklin and Enterprise*, and the new light carriers *Cowpens, Cabot, Independence, Princeton, Langley, San Jacinto, Belleau Wood* and *Monterey*. These ships had 1,000 aircraft between them. The fleet also included six battleships, six heavy and nine light cruisers, and sixty destroyers.

The Seventh Fleet under Admiral Kinkaid included a support force under Vice-Admiral Oldendorf, again with six battleships, four heavy and five light cruisers, and thirty destroyers. This fleet, whose main role was the support of American ground forces ashore in Leyte, had a carrier group with 18 escort carriers under Rear Admiral Sprague, 400 aircraft, and 21 destroyers as escorts.

These ships were the by now familiar combination of the Essex and Independence classes of aircraft carrier. At Leyte Gulf, the ships present included *Essex* herself, *Franklin, Hancock*, while a new *Hornet, Lexington* and *Wasp*, were also of this class.

Altogether, the Third Fleet at Leyte had eight aircraft carriers and another eight light carriers, which operated as Task Force 38, itself divided into four groups, designated 38.1, 38.2, 38.3 and 38.4.

The eighteen escort carriers, CVEs, which were divided into three groups, and as their radio call sign was 'Taffy', these became 'Taffy One', 'Taffy Two' and 'Taffy Three'. Sprague had command of the whole unit and of 'Taffy One', while he had subordinate commanders with the other two groups.

Ise was one of two Japanese battleships modified as hybrids, with a flight deck aft in place of the after gun turrets. Despite the aircraft on the flight deck in this photograph, at Leyte, she was without aircraft, and operations would have been difficult given the turbulence from the superstructure. (IWM MH5924)

Zuiho was a relatively new aircraft carrier, and her flight deck was later extended. (IWM MH6494)

The aircraft had changed as well by this time. In addition to the Grumman F6F Hellcat, which arrived in time for the landings in the Gilbert Islands, two other new aircraft had entered service with the United States Navy, the Curtiss SB2C Helldiver dive-bomber, and the Grumman TBF Avenger, a torpedo-bomber which could also make a highly effective bomber. The Hellcat was by this time the mainstay of the USN's carrier fighters, capable of gaining and maintaining aerial superiority wherever it appeared.

A scout and carrier-borne dive-bomber, the typical Helldiver was powered by a single 1,900 h.p. Wright R-2600-20 radial engine for a maximum speed of 295 m.p.h., and a maximum warload of 2,000 lbs, although this fell to 1,000 lbs if the range of 1,165 miles was to be exploited. The two-seat aircraft had two wing-mounted 20-mm cannon, plus a pair of 0.3-in machine-guns for the observer to use.

Sailing from bases in Japan and Singapore, the Japanese divided their forces, consisting of the First Striking Force under the overall command of Vice-Admiral Kurita, into three.

The Northern, or Mobile Force's primary task was to confront the American carriers under Halsey. It was under Vice-Admiral Ozawa and had four aircraft carriers, including the *Zuikaku*, not long returned to service, and the light carriers *Chitose*, *Chiyoda* and *Zuiho*, with just 116 aircraft between them. The small number of aircraft spread among the Japanese carriers was not simply attributable to the shortage of aircraft, but to a strategic decision to leave most of the aircraft available in Formosa to counter the anticipated invasion there. By this time, the Japanese had extreme difficulty not only in maintaining aircraft production and pilot training at a level which would replace losses, but in delivering aircraft as inexperienced pilots either got lost or succumbed to American mastery of the air.

There were also the hybrid *Ise* and *Hyuga*, battleships partially modified as carriers with a flight deck aft in place of the after gun turrets, which had no planes aboard, as well as three light cruisers and nine destroyers. At the very least the Northern Force was expected to lure Halsey and the American carriers away from the other two forces.

Kurita himself led the Centre Force of the two giant battleships *Yamato* and *Musashi*, three other battleships, ten heavy and two light cruisers, and fifteen destroyers.

The Southern Force was under the command of Vice-Admiral S. Nishimura, with two battleships, three heavy and one light cruiser, and eleven destroyers.

Despite his formidable First Striking Force, which included the *Yamato* and *Musashi*, five old battleships, eleven heavy cruisers, two light cruisers and nineteen destroyers, Kurita was pessimistic. Remembering Guadalcanal, he believed that 'the enemy transports would have to be destroyed completely. However . . . my opinion at that time was that, in view of the difference in air strength of the opposing forces, our chance for a victory after the sortie would be about fifty-fifty. I had also thought that the aerial support would fall short of our expectations.'[1]

There were also another three hundred Japanese shore-based aircraft on Luzon, including both JAAF and JNAF units.

THE ACTION

The Japanese First Striking Force was ordered to arrive off Leyte on 25 October 1944. En route, on 23 October, two American submarines, *Dace* and *Darter*, discovered the fleet and torpedoed three heavy cruisers, two of which, Kurita's flagship *Atago* and the *Maya*, sank almost immediately.

The actual engagement started a day early, when, on the morning of 24 October, aircraft based on Leyte attacked the most northerly of the American carrier groups in the Battle of the Sibuyan Sea, itself regarded as a component part of the Battle of Leyte Gulf. Ozawa's carrier-based aircraft were also intended to take part in the attack, with the intention of drawing the American Third Fleet away, leaving Kurita with a clear run at the invasion force. The aircraft from the Japanese carriers failed to find the American carriers, and then, running short of fuel, attempted to fly on to bases in Luzon. Most of them were intercepted by American aircraft on the way.

Aboard the American light carrier *Langley*, an alert fighter direction officer, Lieutenant John Monsarrat, had noticed the Japanese aircraft on his radar screen and ordered four of her Hellcats to intercept, while asking the *Essex* to send more aircraft. *Essex* immediately sent eight Hellcats on patrol to reinforce *Langley*'s fighters. Unhappy about sending four American fighters to tackle sixty Japanese aircraft, he gave his directions and then added, 'Help is on the way, coming up close behind you.'[2] He need not have worried. The twelve American fighters and their pilots were more than a match for their opponents, shooting down half of them. It was at this stage that the American fighter pilots noticed that the Japanese aircraft had tailhooks, suggesting that they had probably come from a carrier.

The shore-based aircraft only managed to hit one of the American carriers, the light carrier, or CVL, *Princeton*. A single 550-lb armour-piercing bomb hit the flight deck just forward of the after elevator, leaving a small hole in the flight deck as it continued into the ship.

The small hole caused the ship's commanding officer, Captain William Buracker, little concern: 'I saw the hole, which was small, and visualized slapping on a patch in a hurry and resuming operations.'[3] This was the height of optimism, since the bomb had also gone through the hangar deck

[1] Gordon W. Prange with Donald M. Goldstein and Katherine V. Dillon. *God's Samurai*, Brassey's, US.

[2–6] Thomas J. Cutler. *The Battle of Leyte Gulf*, Pocket Books.

and, without any armour, continued to plunge downwards until it hit the ship's bakery, where it exploded, killing everyone present. The explosion ripped open the hangar deck where six aircraft were being refuelled and re-armed, setting them alight, and this in turn exploded their torpedo heads. On the flight deck, Ensign Paul Drury was standing by his Grumman F6F Hellcat of VF-27. He could feel the shock of the explosions below: 'I knew there was no way we were going to get airborne under those circumstances,' he later said.[4] The bomb had struck the *Princeton* at around 09.35. As the fires reached the aviation fuel, the struggle to save the ship went from damage control to Salvage Control Phase I at 10.10, which meant that two-thirds of the ship's company of 1,570 were to abandon the ship, leaving just fire-fighters and gunners. The gunners were ordered to leave as well once the AA ammunition started to explode. A destroyer took the men off.

The fires were slowly brought under control, so that by 13.30 the only area still ablaze was near the ship's aft magazine. *Princeton* was on an even keel without any hull damage. The light cruiser *Birmingham* was ordered alongside to provide assistance and to get the carrier under tow. Warnings of attack from submarines and enemy aircraft delayed the manoeuvre until 15.30, when the cruiser came alongside with many of her crew on deck, either helping the fire-fighters or providing assistance, or simply watching. Without any indication or warning, the aft magazine exploded, tearing off much of the carrier's stern. 'There was a terrible staccato of metal on metal as shrapnel of all shapes and sizes – pieces of *Princeton* – raked across *Birmingham*'s exposed decks like the deadly grapeshot canisters fired from the cannons of yesterday's sailing ships. The effect was the same. Hundreds of men instantly fell dead or horribly wounded. Within seconds, the ship's scuppers ran red with blood as it poured

forth from thousands of grotesque wounds, and severed limbs lay about the blood-smeared deck like the casual droppings on a slaughterhouse floor.'[5]

The *Birmingham* survived, but 233 of her crew did not, and another 211 suffered serious wounds, while another 25 had minor injuries. *Princeton*'s casualty list amounted to 108 killed and 190 wounded. Despite this, *Princeton* eventually had to be sunk by torpedoes from a destroyer.

One of the casualties was intended to be *Princeton*'s next captain, and he was already aboard. Captain John Hoskins lost a foot, but quickly used some rope to tie a tourniquet. Later, after he had recovered from his wounds and had had an artificial foot fitted, he badgered the authorities to allow him to command a new *Princeton* – and succeeded!

Two of the other US carrier groups by this time had located the Japanese fleet and attacked it while the Japanese ships were steaming through the Sibuyan Sea. Four waves of aircraft were sent throughout the day, and the giant battleship *Musashi*, sister of the *Yamato*, and one of the two largest warships in the world at that time, was hit by eleven torpedoes and nineteen bombs, and eventually sank. During the battle, her gunnery officer had pleaded with her commanding officer, Rear Admiral Toshihira Inoguchi, to be allowed to use the huge 18.1-in guns to fire large anti-aircraft rounds which acted like a giant shotgun cartridge, but he was refused since the use of such munitions had been found to cause damage to the barrels, and these were to be kept intact for the expected battle off Leyte. As repeated torpedo attacks started to take a toll upon the ship, flooding an engine room, permission was finally given to use the AA rounds as a fresh wave of attacking aircraft arrived. When all nine guns fired at once, the noise and recoil was so great that some thought that the ship had been hit yet again.

Shrapnel flew through the sky towards the American aircraft, but not one of them was shot down. Afterwards, one of the turrets was found to have been damaged.

'One bomb detonated directly on the pagoda-like tower housing the command bridges. The damage was extensive and for a brief time it appeared that no one was in command of the ship. Then Inoguchi's voice emanated from a speaking tube, saying that all personnel on the main bridge had been killed and that he was shifting to the secondary bridge. Moments later, another series of explosions rained heavy shrapnel on *Musashi*'s command tower. This time, Inoguchi was not so fortunate. His distinctly weakened voiced echoed in the brass speaking tube, saying, "Captain is wounded. Executive Officer, take command." [6]

Eventually, the giant ship, moving slowly in circles because her steering gear was damaged, slipped beneath the waves.

There were other casualties. A torpedo hit so damaged the heavy cruiser *Myoko* that she had to turn back. Although the other giant battleship, the *Yamato* was also hit by bombs, as was another battleship, *Nagato*, both remained operational.

An attack by aircraft from the American carriers on the Japanese Southern Force caused some damage, but without sinking any ships.

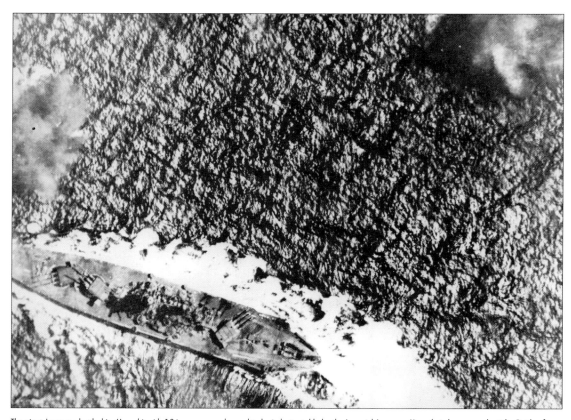

The giant Japanese battleship *Musashi*, with 18-in guns, was deemed to be indestructable by the Imperial Japanese Navy, but she was sunk at the Battle of Leyte Gulf by American carrier-borne aircraft. (IWM NYF47538)

As a defensive move, Kurita temporarily reversed course, a move which Halsey took as a victory for the Americans. He decided to give chase, taking carrier groups 38.2, 38.3 and 38.4, while 38.1 refuelled. This was against the American plans for the battle, since Halsey's forces were supposed to be guarding the San Bernardino Straits, while Kinkaid's Seventh Fleet guarded the Surigao Straits against the Japanese Southern Force. Leaving the San Bernardino Straits unguarded allowed the Japanese to reverse course yet again, and sail through the Straits at night.

That same night, the US Seventh Fleet and the Japanese Southern Force engaged in a night battle in the Surigao Straits. This started with an ineffectual American motor torpedo-boat attack, which damaged just one ship, the light cruiser *Abukuma*. This was followed at 02.00 by a torpedo attack by destroyers, which sank the battleship *Fuso* and three Japanese destroyers. At 04.20, a traditional naval gun battle opened up, and the other battleship, Nishimura's flagship *Yamashiro*, blew up, leaving the two halves of the ship burning furiously: there were no survivors. The cruiser *Mogami* was also damaged. After daybreak, USAAF aircraft found and sank the *Abukuma*, while aircraft from the Seventh Fleet's escort carriers found and sank the *Mogami*, together with a number of destroyers. In the end, two heavy cruisers and some destroyers escaped.

Meanwhile, Kurita's battle fleet had been discovered at 06.45 by American reconnaissance aircraft while the fleet was east of Samar, the large island to the north-east of Leyte. Thirteen minutes later, the Battle of Samar began, as Kurita's battleships found and started to shell the most northerly of the escort carrier groups, 'Taffy One', commanded by Rear Admiral Thomas Sprague. Unable to do anything else, Sprague ordered his ships to fly off their aircraft while the entire force withdrew to the south. Those carriers able to make smoke did so and the remainder did their best by changing the fuel-air mixture in their boiler fires. The smoke was of limited value – some of the Japanese ships, including the flagship, *Yamato*, had radar. A desperate and gallant torpedo attack by American destroyers caused the cruiser *Kumano* to withdraw, but three destroyers were sunk.

George Smith was a member of one of the aircraft maintenance teams aboard one of the escort carriers that morning. He recalled, 'that morning I had a duty on the flight deck . . . he yelled at me he said you'd better get your helmet on and your Mae West – your life belt – because here comes the Japs and about that time I heard an explosion on the fantail. First I thought it was one of our own planes exploding back there and I looked up and saw all this tin foil falling, this tin foil to jam our radar and of course GQ [General Quarters] and everybody manned GQ stations and then they started shooting . . . trying to get our range, our skipper turned the ship . . . zig-zagged it, as we were trying to escape from the Japanese. . . . Then we started laying down smoke . . . trying to blind the Japanese . . . and they pulled pretty fast on us, they caught one of the carriers back there and they sank it . . . they got so close we could even see the Japanese flags flying . . . of course we were opening up with everything we had . . . and of course this was a running battle of about two hours . . . we was going between these two islands and the Japanese decided that it was leading to a trap . . . so they broke off the engagement . . .

'We had funny things happen like one kid . . . was wandering around and one guy asked him where he was going to he said, "Since this battle, sir . . . I've looked over on a ship for a safe place to hide . . . I haven't found one yet and I'm still looking." That's one incident and another incident one of the boys had battened down a hatch and a piece of shrapnel came through the hole and took off his finger and the only thing he could do was say "it was my million dollar finger" . . . we were all pretty tired because it takes a lot out of you when you're actually in a combat condition and they're really throwing the live ones at you. . . .'[7]

Meanwhile, the aircraft from the CVEs attacked the Japanese, although for many their heaviest warload was fragmentation bombs for use against troops. Many had only their guns with which they could strafe the warships, hoping to catch those crew members in exposed places such as the flying bridges. A few did not even have their guns loaded, and could only attempt to distract the Japanese. Most were very short of fuel, having been scrambled with whatever was in their tanks.

George Smith again: 'During this battle . . . we had our pilots making dummy runs on the Japanese fleet . . . our pilots, they were taking any carrier they could get to get back on board and a lot of them ran out of gas and they would come by the carrier and would drop in the water, hoping that our tin cans would pick them up . . . as we was trying to escape from the Japanese.'[8]

As the chase continued, the *Gambier Bay* was sunk, and three other CVEs, *Fenshaw Bay*, *Kalinin Bay* and *White Plains*, were damaged. Then, almost as suddenly as it started, the engagement ended and the Japanese ships turned away.

The Japanese action was a mystery at the time, since they had the advantage and could have destroyed all of the American escort carriers before turning on the transports. Subsequently, it transpired that Kurita was convinced that he was attacking standard battle carriers, and that it would take some time to overtake them, since he was also under the impression that the escort carriers were withdrawing at 30 knots, almost double their maximum speed! Ahead, he mistook a second group of escort carriers for full-sized

carriers. He also expected other American carriers to arrive from the north, and preferred to do battle with these in the open sea rather than be caught in the enclosed waters of Leyte Gulf. Seemingly a pessimist, Kurita said later that he feared that to enter Leyte Gulf 'long after the scheduled time would mean rushing into the enemy, who had completed its defense, and would only result in our becoming easy victims'.[9] So he reversed course, greatly to the relief of the Americans.

As the Japanese Centre Force broke off the engagement, the first properly planned Kamikaze attacks occurred. Four aircraft dived onto the Second Escort Carrier Group, hitting both *Suwanee* and *Santee*, which was also hit by a torpedo from a submarine. Kurita returned to the east of Samar, and further Kamikaze attacks followed, blowing up the escort carrier *St Lo* and damaging *Kalinin Bay* and *Kitkun Bay*. Kurita was completely unaware of the Kamikaze attacks, let alone their successes. At noon, he ordered a withdrawal, scuttling three heavy cruisers. Another two were badly damaged but judged capable of returning to base.

George Smith witnessed these first Kamikaze attacks: 'We thought they was dropping bombs on us because one of the carriers off the port side took a direct hit from a Kamikaze. . . . They hit this carrier just dead centre and as we went by men were abandoning ship . . . and as we got beyond it the whole ship just seemed to explode . . . there was nothing there. And about that time on our ship a Kamikaze came in on us . . . just like a regular landing I guess he was trying to sneak in on us like one of our own planes. . . . And he started to drop in and of course the skipper seen what was going on so he turned the ship hard port . . . the men on the starboard side were banged against there, they swung our guns around and shot across

[7,8] Imperial War Museum Sound Archive.

[9] Gordon W. Prange with Donald M. Goldstein and Katherine V. Dillon, *God's Samurai*, Brassey's, US.

The Grumman Wildcat was known to the Royal Navy as the Martlet, until aircraft designations were standardized. Here a Wildcat gets ready to take off from HMS *Formidable* during Operation Torch, the Allied invasion of North Africa. (IWM TR 285C)

The First USN combat mission of the Korean War was flown by Grumman F9F Panthers of VF-51 from USS *Valley Forge* on 3 July 1950. (Robert F. Dorr)

Landings weren't always so happy, which attracted spectators to view from positions on the island known as 'vulture's row' in the USN and 'goofer's gallery', or sometimes just 'goofers' in the RN. There were far worse results than this one. (Robert F. Dorr)

One of the most potent naval aircraft of its day, the Douglas Skyraider managed to bridge both the Korean and Vietnam wars.

The Vought Corsair in its F4U-4B form was one of the piston-engined aircraft to play a major role in the Korean War, despite the advent of the carrier-borne jet fighter. Here an aircraft takes off from an American carrier — note the wooden deck. (Robert F. Dorr)

One of the most significant advances of the Korean War was the use of the helicopter for rescuing downed airmen, and the USN also loaned helicopters for plane-guard duties aboard British carriers. Here a Sikorsky HO3S-1 of squadron HU-1 prepares to take off from an American carrier. (Robert F. Dorr)

A crowded carrier deck during the Korean War. Vought Corsairs and Douglas Skyraiders predominate, and in the centre is an AD-3Q Skyraider, or 'guppy' to the USN, with its distinctive radar bulge under the fuselage. (Robert F. Dorr)

A rare shot of a Grumman F9F-5P Panther photo-reconnaissance aircraft in natural metal. (Bill Barron/Robert F. Dorr)

On the deck of an American carrier, members of the crew work on an aircraft wing-tank, but weather conditions were not always so good and the same task during the winter was extremely uncomfortable and even hazardous.

A Grumman F9F Panther takes off from the busy flight deck of USS *Bon Homme Richard* during the Korean War. (Robert F. Dorr)

A time of change. Vought F4U Corsairs and Grumman F9F Panthers share the deck of an American carrier at Yokosuka in Japan, home port for the US fleet operating off Korea. (Robert F. Dorr)

American carriers kept a 'box score' to show the damage inflicted on the enemy; here is USS *Bon Homme Richard*'s proud tally. (Robert F. Dorr)

USN Douglas AD-4 Skyraider pilots prepare for a Korean War mission aboard USS *Bon Homme Richard* off Korea in 1953. Nearest the camera is Ensign Bill Barron, USN, who flew many missions and survived being hit by enemy gunfire. (Bill Barron/Robert F. Dorr)

BEWARE
JET INTAKE
JET EXHAUST

A Vought F4U-4 Corsair folds its wings after landing on USS *Valley Forge* in 1951. Members of the ships' company watch from the island – still an exciting

occupation at this time. (Bruce Bagwell/Robert F. Dorr)

The Skyraider managed to soldier on into the early years of the Vietnam War, and in this 1968 photograph aboard USS *Bon Homme Richard*, the aircraft can be seen sharing the flight deck with the Douglas A-4 Skyhawk which, with the A-7 Corsair II, was one of the types to supersede the Skyraider in the attack role. (Robert F. Dorr)

Peaceful days at Pearl Harbor in 1968, as USS *Bon Homme Richard* calls *en passage* to Vietnam. Ranged on the flight deck are two Vought F-8E Crusaders, the mainstay of the USN's fighter force during the early years of the war, until replaced by the formidable McDonnell F-4 Phantom. (Robert F. Dorr)

USS *Shangri-La*, an eight-cruise veteran of the Vietnam War, at speed off the coast in 1970 with a full flight deck. (Robert F. Dorr)

The Douglas A-4 Skyhawk was intended for air-to-ground work, but this aircraft used its Zuni rockets to shoot down a MiG-17 over North Vietnam's Kep airfield. (Roy Lock/Robert F. Dorr)

An aerial shot of USS *Hancock* at speed off the coast of Vietnam, where the ship made no less than twelve cruises between 1964 and 1975. Douglas A-4 Skyhawks predominate on the flight deck, although there are a number of F-8 Crusaders aft of the island. (US Naval Institute)

The aircraft which carried the brunt of the Vietnam War in carrier-based operations was the Douglas A-4 Skyhawk, seen here heavily armed. Skyhawk squadrons made no less than 107 cruises. (US Naval Institute)

Two McDonnell F-4J Phantoms over the United States in 1973, wearing the markings used by VF-114 Aadvarks in Vietnam. The aircraft in the background was flown by Commander Randall Cunningham, USN, and Lieutenant J.C. William Driscoll for the first two of their five MiG kills, and is now preserved at San Diego. (McDonnell Douglas/Harry Gann/Robert Dorr)

A Vought F-8 Crusader ready to take off on a mission over Vietnam. Behind the cockpit, Laotian, South Vietnamese flags and hash marks show the number of sorties over each territory. (Robert F. Dorr)

VF-301 F-14A Tomcat launching from the USS *Enterprise*. (Frank B. Mormillo)

VAQ-309 EA-6A Intruder ready to launch from the USS *Enterprise*. (Frank B. Mormillo)

CVW-2 F-14D Tomcat and F/A-18C Hornet fighters being positioned for launch from the USS *Constellation*. (Frank B. Mormillo)

A Sea Harrier of 800 Squadron equipped with Sidewinder air-to-air missiles. The Sea Harrier was the star performer of the Falklands campaign, with not one being lost to enemy aircraft.

Although the British armed forces played a significant role in the Gulf War, this was a rare occasion when the Fleet Air Arm played a relatively minor role. Here Sea King HC.4s of 846 Squadron arrive aboard RFA *Argus* to provide support for troops ashore. (FAAM Camp/418)

the flight deck hitting the Kamikaze and the Kamikaze he winged over and dropped on the other side . . . into the water and exploded.'[10]

Kurita was the man who had signalled to his ships on the day before that, 'Braving any loss and damage we may suffer, the First Striking Force will break into Leyte Gulf and fight to the last man.'[11]

The action showed both navies operating in confusion. Admiral Chester Nimitz and Admiral Kinkaid believed that Halsey was still guarding the San Bernardino Strait, and sent signals attempting to discover his location once they realized what had happened. Eventually, Halsey was forced to turn and take part of his fleet south.

Halsey had in fact been having a busy day, or at least Mitscher had! Night reconnaissance aircraft from the light carrier *Independence* had located the Japanese Northern Force at 02.08, followed later by the intelligence that the Northern Force had divided in two. Halsey now ordered Task Force 34 with the battleships and cruisers out ahead of the carriers. The report on the battle explained why:

'The Commander Third Fleet's plan for pushing strong surface forces ahead of his carrier groups and toward the enemy was a logical piece of tactics to attempt. Our expectation, based on past achievements, is that in an exchange of carrier attacks between fleets, it will be our enemy's fleet that takes the worst of it, and starts retiring while still at a distance many times greater than gun range. The only possibility then of closing and capitalizing on our gun power is to overtake cripples or ships of naturally low speed.'[12]

At 08.00 Mitscher had sent the first of six waves with a total of 527 aircraft to attack Ozawa's Northern Force of four aircraft carriers in what became the Battle of Cape Engano, on the east of the main Philippine island of Luzon. The Japanese had just twenty fighters left to defend their carriers, and these were soon shot down. *Chitose* was sunk in the first attack, disappearing below the waves at 09.37, and *Zuikaku*, *Zuiho* and *Chiyoda* were damaged, as was a light cruiser. Subsequent raids saw the remaining three carriers also destroyed. *Zuikaku*, no longer Ozawa's flagship, was burning out of control after the third strike by 200 aircraft, and by the afternoon she was gone. A light cruiser was also crippled, and sunk later by an American submarine. Three destroyers and an oiler were also sunk.

Halsey in his flagship, the battleship *New Jersey*, then went hunting for Kurita's Centre Force. At first he failed to find it, as the Japanese sailed back through the San Bernardino Straits. Later that day and during the following day, both the Third and Seventh Fleets found and attacked the Centre Force using carrier aircraft, sinking two Japanese cruisers, one of which was not part of Kurita's force but was escorting a transport to Leyte at the time.

ACES

At the outset of the Battle of Leyte Gulf, David McCampbell, commanding Air Group 15, embarked in the carrier *Essex*, had twenty-one confirmed 'kills', each commemorated with a small rising sun on the side of his Grumman F6F Hellcat, *Minsei III*, named after a girlfriend. On the morning of 24 October, most of McCampbell's fighters were on a sweep over the Philippines and he had just seven aircraft left aboard *Essex* when the call went out for all fighter pilots to man their aircraft. There was no time to check his fuel gauges before take-off, but his plane was in the middle of refuelling – the centre external tank was full, but the two main tanks were only half-full. The flight deck crew were still attempting to pump fuel into

[10] Imperial War Museum Sound Archive.

[11,12] Thomas J. Cutler. *The Battle of Leyte Gulf*, Pocket Books.

the Hellcat as it was positioned on the catapult, and, faced with the threat of the aircraft being struck down if it was not ready, McCampbell waved them away. The seven fighters from *Essex* joined up at 6,000 feet and then started to climb to meet the incoming Japanese at 18,000 feet. McCampbell and his wingman climbed past the Japanese torpedo aircraft and dive-bombers, leaving these to the rest of his flight, while they concentrated on the forty escorting Zero fighters, which seemed to be unaware of their arrival.

McCampbell shot down two Japanese fighters, one after the other, before the Japanese moved into a 'Luftberry' defensive formation, with the fighters flying anti-clockwise in a circle, so that any attempt to attack one fighter from behind immediately put the attacker in front of the next aircraft in the 'Luftberry'. McCampbell's response to this tactic was to dive down on the Japanese in a head-on attack, but the first target fought back, and so did the next, leaving *Minsei III* with holes in her wings. Before McCampbell could decide on his next move, the Japanese broke off and started their return flight to their base on Luzon. As a parting shot, McCampbell shot down seven of them, following until within sight of the coast of Luzon, and only then breaking off. His wingman had by now shot down five aircraft, making him an 'ace' in a single mission.

By now very low on fuel, McCampbell was told by *Essex* that she had her flight deck full of aircraft and he and his wingman, Ensign Roy Rushing, could not land on. Moving on, hoping to find another carrier, he was attacked first by AA fire from other ships, and then by other Hellcats, although these broke off their attack when they realized their mistake. The next carrier, *Lexington*, also had a crowded flight deck, but *Langley* was flying aircraft off and would have room for him within a few minutes – he landed on and his engine stopped before he could switch it off.

The other 'ace' that day was the unknown pilot of the land-based Yokosuka D4Y Suisei, whose single bomb was to cause so much carnage in the destruction of the *Princeton*, and aboard the *Birmingham*.

COMMENT

Kurita's fears were well founded. Leyte Gulf did for Japan's surface forces what the Battle of the Philippine Sea had done for the air arm. They lost three battleships, including the *Musashi*, four aircraft carriers, six heavy cruisers, four light cruisers, eleven destroyers, a destroyer transport, and four submarines. This was for the loss of one American light carrier and two escort carriers, and three destroyers. In the air, the Japanese lost 150 shore- and carrier-based aircraft, and 10,000 men, against 100 American aircraft and 1,500 men.

As it happened, Ozawa's decoy operation was fairly successful. Precisely as the Japanese had hoped, Halsey thundered after Ozawa, but his force, without the strength to challenge the US carrier force effectively, suffered heavy losses – the four carriers, one light cruiser, three destroyers, an oiler, and all but twenty-nine of his aircraft.

He had done well to keep the American fleet carriers away from the main action. Unfortunately for the Japanese, it was a wasted effort. Kurita did not realize that he was facing Rear Admiral Thomas Sprague's escort carriers instead of Halsey's mighty flat tops, and he still had potent firepower left.

The mistake showed that by this time, Japanese naval intelligence was poor, and partly because of this, and partly because of curtailed training, ship recognition was also inadequate. In addition, the plan for Leyte was too late. The Japanese should have brought their battleships to war much earlier, when they could have worked with the aircraft carriers at their peak, putting far greater pressure on the Americans.

Halsey had taken a great risk. He should not have left the San Bernardino Strait unguarded. While his argument about not dividing his forces and not allowing the battleships to remain in the Strait without air cover were perfectly valid, the forces at his disposal were so strong that dividing them would have been logical. Alternatively, he could have communicated his decision so that the Seventh Fleet could have made its dispositions accordingly. That it was all right in the end merely meant that Halsey had been fortunate.

In mitigation, the American commanders and their senior officers were showing great war weariness. Many aboard their ships, of all ranks, had not been ashore for ten months. The strain must have had an impact on the quality of decision making.

KAMIKAZE:
THE DIVINE WIND OF DESPERATION

DEFEAT IN THE MARIANAS RAISES THE IDEA OF SUICIDE

The major defeats in the Marianas led to the adoption of Operation Sho, the Kamikaze suicide attacks. Accounts of the introduction of the Kamikaze missions vary, and this is not so much a matter of incomplete historical records as the fact that a number of people had the same idea at about the same time. The concept of suicide attacks was not unknown to the Japanese, and even before the Kamikaze missions evolved, soldiers with satchels of explosives had been throwing themselves under American tanks, which were invulnerable to the Japanese anti-tank weapons. Japanese civilians had committed suicide rather than surrender to the advancing American forces, or in other cases had been shot by their own forces.

Later, as United States Army Air Force Boeing B-17 Flying Fortress bombers began to roam over the Japanese islands with apparent impunity, defending fighters lacked the ability to climb to the necessary altitude to intercept these aircraft. Without the steady, even one might argue dramatic, technical development which characterized the German war effort, the Japanese opted to strip their fighter aircraft of anything which could be removed, including weapons. The aircraft were then able to climb high enough to reach the B-17s and ram the bombers.

The contrast with the Germans is worth emphasizing. The Germans pioneered remote controlled glider bombs, the Japanese the Kamikaze suicide bomber. The Germans put rocket-powered Messerschmitt Me.163 inceptors into service, the Japanese fighter pilots simply rammed their opponents, which was highly effective but placed little value on the life of a fighter pilot or his aircraft.

By 'suicide' attacks, we mean simply that. In many countries, people have taken great risks, especially to enable other members of their unit to escape. There have also been those who, faced with certain defeat, perhaps badly wounded and with an aircraft on fire, have driven themselves and their aircraft at the enemy. Neither of these compares with the true concept of suicide as the Japanese knew it and used it. The Japanese warrior was expected to die for his country, and his reward was to reach paradise. Some at least were also promised a posthumous promotion.

There were no official Kamikaze attacks from the Japanese aircraft carriers, but the concept has its place here because among the targets of the campaign were the Fifth Fleet's aircraft carriers.

BIRTH OF AN IDEA

One of the first to advocate a policy of Kamikaze attacks was Admiral Arima. The idea was rejected, and Arima was informed that his superior officers were only interested in those means of attack in which the pilot returned alive. Arima was not convinced, and he raised the matter each time the American aircraft carriers scored a fresh success.

Many Kamikaze aircraft were shot down, or completed their final moments before striking the target on fire, and this Yokosuka D4Y3A Suisei, or Comet, was no exception. (IWM HU63019)

Another proponent of the Kamikaze was Ensign Shoichi Ota of the Naval Air Technical Depot, who began to design a human bomb after the invasion of the Marianas by US forces. Ota's bomb was known as the 'Oka', and it first appeared in September 1944. The name 'Oka' was the Japanese word for cherry blossom, because cherry blossom, which falls at the height of its beauty, is associated by the Japanese with the young warrior dying in battle.

In essence, the Oka was a man-carrying bomb, a small rocket-powered aircraft which could fly for up to eleven miles on its five rockets, and then glide or dive onto the target with its 2,600-lb warload. Of flimsy wooden construction, the Oka had to be carried to within range of the target by a land-based bomber. In some cases the pilot flew in the mother plane until close to the target, then climbed down into the bomb and guided it to the target and his own death – in other cases

the pilot had to spend the entire flight in the Oka. The great weakness of the design was that a large and not very manoeuvrable mother aircraft was expected to get past strong fighter defences to within range of the target. As the American fighter pilots increased in number and in experience, this was a tall order.

For some reason best known to themselves, the first fifty Oka rocket bombs were aboard the new aircraft carrier *Shinano*, a new and substantial addition to the Japanese fleet having been converted from the uncompleted third battleship of the giant Yamato class. Launched on 19 November 1944, she was sunk just ten days later by the submarine *Archerfish*, which fired six torpedoes at her shortly after 03.00. The ship finally slipped beneath the waves some seven hours later, due as much to poor damage control and a crew unfamiliar with her as to the effect of the torpedo attack. One can only surmise that

The Oka, or Cherry Blossom, was designed from the outset as a suicide weapon, but few reached their target due to the vulnerability of the heavy bombers used as mother aircraft.

190

perhaps the Japanese planned to use the large ship to launch twin-engined 'Betty' bombers with the Oka human bombs.

In Mitsuo Fuchida's case, the concept came to his attention after Admiral Toyoda, the Combined Fleet's new commander-in-chief passed it to him for comment. The idea had originated in this instance with a Captain Eichiro Jo, who had put the idea forward to his commander, Admiral Jisaburo Ozawa, who gave it his support and forwarded it to Toyoda. Fuchida was not enthusiastic about the concept, not, it seems, so much out of humanitarian scruples, but because he doubted the ability of raw young pilots to handle the project effectively. His attitude sits uncomfortably with that of some of the senior officers who rejected any idea which did not allow the pilots to come back alive. There were also those who, as resources became ever scarcer, used increasingly inexperienced pilots. As time passed, pilots for Kamikaze missions received just enough training for them to reach the target.

Another objection raised by Fuchida was that small numbers of aircraft on a single mission would be unlikely to inflict significant damage and destruction upon the enemy. This point seems to have been missed by senior Japanese officers time and time again. Massed and concentrated aerial attack was the way forward, as shown by the success at Pearl Harbor, and discovered in Europe first by the Germans, and then by the British and Americans. It was not until the massive air battle off Okinawa that massed Kamikaze attacks started to appear.

Fuchida was also right about the lack of experience. As the last few months of the war dragged on and as fuel and material shortages bit ever deeper, the Kamikaze aircrew received less and less. But even from the beginning, the pilots showed little strategic sense. Most of them were senior ratings and junior officers, who went for escort carriers and destroyers, and a single Kamikaze would sometimes hit one of the larger aircraft carriers. If they had been used *en masse* against troop transports in advance of each invasion, they would have inflicted far greater damage. When hitting a carrier, their preferred spot was the join between the island and the deck, which often inflicted terrible casualties on the flight decks of the carriers, yet the hangar lifts, even of the armoured British carriers, would have been far more effective aiming points and would have resulted in heavier British and American losses.

It is difficult to be certain if the preference for attacks on destroyers and escort carriers was due to poor ship recognition, which can be difficult in any event at altitude and high speed, and which could be further hampered by poor intelligence briefing. After all, even such an experienced officer as Vice-Admiral Kurita thought he was chasing fast American attack carriers at Leyte Gulf. On the other hand, perhaps the Kamikaze pilots wished to have the target to themselves, and settled for the glory of being the sole destroyer of a smaller ship rather than play a part in sinking a more substantial, and worthwhile, target. When they did hurl themselves into troop transports, as at Okinawa, they were too late, as the ships were empty. Prompt attacks on unarmoured transports would have done much to undermine the American advance, and damage morale, especially that of troops getting ready to land.

Others also came up with the same idea, and before long Fuchida was on the receiving end of correspondence on this subject. Names varied, and in one instance the suggestion was that the pilots should belong to a 'Hornet' Corps, because when the hornet attacks, both he and his enemy dies. The name Kamikaze was chosen by Vice-Admiral Takijiro Onishi because of the 'Divine Wind' which had sprung up to prevent Japan being invaded by the Mongol emperor Kublai Khan in 1274.

Meanwhile, an improvised programme of Kamikaze attack was instigated by Vice-Admiral Takijiro Onishi, who took command of the Fifth Base Air Force in the Philippines on 19 October 1944. Onishi's plan centred around the use of Zero fighters. Just why he chose the Zero is difficult to understand. The aeroplane was fast and manoeuvrable, but it could only carry a 250-kg bomb, about 550 lb, which was inadequate for use against vessels with armoured decks, such as battleships and the British aircraft carriers, and only likely to cause damage, not a knock-out blow, on unarmoured aircraft carriers. It compared unfavourably with the American Corsair, which when used as a carrier-borne fighter-bomber with the Fleet Air Arm could carry two 500-lb bombs.

THE FIRST ATTACKS

The first group of twenty-three petty-officer pilots was under the command of Lieutenant Yukio Seki. Their aim was to obtain a hit with every attack. Seki himself had to fly four missions before finding a suitable target, and one observer noted that his enthusiasm and morale sank further with each return to base. Before his first flight during the Battle of Leyte Gulf, he sent a letter to his parents, and after the normal family topics, he wrote:

'At this time the nation stands at the crossroads of defeat; the problem can only be resolved by each individual's repayment of the Imperial Benevolence.

'In this the man who has cherished a military career has no choice.

'Kamakura's parents [his wife's mother and father] whom I hold so earnestly dear to the bottom of my heart – I cannot bring myself to write them this shocking news – please confide in them.

'Because Japan is an Imperial Domain, I shall carry out a ramming attack against a carrier to repay the Imperial Benevolence. I am resigned to this.'[1]

The type of attack varied. Having got past the fighter defences, the Kamikaze could either make a high altitude attack, from as high as 20,000 feet, in which case the aircraft could not dive at a very high angle without speed and handling difficulties making accuracy difficult, or dive at a high angle from 3,000 feet or less, facing heavy and accurate AA fire. The manned suicide aircraft were not as accurate as one might have imagined.

Many have suggested that one weakness of the Kamikaze was the lack of feedback, since there were no debriefings. This was not the case. True, the Kamikazes died, but they were usually escorted by fighters which not only provided escort cover, but were also expected to report back. Whether or not the fighters were so preoccupied in fighting off British and American fighters that they did not see what had happened, or whether there was a subconscious desire to boost the performance of those who had just died, the one consistent theme was the exaggeration of the Kamikaze successes. Again, some of this may have been due to poor ship recognition, mistaking escort carriers for larger carriers. Tankers were often mistaken for aircraft carriers, and destroyers for cruisers.

Japanese propaganda boasted that every Kamikaze sank a ship. This was wildly exaggerated, yet Onishi's men were successful enough to cause the US Navy serious concern. At Leyte, four CVEs were damaged and another, *St Lo*, sunk. Overall, about one in four Kamikazes inflicted damage, while one in thirty-three sank its target. The United States clamped a tight lid of censorship on the

---

[1] Kusanayagi biography, itself based on the Onishi biography, *Tokko no Shiso* (*The Kamikaze Idea*), Daizo Kusanayagi, Tokyo Bungei Haru Aki, 1972.

subject lest the Japanese discover just how much damage the Kamikaze were doing. It appeared that Japan had, in Admiral Morison's words, 'sprung a tactical surprise that might prolong the war another year'.[2]

Later, in November 1944, with the Third Fleet operating east of the Philippines, Kamikaze attacks sank a destroyer and damaged the aircraft carriers *Essex*, *Franklin*, *Hancock*, *Intrepid* and *Lexington*, as well as two light carriers, *Belleau Wood* and *Cabot*.

The worst day was 25 November, when the Kamikaze attacks reached a peak. Japanese aircraft had to be scattered around on their airfields, hidden under trees to avoid detection and destruction by the USN, which had complete aerial supremacy. Five bases each contributed five aircraft, and on this occasion the aircraft were bombers rather than Zero fighters, and included some of the new Nakajima B6N Jill bombers. Seventeen Zero fighters acted as escorts and observers.

They found the Third Fleet out to sea, a comfortable 150 miles off Manila. While the escorts tackled the American combat air patrols, the Kamikaze selected their targets before diving onto them. Hancock was first, but the Kamikaze was shot down by intensive AA fire, but as the plane broke up, burning debris hit the deck and started fires, with one large item knocking out an AA gun position.

Intrepid was next, and this time the Kamikaze managed to evade the protecting fighters and the dense curtain of AA fire to crash into an anti-aircraft gun and then through the deck into the hangar, before exploding and bending the deck upwards. Then another Kamikaze crashed into the *Intrepid*, again smashing through the flight deck and into the hangar deck, where it exploded. The large carrier was now out of action as her crew fought fires, and her aircraft still in the air had to find room on the other carriers.

Cabot received a direct hit on the flight deck from one Kamikaze, and then damage

from another which was shot down and crashed into the sea close to the ship.

Essex was luckier. The Kamikaze which struck her went into the flight deck, but the bomb didn't explode.

This was not uncommon. The Kamikaze pilot was supposed to prime the bomb after he had selected his target, avoiding the early problems when Kamikazes who could not find a target either had to waste their bomb by crashing into the sea, or return to land at base with a live bomb under the aircraft. It was not unknown for pilots to forget to arm their bombs, and while the speed of the impact and the fuel left in the tanks meant that some damage would be done, it was far less than when the bomb also exploded.

Despite the large number of American warships and supply vessels present, some of the Kamikaze returned to base claiming not to have found a target. Most, although not all, of the escorting fighters also returned, so that sixteen out of forty-two returned to their bases.

Damage of this kind was a massive shock to the Americans, and the suicide attacks affected morale. In October, it had seemed to be a one-off, perhaps an expression of frustration among the pilots of a single unit, and the ships lost or damaged had been escort carriers. Now, here was evidence of a concerted campaign, and serious damage had been caused to large aircraft carriers; several had to be taken out of service.

After the US landings on Luzon on 9 January, there were more intensive Kamikaze attacks, sinking the CVE *Ommaney Bay* and damaging three others, as well as two battleships and four cruisers. Again, off Iwo Jima, on 21 February 1945, Kamikaze aircraft sank the CVE *Bismarck Sea*, and the *Saratoga* was hit six times, although after a struggle she was saved. Starting on 6 April, a prolonged Kamikaze offensive was conducted against the US fleet off Iwo Jima, which lasted for six weeks and is covered in the next chapter.

[2] Samuel E. Morison. *The Liberation of the Philippines*, Little Brown & Co, Boston, 1959.

The sequence of a Kamikaze attack on *Formidable*, with the aircraft about to strike, exploding on impact, the ship damaged and on fire, and then covered in smoke, but she survived! (FAAM CARS F/127-30)

LIFE UNDER KAMIKAZE ATTACK

Some idea of the impact of the Kamikaze on those aboard the aircraft carriers can be gained from accounts given by those serving in ships of the British Pacific Fleet, which was retitled Task Force 57. Ordered to work alongside the American Fast Carrier Force, TF57 was to neutralize three islands of the Sakishima Gunto, Miyako, Ishigaki and Iriomote whose airfields would be essential if the Japanese defenders of Okinawa were to receive reinforcements and replacement aircraft.

Each day, the four carriers sent their aircraft to the attack, with aircrew, hangar and flight-deck parties awakened at 03.30, with the ship closing up to action stations before 05.00, waiting for possible Kamikaze attacks. During the day, fighter aircraft were ranged, waiting for possible attack, with the ships having three states of readiness, yellow, blue and red, which meant that the fighters were on standby, readiness or had to scramble.

One of the British carriers, *Victorious* was attacked by a Kamikaze on 1 April. Having passed over the carrier at altitude, the Kamikaze went into a nearly vertical dive, but once he was fully committed to his dive and unable to manoeuvre, the ship's commanding officer turned the ship to port, leaving the Kamikaze to crash into the Pacific close to the carrier's starboard bow.

Norman Hanson was a Corsair pilot aboard *Victorious*'s sister ship, *Illustrious*, when a Kamikaze attacked.

'. . . there was a scream of a diving aircraft passing over us. The hell of a bang followed as a suicider slammed into *Indefatigable*, sailing parallel to us about 300 yards on our starboard side. She took the blow in the worst possible place – in the angle between flight-deck and island – and casualties in dead, wounded and missing were heavy. The armour-plated deck protected the hangar from damage, but itself suffered a dent from the sheer impact. . . . Quick-drying cement was poured into the depression and levelled off. Within a few short hours *Indeft.* was operating her aircraft as through she had experienced nothing more than a slight hiccup.'[3]

Later in the day, a Kamikaze narrowly missed *Illustrious* herself, crashing into the sea after being shot down by the ship's AA gunners.

'The wind was from the starboard side and we were immediately inundated with a shower of crankshafts, pistons, sections of fuselage and assorted pieces of Mitsubishi manufacture. The pilot's dinghy, a gaudy red and yellow affair, flew lazily across the deck, inflating itself in transit, and fetched up on the port aerial mast. The pilot's own skull was the first object to land on the deck, to be gathered up quickly by the medical profession.'[4]

Bob Finlay, who was the Captain's Secretary, was captain of a multiple pom-pom when the ship was at action stations. Lieutenant Finlay was sighting his pom-pom through the ring-sight further up the gun as a second Kamikaze appeared and started to dive. 'Bob opened up again, but had to cease fire momentarily to flick away, somewhat petulantly, something which partially obscured the ring-sight. He didn't feel very well two minutes later when he realised that what he had removed so peremptorily was a slender strip of Japanese flesh, about half a rasher . . .'[5]

At the start of the attack, *Illustrious* had had two Corsairs ranged on the flight deck, ready to take off. As the pilots left their aircraft, one forgot to switch off his engine. The explosion of the Kamikaze in the sea, which Norman Hanson had at first thought to have been a torpedo hit, and the vibration from the AA fire, dislodged the chocks and the aircraft started to move. As the aircraft rolled towards the side of the flight deck, one

3–5 Norman Hanson. *Carrier Pilot*, Patrick Stephens, 1979.

The scene on the flight deck of *Formidable* after the fires had been extinguished on 4 May 1945. (FAAM CARS F/36)

Formidable again, but five days after the previous photograph and after a further Kamikaze strike. The damage was extensive, but the ship was soon operational again. (IWM CARS F/39)

of the ship's electricians ran from the island, jumped into the aircraft, and hit the foot brakes before switching the engine off. Then, amidst the heat of the battle, he sat waiting until two of the flight deck crew ran across with a set of chocks.

Hanson tried to get a DSM for this brave young man, but in vain, although he was at least mentioned in despatches.

The end of the war with Japanese surrender hit the Kamikaze units particularly hard, since surrender was a concept which they treated with contempt. It was not for Japanese warriors.

Admiral Ugaki, commander of the remaining Kamikaze force, took off in the lead bomber of eleven aircraft intending to make one final Kamikaze mission against American forces in Okinawa. Four of the aircraft returned later, the pilots claiming engine trouble, which may seem a happy coincidence but which was also possible, given problems with spares and fuel supplies. Four hours after the bombers had taken off, Ugaki sent a final message:

'I alone am to blame for our failure to defend the homeland and destroy the arrogant enemy. The valiant efforts of all officers and men of my command during the past six months has been greatly appreciated.

'I am going to make an attack at Okinawa where my men have fallen like cherry blossoms. There I will crash into and destroy the conceited enemy in the true spirit of

Bushido, with firm conviction and faith in the eternity of Imperial Japan.

'I trust that the members of all units under my command will understand my motives, will overcome all hardships of the future, and will strive for the reconstruction of our great homeland that it may survive forever.

'Tenno heika. Banzai!'[6]

That night Admiral Onishi, instigator of the Kamikaze, committed hari kiri, the Japanese way of suicide. He made the ritual cut across his abdomen with his short sword and brought the weapon up. He then tried to cut his throat but failed. Weak from loss of blood he lay back and waited. The following morning a servant found him lying in a growing pool of blood, but still conscious. Onishi refused offers of medical assistance and asked to be left alone to die. It took him until six o'clock that evening.

COMMENT

The adoption of Kamikaze tactics was an act of desperation, and one which alarmed the Americans at first, until they realized that their defences were capable of handling such tactics. The Kamikaze attacks were never in sufficient strength to overpower the defences of the American and British warships which were their targets. Even if they had been, the question arises over the waste of men and equipment which the strategy implied. True, at first the attacks scored greater successes than the Japanese had experienced since Pearl Harbor, but this says more about the overall strategy of the Japanese than about the value of suicide attacks.

[6] Based on the Onishi biography, *Tokko no Shiso* (*The Kamikaze Idea*), Daizo Kusanayagi, Tokyo Bungei Haru Aki, 1972.

BATTLE FOR OKINAWA

1–11 APRIL 1945

THE BUILD-UP

As the advancing Fifth Fleet moved ever closer to Japan, the Imperial General Headquarters identified the vital defensive position as Okinawa, which if lost would enable the Americans to intensify their air raids against the home islands. The Americans had already taken Iwo Jima for the express purpose of providing a base for fighter aircraft to escort bombers flying from the Marianas on raids over Japan.

Admiral William 'Bull' Halsey, played a decisive part in the Pacific War. (IWM NYF4764)

Preparations were laid for a strong defence, but even within this plan the tone was pessimistic: 'When the enemy penetrates the defence zone, a campaign of attrition will be initiated . . .' It was to be a battle to see which side could wear the other out first. All hopes of victory or even of breaking the American will were gone. On 6 February, the army section of the Imperial General Headquarters published an implementing directive, 'outline of Air Operations in the East China Sea Area'. This became known as the 'Ten-go Operational Plan'. It was generally agreed that the East China Sea, lying between the China coast and the Ryukus, would be the main area, so Ten number 1 covered Okinawa, Ten number 2 Formosa, Ten number 3 the south-east China coast, and Ten number 4 Hainan Island. The navy viewed Okinawa as being of overwhelming importance, and completely ignored Ten numbers 2 and 4. This was not unusual. Even if the army and the navy agreed to act together, individual commanders often did as they wished.

On 16–17 February 1945, in the first large-scale United States Navy attack on the home islands, Mitscher's carrier aircraft in Task Force 58 attacked 'vast areas' in the Tokyo region. This attack, and those of the succeeding days, destroyed as many as 500 army and navy planes on the ground and in the air, for the loss of 88 American aircraft. By this time, TF58 had sixteen aircraft carriers, including no fewer than ten large carriers, *Bennington*, *Bunker Hill*, *Enterprise*, *Essex*, *Franklin*, *Hancock*, *Hornet*, *Intrepid*, *Wasp* and *Yorktown*, and six light carriers,

Bataan, *Belleau Wood*, *Cabot*, *Independence*, *Langley* and *San Jacinto*, with a total of 1,200 aircraft between them. Alone in this massive fleet, *Enterprise* was the last of the pre-war American carriers. In a further assault on the home islands on 18/19 March 1945, the fleet came under severe Kamikaze attack from the Japanese Fifth Air Fleet, commanded by Vice-Admiral Ugaki. Although none of the carriers was lost, *Franklin*, *Enterprise*, *Wasp*, *Intrepid* and *Yorktown* all received hits, with 1,000 casualties on *Franklin* alone.

SHIPS AND AIRCRAFT

In addition to most of the warships mentioned, the US Fifth Fleet had eight battleships, two battlecruisers and sixteen cruisers, as well as sixty-four destroyers. By this time, the carriers were operating Grumman F6F Hellcats, a number of Vought Corsairs, and the Helldiver and Avenger strike aircraft. In addition, the landing fleet for Okinawa, Task Force 51, under Vice-Admiral Turner, had ten battleships, thirteen cruisers, eighteen escort carriers, and more than five hundred aircraft.

Having learnt the skills of massed air attack, the new British Pacific Fleet was operating on what was known to the Admiralty as Operation Iceberg, as Task Force 57 under Vice-Admiral Rawlings, as part of the US Fifth Fleet. Rear Admiral Sir Philip Vian commanded the British carrier force and for Okinawa had four carriers: *Indomitable* with twenty-nine Hellcats and fifteen Avengers; Victorious with thirty-seven Corsairs, fourteen Avengers and two Walrus amphibians; *Indefatigable* with forty Seafires,

Rear Admiral Sir Philip Vian (right) with a cynical-looking group of war correspondents. (IWM A28072)

twenty Avengers and nine of the new Fairey Fireflies; and *Illustrious* with thirty-six Corsairs and sixteen Avengers. During the Okinawa campaign, *Formidable* was to replace *Illustrious* after she suffered heavy damage from aerial attack.

As well as practising mass air attack, the British Pacific Fleet had to adjust to extended operations, but had just three tankers for fleet replenishment initially. This later rose to five, but these could not refuel ships as efficiently as the American tankers. While the Americans replenished abeam, the British used the much slower system of refuelling astern, which was slow and affected station-keeping.

David Devine was a war correspondent for Kemsley Newspapers who had just transferred to a British ship:

'I had just come from the USS *Lexington*, the second *Lexington*. I'd been living in her for a long time. *Lexington* would fuel willingly in a wind of Force 6 provided the sea wasn't up to the wind yet. The American tankers would take a ship on either side in that kind of weather. They would have everything aboard, three lines pumping, in twenty minutes . . . *KGV* [the battleship, *King George V*] went up astern of one rusty old tanker, which appeared to be run by two Geordie mates and twenty consumptive Chinamen and it took us, I think, an hour and a half to pick up a single buoyed pipeline, fiddling around under our bows.'[1]

In fact the Royal Navy had a long way to go.

Before sailing for Okinawa to replace *Illustrious*, *Formidable*'s ship's company had been in Sydney where they saw *Fighting Lady*, a story about a US carrier in the Pacific. Geoffrey Brooke was the ship's Fire and Crash Officer.

'I came to the unpalatable conclusion that our fire-fighting equipment was totally inadequate and was shocked to discover that there was no more left in the dockyard store

Vice-Admiral Sir Henry Rawlings (left), in command of the British Pacific Fleet, with Admiral Chester Nimitz, who masterminded the crucial stages of the Pacific War. (IWM A29263)

. . . in some trepidation I went and bearded Captain Rock-Keene, who, hardly looking up from his papers, said "Are you sure? Then buy some!" Knowing better than to ask how, I took myself off to the largest store in Sydney and asked for the fire-fighting department. To my surprise, there was an excellent one, full of the latest American gear, I ordered a variety on approval, and had a field day testing them on the flight deck and invited the Skipper to witness a demonstration of the choicest items. On completion, he said, "Come ashore with me in half-an-hour," and I found myself the rather embarrassed third party to a verbal meal, with much table thumping, of the unfortunate Captain of the Dockyard, By the end of it he was only too glad to get rid of us

[1] John Winton. *The Forgotten Fleet*, Coward McGann, 1970.

by underwriting the expenditure of many thousands of pounds.'[2]

After Leyte, the Imperial Japanese Navy was also short of ships, with the carriers *Amagi*, *Katsuragai*, *Ryuho* and *Junyo*, three battleships, a cruiser and ten destroyers, comprising the Second Fleet under Vice-Admiral Seiichi Ito.

THE ACTION

The role of the aircraft carriers in TF58 was to secure and support the operation, with the carriers in TF57 protecting the left flank of the US Fifth Fleet and especially that of TF51, by suppressing enemy airfields in the Sakishima Gunto islands, both to prevent the Japanese from using these as bases and to prevent replacement aircraft being ferried to Okinawa. TF51, of course, had the by now well-established role of providing air support for the landings, including reconnaissance and ground attack. Ashore, the Japanese had almost 80,000 soldiers, as well as another 10,000 naval personnel who would certainly join the ground fighting as required. The defending forces were initially mainly concentrated in well-prepared defensive positions on the southern part of the island.

The landings were scheduled for Easter Sunday, 1 April 1945, and the troops arrived after their ships had struggled through heavy seas and gale-force winds. Mitscher's TF58 was eighty miles east of Okinawa, providing air and surface protection for the expeditionary forces, which were expecting attack from Kyushu and Okinawa.

Initial resistance proved to be light when the United States Tenth Army, under Lieutenant General Buckner, landed on the west coast of Okinawa with four divisions in the first wave on 1 April. The main reason for this was that in an amazing display of incompetence, Lieutenant-General Mitsuri Ushijima, commander of the Thirty-Second Army on Okinawa, failed to follow the joint army-navy defence agreement, which required the army to keep the landing forces on the beachheads long enough to give the navy time to amass both a Kamikaze attack and heavy gunfire from the battleship *Yamato*. Instead, Ushijima abandoned the coastal area and retired to the mountainous interior to dig in. This situation was compounded to the benefit of the Americans by details of the actual landing points not reaching the Imperial General Headquarters in time for action to be taken. When the first Kamikaze attacks were launched on 6 April, the landings had been completed and many suicide pilots wasted themselves against empty ships. When fierce fighting eventually did break out, this was largely concentrated in the southern part of the island.

Admiral Soemu Toyoda had overall command of air forces for attacks on the Allied fleet. The air offensive began on 6 April, and by the end of that day some 900 aircraft had attacked the fleet, of which 355 were Kamikaze. TF58 claimed to have shot down 249 aircraft, and of the 182 estimated to have struggled through the fighter cordon to the air over the fleet, 108 were shot down. That same day the giant battleship *Yamato*, with 18.1-in guns, put to sea for Okinawa, escorted by a cruiser and eight destroyers. The following day, 7 April, 280 USN aircraft sank the *Yamato* as well as the cruiser and four of the destroyers. Nevertheless, following the invasion, a grim war of attrition emerged, with the Japanese mounting a major air attack every few days in addition to frequent nuisance attacks.

Between 6 April and 29 May, 1,465 aircraft from Kyushu, one of the home islands, were used in ten massed Kamikaze attacks, with 860 of these aircraft coming from the JNAF's Fifth Air Fleet and the remainder from the JAAF's Sixth Air Army. Another 250 aircraft appeared from Formosa, with about 50 of these being JAAF and 200 JNAF. In addition, there were 3,700 JNAF and 1,100 JAAF conventional sorties.

[2] Geoffrey Brooke. *Alarm Starboard: A Remarkable True Story of the War at Sea*, Patrick Stephens.

Over the first six weeks, the attacks on British and American ships resulted in 26 ships of destroyer size and smaller sunk, and another 164 damaged, including the carriers *Bunker Hill*, *Enterprise* and *Intrepid* in TF58, and *Illustrious*, *Formidable*, *Indefatigable* and *Victorious* in TF57.

Enterprise was hit by a suicide aircraft on 11 April, and had to suspend flying operations for forty-eight hours. *Franklin* was also badly hit by Kamikaze attacks, losing more than 700 members of her crew, with many more badly injured.

Before this, on 9 April, TF57 was called upon to attack airfields in northern Okinawa, while American escort carriers of the Support Carrier Group in TF51 took over pounding the air bases on the Sakishima Gunto. TF51 had to do all of the odd jobs. It '. . . was the backbone of the attacks against the defence installations, and provided the close support for the assault of the western islands. . . . It was apparent that this force realised what was required of it far better than did the fast carrier force, and its pilots were far more assiduous in engaging concealed defences.'[3]

ON THE FLIGHT DECK

In any prolonged carrier campaign, ships have to be rotated out of the battle area for replenishment. This could mean every few days if operations were intense enough. By 4 May, TF57 was off Miyako in the Sakishima Gunto again, when a Kamikaze attacked. This was witnessed by Geoffrey Brooke: 'It was a grim sight. At first I thought that the Kamikaze had hit the island and those on the bridge must be killed. Fires were blazing around several piles of wreckage on deck and a lift aft of the island and clouds of dense black smoke billowed far above the ship. Much of the smoke came from fires on deck, but as much seemed to be issuing from the funnel, which gave the impression of damage deep below decks.'[4]

The attack happened while the battleships with their heavy AA armament were away from the carriers, shelling coastal targets, following a request from the forces ashore, to which the British commanders had willingly agreed. Some view this as a mistake, but some Kamikaze attacks did get through, and there could be no guarantee that this would not have happened even if the battleships had been present.

Formidable had been hit at 11.31 by a Kamikaze which managed to put a 2-foot dent in the flight deck, although without bursting through into the hangar. The flight deck had been crowded at the time, as aircraft were being ranged ready for launching, so eight men were killed and forty-seven wounded, many of them badly burned. The only consolation was that it could have been so very much worse. The Medical Officer had decided to move the flight deck sick bay from the Air Intelligence Office at the base of the island where the Kamikaze had struck. As it was, two officers were killed in the AIO, and the others with them were all horribly burned.

Five days later, on 9 May, *Formidable* was hit yet again, and this time the Kamikaze hit the after end of the flight deck and ploughed into aircraft ranged there. A rivet was blown out of the deck and burning petrol poured into the hangar, where the fire could only be extinguished by spraying, with adverse effects even on those aircraft not on fire. Seven aircraft were lost on deck, and another twelve in the hangar, leaving the ship with just four bombers and eleven fighters.

By this time, *Formidable* must have appeared jinxed. After refuelling and accepting replacement aircraft, on 18 May an armourer working on a Corsair in the hangar failed to notice that the aircraft's guns were still armed. He accidentally fired the guns into a parked Avenger, which blew up and set off yet another fierce fire, this time

[3] Admiralty, Naval Staff History, Battle Summary No. 47 'Okinawa'.

[4] John Winton. *The Forgotten Fleet*, Coward McGann, 1970.

A familiar sight during the Pacific War, as a Corsair lands on *Illustrious*, note the batsman just ahead of part of the ship's AA armament. (IWM A20995)

destroying thirty aircraft. Yet, by that evening, the ship was fully operational once again.

An American observer took a charitable view of the mayhem aboard the British ships: 'When a Kamikaze hits a US carrier, it's six months repair at Pearl. In a Limey carrier, it's a case of "Sweepers, man your brooms!"'[5]

Among those who witnessed the campaign was the New Zealander 'Cappy' Masters, whom we met at Salerno. By this time Masters, despite his protests, had been trained as a carrier deck landing officer, or 'batsman'. After completing his training for this unwelcome task, he soon had to teach other batsmen aboard British carriers, as the fleet expanded with the arrival of the escort carriers. If reluctant to be a batsman, he was not at all enthusiastic about his posting to the British Pacific Fleet, having been recalled while on leave in New Zealand and in the

middle of his honeymoon, to replace another carrier deck landing officer who had been taken ill. By this time promoted to Lieutenant, he was assigned to *Indefatigable*, and joined her at Leyte on 28 April, four weeks after the initial landings.

Apart from the obvious dangers of being struck by an aircraft wing and decapitated, life as a batsman during a major operation was not for the weak.

'Cappy' Masters recollections of the campaign were not enjoyable.

'. . . I was to stay on board for just over one month before a replacement batsman was appointed. Those four weeks were the toughest constant physical exercise I have ever experienced. Although there were three batsmen to share the deck landing duties, the hours of duty were particularly demanding. On strike days we would be aroused by the Royal Marine servant at 03.00 hours. We did

[5] US Navy Liaison Officer aboard HMS *Indefatigable*.

not work watches (four hours on, four hours off) like the seaman branch – we were on call from the first range of aircraft at about 04.00 hours to 18.00 hours in the evening. In my own case, I was required to be the standby night batsman in case of any deck landing accidents on HMS *Indomitable*, in which case we would have to take one or more of their night fighter Hellcats on to our deck . . .

'That routine meant that apart from the odd rest that I could have during the day in the aircrew room on the island, I was on call for seventeen hours on each strike day, during which I would be required to hold the bats in a 30 knot wind, to control as many as forty-eight landings in a day. This was as tough as being a boxer in a 12–15 round contest.'[6]

Ranging the aircraft was also part of the batsman's duties. Some idea of the pressure on the batsman can be taken from the fact that on 8 May 'Cappy' handled thirty Seafires and twelve Avengers, while on 12 May he had twenty-four Seafires and six Avengers, with twenty-eight Seafires and twelve Avengers on 16 May, a day which had been especially difficult. He recalls:

'On this last day the wardroom had been hit by food poisoning. Many aircrew were unable to fly, so those who were fit had to fly double the number of normal sorties.' His two colleagues were among the officers struck down with food poisoning, '. . . so for that day I was the only batsman on duty'.[7]

The best performance for landing on was *Implacable*'s aircraft, which had an average landing interval of 42.8 seconds, but even this was exceeded on one occasion when a nineteen-aircraft strike returned to the ship, with an average 31.8 seconds between aircraft, something which took good airmanship with excellent deck landing techniques, great confidence in the batsman and, last but by no means least, well-trained and energetic flight deck parties.

6–10 A.O. 'Cappy' Masters. *Memoirs of a Reluctant Batsman*, Janus.

STRIKING AT THE ENEMY

One of Masters' fellow countrymen was Lieutenant Donald Cameron, also a New Zealand volunteer reservist, although he later became a regular officer in the Royal Navy. He was in *Victorious* at the time of TF57's raids on Sakishima Gunto. He recalls one operation which was particularly ill-starred on 9 May 1945.

That afternoon, Cameron was due to take his flight of four Corsairs to escort a raid by a squadron of Avengers against airfields on the island of Miyako. As had become standard practice, once the Avengers had finished their work, if there was no apparent threat from enemy fighters, the fighter aircraft were free to look for targets of opportunity.

The flight took off at 15.30, leaving one of the aircraft behind with engine trouble. As they escorted the Avengers to the target, another aircraft had to return to *Victorious* with low oil pressure. The Avengers did their work, and Cameron and his wingman decided to attack the airfield at Ishigaki, which appeared to be busy and Cameron himself thought he had just seen a aircraft land. Cameron's aircraft was not carrying bombs, but his wingman had a 500-lb bomb under each wing, so he was invited to pick his target, and to let Cameron know when he was ready to dive so that he could accompany him to divide the anti-aircraft fire between the two aircraft.

'"Going in now, 501,"' my No. 4 called, and we both winged over together. At about 2,000 feet I pulled up to port in a skidding climbing turn and see-sawed my way back to 15,000 feet. No sign of No. 4. I called again, but no reply. Slowly circling I saw a large fire burning among the hangars of the airfield.

'That had to be No. 4 . . .'[8]

Cameron looked around the airfield, and saw what appeared to be a large aircraft at the corner of two hangars. He dived down

If all goes well, this Hellcat's arrester hook will catch the wire . . . (FAAM Hellcat/125)

. . . but if not there is always the crash barrier . . . (FAAM Hellcat/114)

. . . unless the undercarriage fails! (FAAM Hellcat/105)

once again as fast as the Corsair would go, just over 400 m.p.h., and reached the airfield at about 45 degrees to the main east–west runway, and at low altitude raced across the airfield firing continuously as the hangars rushed towards him. He had a fleeting glimpse of men running and jumping down from an aircraft outside a hangar, before he was climbing again and over the sea. He decided to repeat the exercise.

'I streaked up the runway at nought feet and as I passed the hangars at the far end there was a terrible bang and the aircraft seemed to jump sideways. Bits of cowling shot over the hood and the cockpit filled with smoke.

'Keeping low I shot the hood back with my left hand and the airflow enabled me to see ahead. I was by this time out to sea . . . the aircraft still handled normally apart from the burning smell . . . no oil pressure at all . . . cylinder head temperature was off the clock.

'I eased the throttle back, eased the nose up a little and tried to get what height I could. At about 2,500 feet I called "Mayday, Mayday, 501 ditching 20 miles west of Ishigaki."'[9]

He repeated the call, held the hood back and prepared to ditch.

'Off harness, out on wing, reach in and tear dinghy off bottom of parachute, turn on a small CO_2 bottle, the dinghy inflates, and I jump into the sea with it.

'Now comes the hard part, trying to get in the small dinghy. I had to let the air out of my Mae West and after repeatedly tipping the dinghy over onto myself managed to hold one end under the water while I got the top of my body on top by kicking my legs, raising my behind, and pulling towards my knees with both hands, I finally flopped into the bottom of the dinghy . . .'[10]

Cameron had made the mistake of repeating a strafing run across an enemy airfield, something which was discouraged as

After raiding the islands in the Sakishima Gunto, the British Pacific Fleet went to attack the Japanese home islands, including Matsushima Airfield on Honshu, seen here burning after an attack by Avengers on 9 August 1945, the same day that an atomic bomb was dropped on Nagasaki. (FAAM Camp/463)

each successive run became more dangerous. In his case, the mistake was not fatal, but it could have been indirectly, as he suffered barbaric treatment from his Japanese captors.

SUMMING UP

A change of command at the US Fifth Fleet saw Spruance replaced by Halsey. He signalled the British admiral, Rawlings:

'I wish to express to you and to the officers and men under your command my appreciation of the fine work you have done and the splendid spirit of co-operation in which you have done it. To the American portion of the Fifth Fleet, TF57 has typified the great tradition of the Royal Navy.'[11]

The Okinawa campaign had seen the British Pacific Fleet at sea for sixty-two days, apart from an eight-day replenishment at Leyte. Strikes had been flown from the carriers on twenty-three days, giving a total of 4,691 sorties, dropping 927 tons of bombs and firing 950 rocket projectiles. Estimates of the numbers of Japanese aircraft destroyed vary between 75 and 100, but airfields and shore targets also received attention. Twenty-six aircraft had been shot down by the enemy, but another seventy-two were lost for operational reasons, and sixty-one of these while landing on! Thirty-two aircraft had been lost to Kamikaze attacks, and another thirty in *Formidable*'s fire.

That there was room for improvement can be judged from the fact that the British lost 72

[11] Admiral Sir Philip Vian. *Action This Day*, Muller, 1960.

out of 218 aircraft for operational reasons, over a period of 54 days, while the Americans lost 231 out of 919 over a period of 80 days.

COMMENT

The Okinawa campaign was an essential preliminary to any invasion of the Japanese home islands, which at the time seemed to be the only certain means of ending the war, since those in command were not aware of just how quickly the atom bomb would be available. The fanatical defence by the Japanese also served as a warning that any invasion of Japan herself would be bloody, to an extent unprecedented in history.

The basic technique, of softening up the enemy defences before the attack, providing good combat air patrols over the fleet and also having aircraft dedicated to the support of troops on the ground, cannot be faulted.

Weaknesses, if there were any on the Allied side, lay in training and equipment among the Royal Navy ships, which had to learn the techniques of massed air attacks, and of maintaining a substantial fleet far from its usual base facilities. Against this, many of the aircraft were modern capable naval types, designed for carrier operation, while the ships were fast and robust, and this was also an essential characteristic of their crews.

As for the Japanese, their armed forces, while still determined and willing to fight regardless of cost, seemed time and time again to be deteriorating into a loose assortment of warlords rather than an integrated defence. Commanders in the field did as they thought best, regardless of the overall strategic situation. As with the Germans and Italians, war was a series of tactical events rather than a grand strategy, with all too few considering the consequences of each move.

PART SIX

CARRIER WARFARE IN PEACE

AN UNEASY PEACE

THE CHANGING ROLE OF THE CARRIER

The aircraft carrier emerged from the Second World War as the undisputed capital ship, with a potency far beyond that of any battleship. The outcome of the war at sea had been dictated by the aircraft carrier and the submarine, and indeed one could argue that the outcome of the war in the Pacific had depended almost entirely on these comparatively recent additions to the fleets of the world. It was the aircraft carrier that enabled the Americans to fight back across the vast reaches of the Pacific, while the United States Navy's use of the submarine against Japanese shipping of all kinds should be legendary, surpassing even the effectiveness of the deadly German U-boats.

The other big development of the war years had been the amphibious operations, essential in regaining territory and then carrying the war to the enemy. The roles of the aircraft carrier and of amphibious operations were to become much closer in the post-war world.

A new and even more dangerous order came into being after the war years. Those who had doubted the good faith of the Soviet leaders were not long in having these doubts confirmed, as Russian and then Chinese communists worked to ensure that a new empire was created. The aircraft carrier was soon to prove just how adaptable it could be. Unlike the submarine, which is a weapon of all out warfare, the carrier can scale its operations up or down to suit the occasion. With the arrival of larger ships, and aircraft designed for carrier operations, the aircraft carrier became a potent weapon. Both the Royal and United States Navies were eventually to have nuclear-capable aircraft aboard their ships, a part of the nuclear deterrent forces upon which the safety of the western democracies had to rest during the so-called 'Cold War'.

Yet, for other operations in more localized conflicts, the aircraft carrier was just as effective, offering the security against terrorist attack which was often impossible at airfields ashore, even when large numbers of troops were deployed to patrol airfield perimeters. In extremis, the aircraft carrier was the ship of choice to evacuate civilians from a crisis zone, not only in the closing days of the Vietnam War, but in other conflicts with a lower profile, such as the evacuation of British holidaymakers after the Turkish invasion of Cyprus in 1973.

In short, the initial outlook for naval aviation at the end of the war was good. With a couple of exceptions in the United States Navy, all other navies scrapped their battleships during the first fifteen years or so after the war ended. The helicopter meant that even smaller navies which could not afford aircraft carriers could take aircraft to sea, primarily for anti-submarine and anti-shipping duties. Had such machines been available during the war years, submarines would probably not have got close enough to *Courageous*, *Eagle* or *Ark Royal*, and the Arctic convoys to Russia would have been much safer. The helicopter also prolonged the useful life of some of the smaller aircraft carriers in many navies. After the disastrous decisions which resulted in the Royal Navy going to battle in the Falklands without airborne early warning cover, the helicopter was to fulfil this role as well. Cruisers soon boasted platforms and even hangars for helicopters, with the Italian Navy taking this to considerable lengths with the *Vittorio Veneto*, capable of taking up to nine helicopters. By the early 1960s, all new frigate and destroyer designs accommodated at least one helicopter.

Of course, the first sign of peace meant a substantial reduction in the number of aircraft carriers and their aircraft, as the United States Navy statistics show:

USN carrier force 1 July 1945:

20 Essex class CVs
8 Independence class CVLs
70 escort carriers CVEs

Total aircraft of all types: 40,912

USN carrier force 1 July 1946:

12 CVs
1 CVLs
10 CVEs

Aircraft available, 24,232, many of which were in storage or reserve.

The Royal Navy, which had invented the aircraft carrier but which had allowed its lead to falter between the wars, was to the fore again in the new era. Innovations such as the angled flight deck and the mirror deck landing system were British, just as later, out of cruel necessity, were carriers for vertical and short take-off and landing, V/STOL, aircraft.

The angled flight deck meant that aircraft landing on could 'go round' safely if the pilot missed the arrester wires. Even if the aircraft ditched, it would do so clear of the ship. It also meant that carriers could launch and recover aircraft at the same time, something which could have made a difference to the outcome of the Battle of Midway! Landing on itself became easier with another British invention, the mirror deck landing system which meant that a pilot could see for himself whether his aircraft was on the right approach path, neither too high nor too low.

Yet another British invention, the ejection seat, also meant that getting out of an aircraft in trouble became safer, and before long ejection seats which could be used at zero altitude or under the water became available.

The post-war years saw many other navies take to the aircraft carrier. The Dutch borrowed an escort carrier, which they renamed *Karel Doorman* after the admiral lost in the Battle of the Java Sea for the want of carrier air power, before buying a light fleet carrier, which they also named *Karel Doorman*. Canada and Australia, and then India, Argentina and Brazil all followed, while Spain was loaned the Independence-class light carrier *Cabot*, which was renamed *Daedalo*. The French started to modernize and rebuild their air arm, the Aéronavale, around two leased American Independence-class carriers and a light fleet carrier of their own, *Arromanches*.

The vessels which launched so many navies into operating their own fleet air arms were of the Colossus class, designed for the Royal Navy during the war years. A purpose-designed light fleet carrier, this was one of the most successful warship designs ever in terms of exports. Displacing 16,000 tons (20,000 tons full load), these ships had a maximum speed of about 25 knots. Aircraft accommodation varied, depending on the size of the aircraft, but they could accommodate twin-engined aircraft, such as the Grumman S-1 Tracker anti-submarine aircraft. Most important of all, on 3 December 1945, Lieutenant-Commander Eric 'Winkle' Brown made the first landing of a jet aircraft on a carrier, landing a de Havilland Vampire jet fighter on the Colossus class aircraft carrier *Ocean*.

These ships also provided the backbone of the Royal Navy's carrier fleet in the immediate post-war years while two new classes of carrier were being built. The Illustrious class ships had suffered during the war from enemy action and neglect, with normal refitting rarely possible, while the ships were expected to perform at maximum speed for long periods without relief. *Victorious* eventually benefited from a major refit, including fitting a half-angled flight deck and three-dimensional radar, while *Illustrious* was scrapped after some years as a trials and training carrier.

Dennis Sutton worked in the engine room of *Illustrious* after the war. 'She was a fantastic ship, but living conditions were atrocious,' he recalls. 'I have never seen so many cockroaches in my life.

'She was absolutely clapped out, but although she was a training carrier, she still had to do 30 knots for flying operations, so we still had to get the speed up. We could see where she had been damaged during the war, and where she had been repaired.'[1]

Not all of the improvements came immediately. Many carriers had 'half-angled' flight decks fitted, either because they were too small for the fully-angled deck, or as an interim measure until a major refit could be justified.

Eventually, in the early 1960s, the French introduced the first purpose-designed and built carriers to enter service with the French Navy. More than twenty years more had to pass before the Spanish and Italian navies introduced their own aircraft carrier designs.

Vertical take-off was not confined to the helicopter. The Hawker Siddeley P.1127 Kestrel was intended to provide tactical close air support for armies in the field, and was tested as such by a joint RAF, Luftwaffe and USAF squadron. Inevitably, someone tried to operate from the deck of a ship, initially believing that helicopter cruisers and other smaller ships could in this way have fighter protection. Instead, vertical and short take-off, or V/STOL, saved the aircraft carrier from extinction in the Royal Navy, and encouraged Spain to retain aircraft carriers and the Italians, at long last, to introduce an aircraft carrier, after much debate and rivalry between air force and navy! Oddly, the United States Marine Corps and both the Spanish and Italian Navies used Harrier-type aircraft, with only the Royal Navy and Indian Navy using the Sea Harrier. This is because while the USMC has experimented with using the Harrier as a fighter, the corps prefers to use it in the same way as the RAF, in support of ground troops. The Harrier's capability dispenses with the need for runways, although USMC AV-8s operate from carriers as well as from ashore.

After their experience in the Suez Campaign, the Royal Marines also adapted to the changing world, and obtained their own commando carriers, initially by converting two light fleet carriers, *Albion* and *Bulwark*. These ships improved the strategic mobility of the 'Royals', which now arrived fully-equipped and supported, with Westland Wessex, and later Westland Sea King HC.4, helicopters for rapid deployment and resupply. Once in position they provided a secure offshore floating base. Even so, their introduction was not without controversy. The Admiralty thought that the Royal Marine Commandos should be permanently based aboard the carriers. Fortunately, the then Commandant-General of the Royal Marines, General Sir Ian Riches, whose task it was to introduce this exciting development, objected.

'While conceding that the Commando might have to stay in the ship for long periods, depending on operational requirements, he insisted that a Commando was still an individual military unit, with its own identity, and thus would need proper military training, based on shore with its own accommodation, so as to be able to give a good account of itself.'[2]

---

[1] Interview with the author, November 1995.

[2] *Daily Telegraph*, 30 December 1996.

The General's view prevailed, and the Royal Marines were soon using their new ships, with a deployment to Kuwait in 1961, and later in the confrontation between the newly independent Malaysia and Indonesia.

Naval aircraft became larger and faster, and more capable. In the case of the McDonnell Douglas F-4 Phantom and LTV A-7 Corsair, carrier-borne aircraft were adapted for use by air forces, in a complete reversal of the situation which had prevailed between the wars!

The Soviet Navy eventually took an interest in the aircraft carrier, after first developing large helicopter cruisers. Eventually four 43,000 ton aircraft carriers of the Kiev class were introduced, with the first vessel commissioned in 1976, able to accommodate up to thirty-five aircraft. These ships operated the Yakovlev Forger A vertical take-off aircraft. The collapse of the Soviet Union and the resulting economic chaos has meant that just one of these ships is now believed to be operational.

Despite the growing interest in aircraft carriers which saw new ships enter service in countries without a history of carrier operations, first Canada, then the Netherlands and finally Australia abandoned the aircraft carrier, ignoring the lessons of naval history. Although outright abandonment was avoided by the Royal Navy with the introduction of the Invincible class ships, it nearly happened, and initially *Invincible* was described officially as a 'through deck cruiser' to avoid RAF opposition to a fixed-wing Fleet Air Arm. A defence review did attempt to cut the Invincible class from three ships to two, but the Falklands Campaign prevented this, although now further cuts have meant that only two of the Royal Navy's carriers are operational at any one time.

The United States Navy has kept faith with naval aviation, with ever larger carriers, and a steady move to nuclear propulsion, extending the range of these ships to years rather than miles! The high cost of nuclear-powered warships has, on the other hand, forced the French, who are also following this course, to have just one carrier to replace both *Clemenceau* and *Foch* around the turn of the century.

THE KOREAN WAR

NORTH KOREA INVADES THE SOUTH

The Korean War was the first of many post-Second World War conflicts, during what has been variously described as 'war in peace' or, more usually, the Cold War, between the Soviet Bloc and the Western Allies. Many of these wars were superpower conflicts fought by proxy. Korea was different, in that it was one of just two instances in which the United Nations was involved against the aggressor, and that was only possible because at the time the Soviet Union was boycotting the UN Security Council, and could not use its veto against UN military action.

The conflict had its origins in the preparations made for the end of the war against Japan. It was agreed in 1945 that the Soviet Union would take the Japanese surrender in Korea north of the 38th parallel, and the United States would take the surrender south of this line. In the post-war world, this arrangement solidified into a 'People's' republic in the north, backed by the Soviet Union and Communist China, still allies at that time, and a pro-Western regime in the south.

Many conflicts start by mistake, the usual mistake being that the aggressors believe that they can get away with it. In the case of Korea, the mistake was for the South Koreans, and their allies, to drop their guard. North Korea claimed that it had invaded South Korea because it had just repelled an invasion by South Korean forces. This was a lie, and a transparent one since no army has ever managed an immediate counter-attack. What had happened was that the invasion came immediately before the start of the wet season, when no one in South Korea was anticipating any military activity, and so the South Koreans were caught off their guard. The initial attack, early on a Sunday morning, found most South Korean troops off duty and most of them well away from their barracks. Before long, North Korean troops had pushed the South Koreans back to a small pocket of territory around Pusan, having overrun the capital, Seoul.

The situation worsened with the sudden entry of China into the war in October 1950, sending large numbers of 'volunteers' to swell the forces of the North Koreans.

While most of the aerial operations over Korea were by land-based aircraft, the aircraft carrier played a significant part, especially in the early days when the number of secure airfields was limited. The Royal Air Force played little part in the Korean War because of heavy commitments elsewhere, and so the British contribution to the air war fell mainly on the Fleet Air Arm.

SHIPS AND AIRCRAFT

The ships were primarily those of the latter part of the Second World War, the American Essex class aircraft carriers and the development of the *Essex*, the Midway class, some eighty feet longer. There were usually three American carriers on station, and, for example, for the landings at Inchon on 15 September 1950, which marked the start of the UN fight back, the US carriers included *Boxer*, *Philippine Sea* and *Valley Forge*, as well as the British light fleet carrier, *Triumph*.

This was what could be described as an 'interim' period for British carriers. The six large, fast, armoured carriers of the Second World War had taken much punishment. *Illustrious* was a trials and training carrier, while *Victorious* was waiting for a lengthy major refit. In their place were the small carriers of the Colossus class. In some navies such ships would have been confined to anti-submarine duties, but the British term 'light fleet carrier' meant just that. Such ships were meant to undertake a wide range of duties. Four ships were rotated for duties off the Korean coast, *Ocean*, *Triumph*, *Glory* and *Theseus*, while the Australian sister of these four ships, *Sydney*, also put in an appearance. *Unicorn*, the Royal Navy's maintenance carrier, also supplied aircraft for the light fleet carriers.

For the most part American aircraft carriers operated off the east coast of Korea in the Sea of Japan, while the British and Australian ships operated off the west coast in the Yellow Sea.

The United States Navy was in a period of transition at the time, with piston-engined and jet aircraft operating alongside each other. Because of the success of the Douglas Skyraider, this was a situation which was to last until the early years of the Vietnam War, until 1968. The practice which was adopted almost from the outset was for piston-engined strike aircraft, such as Avengers, Skyraiders and Corsairs, to take off before the jet aircraft, which then caught up before the target was reached. This was a practical approach, avoiding wasting jet time and fuel, not least because many of the early jet fighters were extremely short on endurance.

Aircraft included the first operational naval jet aircraft to enter service, and see combat, the Grumman F9F Panther, a single-engined straight-winged fighter capable of flying at almost 600 m.p.h. The ex-wartime aircraft included the Grumman Avenger, Vought F4U Corsair and the Douglas A-1 Skyraider, or A4 as it was sometimes called at

this time when standardization of USN and USAF designations was still in hand. The Skyraider was used both as a bomber, carrying up to 8,000 lbs of bombs and rockets, and as an airborne-early-aircraft, in its A4W, or EA-1E and EA-1F forms, giving coverage up to two hundred miles away. A single Wright R-3350 radial engine powered this versatile aircraft.

The Fleet Air Arm had its Avengers and Fireflies, which had appeared in the last two years of the Second World War, as well as many Supermarine Seafires. They also had the potent Hawker Sea Fury, a single piston-engined monoplane fighter-bomber developed from the RAF's Tempest fighter. A single Napier Sabre engine of up to 2,825 h.p. could power this aircraft at speeds of 450 m.p.h. and more. The Fleet Air Arm was moving rapidly in favour of conversion to jet aircraft, and had it not been for the Korean War, this could have been another promising aircraft which missed its chance of seeing combat.

These aircraft had to face Russian-built Yakovlev 'Yak' piston-engined fighters of various marks, which they soon mastered, as well as the new Mikoyan MiG-15 jet fighter, which was at first unexpected because few in the west were sure that the Soviet Union had jet fighters.

One innovation which did reach the Korean War was the use of helicopters for plane guard and transport duties. Although the Royal Navy had helicopters of its own at the outbreak of the Korean War, the first British aircraft carrier on the scene lacked a helicopter of her own for plane guard duties and was loaned a USN Sikorsky S-51, with a pilot, for this task. The helicopter was faster and more efficient than a plane guard destroyer.

The S-51 had flown in prototype form in February 1946, and was known to the USN as the HO2S-1. It used a single Pratt & Whitney R-985 piston engine of 450 h.p., and had a maximum speed of 110 m.p.h.

There were other helicopters in use ashore with the air and ground forces, but the main machine afloat was the Sikorsky S-55, which was a larger helicopter with an 800 h.p. Wright R-1300-3 piston engine, and which could accommodate up to ten passengers in addition to its crew of two.

ACTION

At the outbreak of war, the United States Navy had one attack aircraft carrier, or CVA, group centred around the aircraft carrier *Valley Forge*. A blockade and escort force were in position on 3 July, with amphibious, reconnaissance and anti-submarine warfare, ASW, units. The Royal Navy had a light fleet carrier, *Triumph*, with two cruisers and eight destroyers in position on 12 July. Australia had two destroyers on 28 July, with the light fleet carrier *Sydney* and a frigate the following day.

The reason why British naval forces were so quickly on the scene was that *Triumph* had been visiting Japan, and was returning home at the time of the invasion. Frank Taylor was a young Royal Marine aboard the carrier.

'We were on the way home, off the Korean coast, when the skipper came on the tannoy and told us that the North Koreans had crossed the 38th Parallel. We had to return to Kure to collect our aircraft. Many of us hadn't heard of Korea until that time. Anyway, as a young man, I was in no hurry to get home.

'*Triumph* was a happy ship, and there was always something going on. There was nearly always a crash. The Seafires and Fireflies would cut their engines and bounce as they landed on deck, and if they missed an arrester wire, they would go into the crash barrier.

'When *Triumph* came home, I got a draft and transferred to *Unicorn*, which acted as a maintenance carrier supporting the aircraft for *Theseus* and *Glory*. Now that was boring.'[1]

[1] Interview with the author.

The conflict was spread over three years, and we have a selection of eye-witness accounts as British and American forces fought first the North Korean Air Force and then the Chinese, after they joined the conflict.

Lieutenant J.G. Leonard Ploy was flying a Grumman F9F-3 Panther of VF-51 from the carrier *Valley Forge* on 3 July 1950.

'The 3rd July mission was the first take-off and initial mission of the Navy in the Korean War. We launched at about 07.30. The mission was a fighter sweep over the airfield at Pyong Yang, North Korea. . . . Quite a job for the eight of us since intelligence had briefed us that there were more than a hundred Soviet fighters in the area . . . as we circled the airfield, we could see many enemy aircraft taking off. Finally, we were cleared to strike targets of opportunity. Just as I was beginning my strafing run, I saw a Yak heading for the runway. He was ahead and to my right and starting his take-off roll. I banked over to my right and pulled up behind him. By the time I got into firing position he was well airborne, about 350 feet in the air.

'As I was closing on him, I looked to my left and saw another Yak shooting at me. . . . He had a perfect run on me but had evidently never shot at anything moving that fast before. I pulled up, watching him firing at me all the time. Then I saw Ensign Brown pull in behind him very close. The next thing I saw was a terrific explosion and Yak parts flying around. Sections of the starboard wing separated and the Yak rolled and went straight into the ground. We were less than fifty feet in the air as I passed over the wreckage.

'I looked back at 'my' Yak. I was in perfect position and let loose a short burst from the four 20-mm cannon. I got a couple of lucky hits on the starboard wing and it just peeled away. The Yak flopped over and crashed into the ground . . .'[2]

[2,3] Larry Davis. *MiG Alley: Air-to-Air Combat Over Korea*, Squadron/Signal Publications.

The Korean War saw jet aircraft and piston-engined aircraft in combat again, as in the closing stages of the Second World War in Europe. The Grumman F9F Panther was involved in one of the early engagements. (United States Naval Institute)

The eight aircraft then shot up the airfield, striking at the control tower, fire engines and a power substation.

'As we were getting pretty low on fuel by this time, we turned and headed for the carrier. We returned to the "Happy Valley" at about 09.00. The first Navy combat jet strike had been a very successful one.'[3]

This type of action was to be typical of carrier air operations throughout the Korean War. The aircraft which mattered in Korea was to be the fighter-bomber, both in close support roles for the ground forces, and as inderdictors, attacking the supply lines of the North Koreans. The Fleet Air Arm in particular was to enjoy considerable success in its strikes against railway bridges, but the North Korean infrastructure was relatively primitive, and ox-carts were also to be worthwhile targets. Soon, the Yak piston-engined fighters of the North Korean air force were cleared from the skies. As 1950 drew to a close, land-based aircraft were flying some seven hundred fighter-bomber sorties a day, with a further three hundred from the aircraft carriers steaming offshore. In total, UN forces were to fly 1,040,708 sorties during the war. The casualty rates were good by the standards of previous conflicts, with the UN forces losing 343 aircraft with a further 290 damaged. Most of these aircraft were, as one might expect, the ubiquitous fighter-bomber.

THE HELICOPTER GOES TO WAR

Korea offered a difficult terrain, extremes of weather conditions and a poor infrastructure. It is not surprising that, in these circumstances, the conflict was to see the first mass transport of troops by helicopter. On 20 September 1951, twelve USN Sikorsky S-55s airlifted a company of 228 fully-equipped US Marines to the top of a strategically important 3,000 foot hilltop. The helicopters then kept the marines resupplied, and eventually laid a telegraph wire back to their headquarters. The entire operation took just four hours, against estimates by commanders in the field that the operation could have taken two days travelling over the ground, during which the men would have been easy prey for enemy air attack.

A month later, the same helicopters moved a battalion of a thousand marines to the front line, in full view of the enemy. The operation in this case took 6 hours, 15 minutes, which was 25 minutes less than the marines had planned!

A DIFFERENT KIND OF CARRIER WAR

In contrast to the Second World War, carrier operations off the coast of South Korea were, as some have described them, 'curiously unreal'. The enemy lacked the means to carry the war to the aircraft carriers. There were none of the bombing and torpedo attacks against the carriers which had so characterized fighting during the Second World War. True, the smaller warships, and especially the minesweepers who had much work to do to counter North Korean mining of ports and coastal waters, found themselves under fire from enemy shore batteries from time to time, but the large cruisers bombarding North Korean and Chinese positions were safe. Even safer were the aircraft carriers on their monotonous steaming patterns, launching and recovering aircraft. Life aboard these ships meant much hard work, the boredom of off-duty hours and a steady routine, and little chance of enemy action.

The exceptions to this rule were, of course, the naval aircrew, who daily risked death and injury, and the chance of becoming a prisoner of war, as they carried the war to the enemy. The newer aircraft were, for the most part, stronger and faster than those used even in the closing stages of the Second World War, but aircraft still had to become airborne off

Lieutenant Peter Carmichael of the Fleet Air Arm shortly after shooting down a MiG-15 jet fighter in his piston-engined Hawker Sea Fury. (IWM A32268)

flight decks which had changed little since wartime. The angled flight deck and other innovations were still some years away from fleet use. The Colossus class carriers were not the fastest, managing 25 knots at most.

On the other hand, thanks to the helicopter and to strong UN naval forces, search and rescue services were far better than in any preceding conflict. This was true for those ashore as well, with wounded soldiers being airlifted by helicopter to field hospitals, vastly improving their survival rate.

Weather was another problem. The winters were harsh and cold, reminiscent of those endured by ships on the Arctic convoys to Russia. By contrast, the summers were hot, and many of the fliers believed that this was worse than the winter.

[4,5] Fleet Air Arm Museum.

Operations from the aircraft carriers were intensive, as this routine signal from *Ocean* on 17 May 1952, relates:

'Our pilots today have broken all existing records for British light fleet carriers in flying 123 sorties over our operating area. From dawn to dusk, the area has been pounded by rocket and bomb attacks. The destruction included three bridges downed, four coastal gun emplacements shattered, fifteen ammunition laden ox-carts exploded, an oil dump fired, smoke and flames have been billowing from this for most of the day. . . . Serviceability has remained excellent and we continue with sixty-eight sorties tomorrow.'[4]

There was also a generous response from the USN commander when *Ocean* moved off station:

'The unprecedented record set by the Ocean evokes pride and admiration in us all. This is the kind of warfare by the UN which the Commies do not mention in the Truce negotiations.

'Aggressiveness and top drawer training of pilots, ground crew and ship's company reflected in your operations are noted with profound pleasure. To the commanding officer and each man of the *Ocean* and her squadrons, Rear Admiral George C. Dyer sends "Well Done".'[5]

Some have suggested that the mix of intense danger and peaceful shipboard conditions placed a strain on many of the naval aircrew. Not all of the aircrew agreed with this. As a British Fleet Air Arm pilot put it, 'You could fly four sorties in a day; then come below, change into mess dress, and sit down for an evening of sherry, bridge and brandy.' The US Navy and Marine pilots, of course, on their 'dry' ships, were denied the Royal Navy's alcoholic refinements.[6]

If anyone felt that the odds were stacked against the Fleet Air Arm pilots once the MiG-15 fighters arrived in the skies over Korea, they were soon put right. At 06.00 on 9 August 1952, flying north of Chinimpo,

[6] Max Hastings. *The Korean War*, Michael Joseph, 1987.

A cartoon celebrating the first train hit by 802 Naval Air Squadron on a pre-dawn reconnaissance flight. (FAAM Camp/245)

four Sea Furies were returning from a raid against railway lines and trains when they were attacked by eight MiGs at 3,500 feet. In the ensuing battle, one MiG was shot down by Lieutenant Peter Carmichael, and another two were damaged. He later told a newspaper reporter, 'The MiG is a beautiful aircraft. . . . Though the piston-engined Sea Fury is about 200 m.p.h. slower, it can cope so long as the MiG can be seen. If the MiG comes in and fights, we are confident of the result.'[7]

Routine for the Royal Navy's aircraft carriers meant a nine-day cycle of operations, with four days' flying followed by one day's replenishment at sea, and then another four day's flying, before a brief trip to Japan. They aimed to fly 544 sorties in nine days, 68 a day. Each aircraft might be called upon to fly up to 120 miles from the ship, and to remain in the air for up to two hours. Aircraft took off in waves every two hours throughout the day, generally in flights of five or six aircraft each. The crews were briefed the previous night for the next day's operations. If it was summer, with dawn around 05.00, soon after 04.00 a Chinese steward might be shaking his officer awake: 'Must have blekfuss, Mr Jacob. Otherwise other officer have two blekfuss.'[8]

Lieutenant William Jacob was a pilot in a Firefly squadron aboard the 20,000-ton full load displacement light fleet carrier *Ocean* in the spring of 1952. The son of one of Winston Churchill's best-known wartime staff officers, Sir Ian Jacob, had, as a boy, attended the Royal Navy's officer training college at Dartmouth, and was disappointed that the Second World War should have ended when he was seventeen, just too young to take part. No doubt as a consequence of this, he was delighted to receive a posting to Korea: 'I simply loved the flying.'[9]

[7] Unidentified newspaper cutting, Fleet Air Arm Museum.

[8–13] Max Hastings. *The Korean War*, Michael Joseph, 1987.

Log book of Lieutenant, later Captain, D.T. McKeown, RN, for 9–16 August 1952. Note that the pilot passed through his hundredth sortie and his eighth bridge! (FAAM Camp/158)

Warmly welcomed when first introduced as an improvement on earlier naval fighters, by the time of the Korean War the Fairey Firefly was obsolescent. It was slow and in common with many carrier fighters and fighter-bombers, notoriously prone to bouncing when landing on. Advice to the pilots was scarcely reassuring. If they met a MiG jet fighter over Korea, they had to cut their speed to 125 knots, put their flaps down, and turn tightly, in the hope that the jets should then have great difficulty in flying slowly enough to hit them. Obviously, no one thought that a Korean MiG pilot would fly past, firing as he went! Nevertheless, the Firefly was a good ground support aircraft, being able to carry an effective load, usually sixteen rockets and four 20-mm cannon. *Ocean* also carried a squadron of the newer and faster Sea Furies, far more attractive and dashing than a Firefly by this time.

As always with carrier operations, take-offs provided some of the most dangerous moments. The Fireflies needed 30 knots of wind over the deck to get airborne once fully armed and fuelled. Unfortunately, a fully laden *Ocean* could barely manage 24 knots, and on a still day the aircraft would sink alarmingly over the bows as it bolted from the catapult, then lumber uncertainly upwards towards 10,000 feet, collecting the two or three other aircraft in the flight as it climbed.

This was the case when being detailed to make a sortie against enemy targets ashore, but throughout the day one aircraft was always on anti-submarine patrol ahead of the carrier, a dull and monotonous task, even though it was essential. The equivalent task for the Sea Furies was for a flight to be on combat air patrol, just in case the enemy decided to attack – they didn't.

'Operating in summer was the worst, with the temperatures in the glasshouse cockpit soaring to 140 degrees, the crews flying in underpants and overalls, soaked in sweat from

The Korean War saw British and American naval aircraft disrupting North Korean communications through attacks on bridges, such as this, destroyed by aircraft from *Theseus*. (FAAM Camp/23)

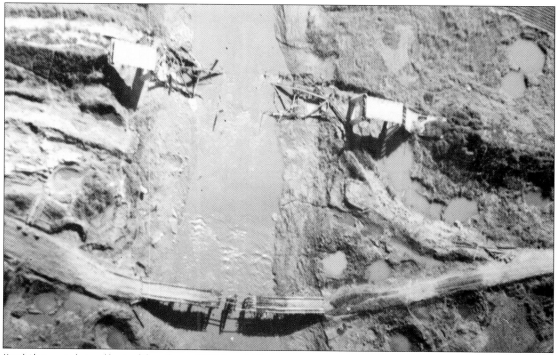

More bridges, again destroyed by aircraft from *Theseus*. (FAAM Camp/167)

take-off to landing. Yet still they wore their chamois leather gloves and scarves, and covered every inch of exposed flesh against the dreaded risk of fire. Accidents accounted for a high proportion of carrier casualties – such daily mishaps as that of a man on *Ocean* who was blown overboard one morning and never recovered when a pilot ignited his Rocket Assisted Take-off Gear without warning. Somebody had changed the positions of his RATOG and radio switches without telling him. Over the target, the tail fins of their 3-inch rockets were prone to break off after launching, and could hole the radiator with fatal consequences. And always, landing and take-off errors could prove fatal. On the ship, the intense physical demands of what the aircrew were doing magnified small irritants: the delayed arrival of mail, the absence of new wardroom movies, an argument over who should lead a given sortie.'[10]

Nevertheless, for those who felt that they were in effect fulfilling their destiny, doing the job which they had chosen and had trained for, life had its satisfactions, as Jacob recalls: 'I adored it. We had a marvellous time. It was so good to be doing it all with friends.

'I strafed an ox-cart and I think hit it while I missed another. Each of the two runs I did and also Purnell's runs left the cart surrounded in dust and smoke from which emerged an ox-cart going like a train. The man, however, was killed. . . . My landing was good for a change . . .'[11]

Ocean at speed, albeit just 24 knots, with Hawker Sea Furies ranged on her deck. (IWM A32243)

Arming a Sea Fury aboard *Ocean* during the Korean War. (FAAM Camp/165)

On 27 August, Jacob identified and photographed a communist radar station, and as had become the usual practice, the following day he was assigned to this target. Unfortunately, heavy anti-aircraft fire holed his radiator and fractured his coolant pipe. Realizing that the aircraft's engine would soon fail, he pulled back the control column and climbed to 6,000 feet before the inevitable happened and the engine failed. The Firefly began to drift downwards, trailing smoke. Jacob was undecided over what to do next. 'Prepare to bale out,' he told his navigator. 'No we'll take her down and ditch.' 'No, let's bale out.' In the back seat was a chief petty officer with vast experience and two Distinguished Service Medals,

named Hernshaw. The CPO was not impressed. 'Make your mind up,' he told Jacob crossly. 'I've been shot down seven times and I don't mind what you do as long as you make your mind up.' Jacob ditched. [12]

On hitting the water, the Firefly cartwheeled, but eventually stopped the right way up, enabling the two airmen to scramble out and slip into the warm water. They were just offshore and close to the island of Chodo, home of the UN's search and rescue service. As British and American aircraft circled overhead, they swam ashore, where Jacob was interrogated by an American radar officer on the island. Afterwards, Jacob swam back to his aircraft in the shallow water, to dive for his radio set, gyro gunsight and other

One of the innovations of the Korean War was the widespread use of airborne early warning aircraft such as this USN Douglas AD4W Skyraider, known as a 'guppy'. (United States Naval Institute)

secret equipment, which was brought ashore in a dinghy. That night, Jacob and Hernshaw were back on *Ocean*. The following morning they were sent to attack the radar station again. It was Jacob's 121st sortie: 'I thought that my luck must be beginning to run out.' But it did not. A few weeks later, he completed his tour in one piece, and was posted home.[13]

Not all of the flying was on combat missions, and the arrival of radar picket aircraft such as the Douglas Skyraider meant that the fleet had the reassurance of being able to keep an eye open for attacking enemy aircraft. One witness of this aspect of modern warfare was Jack Sauter, who served aboard *Lake Champlain*, an Essex class aircraft carrier which had joined the fleet in August 1945, and instead of taking part in the final attack on Japan, brought American troops home from Europe. She was known affectionately to her ship's company as 'The Champ'.

'The Champ' entered the Korean War Zone on 14 June 1953, by which time the war had been in progress for almost three years. She entered the zone just after midnight and at 13.00 joined Task Force 77 operating off the coast. Relieving the *Valley Forge*, she operated alongside the *Philippine Sea*, *Boxer* and *Princeton*, a cruiser and nine destroyers. The first operational flights were made that same day. Jack Sauter recalls:

'All of our planes returned safely and were taxied forward of the barriers. When the last plane had been recovered, the plane captains secured the control sticks with the pilots' safety belt to lock the elevators. This prevented wear on the control cables from the strong gusts on the flight deck. On one of the Banshees of VF-22, the arming circuit had not been de-activated, and when the stick was pulled back, several rounds of 20-mm were fired into a jet parked forward.

'The aircraft caught fire in its fuel tank, which fortunately didn't explode. As alarms sounded and scores of flight deck personnel raced up with foam and fog hoses, the flames roared like a blowtorch. The burning plane was parked in the middle of gassed aircraft, and it was only by the grace of God that everything else didn't explode. About half a dozen men from the flight deck crew crawled right under the flaming jet and directed a stream of foam right into the blaze. If the main tank had blown, they would have been instantly incinerated. I witnessed this from the 0-5 level, and it was about the bravest thing I'd ever seen. I wouldn't have gotten within a hundred feet of that fire.

'It took an hour, but the fire was brought under control without the loss of any more aircraft . . .'[14]

After this incident, the ship was ready for operations the following day. Fifteen men received the Medal of Honor for their bravery in fighting the fire.

Sauter was a radar operator in an airborne early warning and control aircraft, a Skyraider fitted with an APS-20 radar. His squadron was VC-12, a so-called 'composite' squadron with fifty aircraft in flights of three, spread around the fleet. The APS-20 radar had a range of 200 miles, giving that much of an extension to the carrier's 'eyes'. On 14 June he flew his first operation, and on returning to the ship, hurried below to snatch a late lunch. On entering the messdeck, he was surprised to find that many of the tables and benches had been replaced by bombs, rows and rows of bombs ranging from 250 lb to 2,000 lb, and among these men were happily eating their food!

Back in the air, Sauter again:

'On a more serious note, this threat of Chinese bombers (and their accompanying fighters) kept us ever alert at our radar screens, even after four hours of eyestrain. We lacked guns and speed, but our mission was critical to the security of the fleet. Our sole

14–16 Jack Sauter, *Sailors in the Sky*, McFarland & Co.

A development of the Panther was the Cougar, seen here landing on an American carrier. (FAAM Grumm/213)

defense, and only chance of survival, lay in that five-inch screen, for our job was to find them before they found us. Our guppies were the unarmed sentinels of Task Force 77.'[15]

On 25 June: 'At 02.45 on a pitch-black flight deck, an AD4W from our sister detachment, VC-33, was catapulted. Immediately, something in the catapult machinery failed, and Bill Naster . . . knew they were going in the drink. Lieutenant Fletcher [the pilot] desperately tried to stop the slewing Skyraider, but it was hopeless. There just wasn't that much deck space. In a catapult shot, you either made it or you didn't, and they weren't going to make it.

'With full power, they didn't fall over the edge of the flight deck. Instead, they pancaked about 100 yards off the port bow, directly in the path of 40,000 tons of aircraft

carrier moving at close to 30 knots.

'The landing, Bill thought, wasn't much different than a normal recovery. In fact, there wasn't even the expected jolt, just a deadly sinking feeling as the AD4W mushed in. Even in the pitch-black compartment, the two aircrewmen had no difficulty in disconnecting their headsets and safety harnesses. It was as if they had been doing it every day.'[16]

The pilot and the aircrewman left by the port side of the aircraft, leaving Bill to climb out on the right, the side closest to the rushing aircraft carrier. He felt that he could almost touch the grey hull, and then realized with alarm that the deadly screws were seconds away. Suddenly, the ship moved away, leaving him gasping in its wake. Someone on the bridge had been alert, and had saved his life.

COMMENT

The outbreak of the Korean War showed just how much deterrence depends on vigilance and a high state of readiness. In retrospect, it was a war that should never have happened, but in an uncertain and uneasy period, it was also a war waiting to happen. What the war did show, nevertheless, was unity among the western democracies and a willingness to participate in a major conflict over a prolonged period. Had they failed to do so, the risk of war breaking out elsewhere would have been heightened.

It was chance which meant that British and American aircraft carriers were close by, and could be in action quickly.

As in so many instances, the success of the Sea Furies showed that victory does not always belong to those with the fastest aircraft. Skill and good airmanship are more relevant to battles in the air.

OPERATION MUSKETEER: ANGLO-FRENCH LANDINGS IN THE SUEZ CANAL ZONE

31 OCTOBER – 6 NOVEMBER 1956

ANGLO-FRENCH WEAKNESS AND MUDDLE DELAYED PROMPT ACTION

Britain had maintained an armed presence in Egypt from 1882, mainly to protect the Suez Canal Zone, with the country being run effectively as a colony until 1922. During the Second World War Britain's main naval base in the Mediterranean had been at Alexandria. After the Second World War, Britain agreed to evacuate troops from Egypt, but this took place slowly and was not completed until 1956, by which time a complacent monarchy had been ousted by Gamal Abdel Nasser, a nationalist army officer.

Nationalization of the Suez Canal in July 1956 by Gamal Abdel Nasser, the new nationalist president, caused alarm in a number of countries. Most affected were the United Kingdom and France, who had owned most of the shares in the Suez Canal Company and were concerned about this short cut to their traditional trading partners in East Africa, Asia and Australia, and the Israelis, who viewed the prospect of a ban on their shipping in the canal with alarm.

The Skyraider also found its way into other navies, including the Fleet Air Arm, one of whose airborne early warning aircraft is seen here taking off on a half-angled deck. (FAAM Skyraider/26)

Initially, world reaction favoured an armed response by the two main powers affected, but neither country had the organizational ability and the manpower or equipment to respond quickly, even though British bases in Cyprus were within flying distance of the Suez Canal Zone.

Delay in mounting the operation saw international support eroded, and by the time Britain and France were ready, in early winter, the mood had swung against the operation, especially in the United States. American opinion was also alarmed by an Israeli attack on Egypt, secretly prompted by the British and French as a pretext for their intervention to secure the Canal Zone.

In practice, the Israeli diversion hindered rather than helped the operation. British and French forces planned on a six-day air campaign against Egyptian airfields and military installations as a softening up before an invasion. This could not take place for six days because this was the time it would take the slowest vessels to reach Egypt from Malta; and, of course, the ships could not leave Malta until the Israeli attack and the resultant British and French ultimatum to the Israelis and Egyptians.

SHIPS AND AIRCRAFT

Seven aircraft carriers were employed in the Suez Campaign, five of them British and two French. Two of the British carriers were the light fleet carriers, *Ocean* and *Theseus*, both of which had been in action during the Korean War. They were joined by two larger vessels, *Albion* and *Bulwark*, and by the still larger *Eagle*. The French aircraft carriers were the *Arromanches*, a sister ship of Ocean and *Theseus*, and *La Fayette*, a loaned Independence class aircraft carrier.

Albion and *Bulwark* were heavier developments of the original light fleet carriers, and have often been referred to as the 'Hermes class', even though the nameship was

last to enter service because of delays during construction resulting from adjustments to the defence budget. The fourth ship was *Centaur*, the first British carrier to have the interim half-angled flight deck, which conveyed some of the benefits of the angled flight deck, albeit at lower cost because relatively little conversion work was needed. Able to steam at 28 knots, these four ships were originally intended to displace 23,300 tons and have an overall length of 737 feet, although *Hermes* was slightly longer once completed at 744 feet, displacing 27,000 tons. Once again, aircraft sizes increased during the lifetime of these vessels, and although *Hermes* eventually had capacity for twenty-eight aircraft, at the time of the Suez Campaign, *Albion* and *Bulwark* would have accommodated nearer forty.

Eagle, commissioned in 1952, was one of the two largest aircraft carriers to enter service with the Royal Navy. At 43,000 tons and with a length of 803 feet, she could steam at more than 30 knots. Aircraft capacity, eventually down to forty-two by the early 1970s, would have been well in excess of sixty at the time of Suez. Essentially, *Eagle* and her sister-ship *Ark Royal* were developments of the Illustrious class of World War II. *Eagle* entered service with a straight flight deck, but by the time of Suez had a half-angled deck; a fully-angled deck was fitted later.

At Suez, the French aircraft carriers and the three larger British carriers were to act as attack carriers, while *Ocean* and *Theseus* were to carry 600 men of No. 45 Commando, Royal Marines and helicopters, although the small size of these ships, and the need to transport a unit of the Royal Air Force Regiment, meant that the marines had to be split between the two ships, as did the aircraft.

Aircraft had changed as well. The Royal Navy had fourteen squadrons of aircraft embarked aboard the three larger ships

Few conflicts have had such a prolonged build-up as Operation Musketeer, the Anglo-French landings in the Suez Canal Zone. Here in early October 1956 are British and French warships in Toulon. Nearest the camera is the French *Lafayette*, a loaned Independence class carrier; followed by the Royal Fleet Auxiliary *Tiderange*; *Eagle* with her half-angled deck; the cruiser *Georges Leygues*; *Arromanches*, a Colossus class carrier and finally the cruiser *Colbert*. (IWM A333593)

A Sea Hawk races over Egyptian territory. (FAAM SeaH/62)

bound for Suez, and these would have included Fairey Gannet turbo-prop anti-submarine aircraft and the now familiar Douglas AD-4W Skyraider airborne-early-warning aircraft. Of greater significance were the Armstrong-Whitworth Sea Hawk, de Havilland Sea Venom and Westland Wyvern fighters and strike aircraft.

The Westland Wyvern was the world's first, and only, turbo-prop-powered naval strike aircraft, and *Eagle* had embarked the Wyverns of 830 Squadron. The single-seat Wyvern used a single 3,760 s.h.p. Armstrong-Siddeley Python turbo-prop, which provided a maximum speed of 383 m.p.h. The aircraft had first entered service with the Fleet Air Arm in 1953. Four wing-mounted 20-mm cannon provided the basic armament, but the aircraft could carry a variety of munitions, including rocket projectiles or three 1,000-lb bombs.

Originating as a Hawker design, development and production of the Sea Hawk was transferred to Armstrong-Whitworth after delivery of the first thirty-five aircraft to the Fleet Air Arm. A single Rolls-Royce Nene turbojet of 5,400-lb thrust powered the Sea Hawk, giving this straight-wing single-seat jet fighter a maximum speed of 590 m.p.h. In common with the Wyvern, the aircraft had four 20-mm cannon, although these were mounted in the fuselage. Bombs and rockets could be carried on the four underwing strongpoints.

A modified version of the de Havilland Venom jet fighter, the Sea Venom was a twin-boom jet fighter with a single 4,850-lb thrust de Havilland Ghost turbojet, which provided a maximum speed of around 600 m.p.h. Four 20-mm cannon were fitted in the nose while the aircraft could carry rockets or up to 2,000-lb of bombs on underwing strong-points. Among the aircraft embarked aboard the French carriers were Sea Venoms built under licence in France.

Helicopters were of considerable importance in this campaign. The Royal Navy was using licence-built versions of the

Under way at sea, *Eagle's* flight deck is crowded with de Havilland Sea Venoms and Armstrong-Whitworth Sea Hawks, while *Bulwark* and *Albion* are in the background. (IWM A33599)

Aircraft from 830 Squadron from *Eagle* destroyed Gamil Bridge, near Port Said. (FAAM Camp/14)

Sikorsky S-55 helicopter, the Westland Whirlwind, with a 750 h.p. Alvis Leonides Major piston engine. There were also a small number of the small Bristol Sycamore helicopter.

ACTION

The Royal Air Force, Aéronavale and Fleet Air Arm commenced their attacks on Egyptian airfields on 1 November, and within forty-eight hours had control of the skies. The initial attacks were at night, and one British instructor, still with the Egyptian Air Force, later explained that the 'Egyptians had thought it thoroughly unsporting of the British to attack at night, since they didn't like night flying!' Sea Hawks, Sea Venoms and Wyverns were embarked aboard *Eagle*. The carrier's Wyverns made bombing and strafing attacks on Dekheila airfield on 1 November. The following day they made further attacks on the airfield and also on army vehicles near Cairo, before moving on to attack targets west of Port Said, including Gamil bridge. It was during this attack that

A successful attack on an oil storage depot at Port Said. (FAAM CM.24)

The Suez Campaign was also notable for an airborne assault by Royal Marines of 45 Commando from the carriers *Ocean* and *Theseus* using Westland Whirlwind and Bristol Sycamore helicopters, both of which are shown here. (IWM HU6447)

the squadron suffered its first casualty, when a Wyvern was hit by flak, but the pilot, Lieutenant McCarthy, managed to drop his bomb and then glide three miles offshore, where he was picked up by *Eagle*'s search and rescue helicopter. On 5 November the squadron was in action again, supporting army units, with bombing and rocket attacks against sniper positions. A second Wyvern was lost during this operation, although the pilot, Lieutenant-Commander W.H. Cowling, managed to eject safely and was picked up by an SAR helicopter.

Bulwark had been acting as training and trials carrier in home waters when the Suez Canal was nationalized. In just a few days, the ship was brought up to her full complement, refuelled, stored and ammunitioned for war, embarked three Sea Hawk squadrons and set off for Malta, where she arrived in early August. There was then some considerable delay, before finally in October she sailed to the Suez Canal Zone for 'Anglo-French' naval exercises. During the six days of air operations, *Bulwark*'s aircraft flew nearly 600 sorties.

Suez gave the Royal Navy and Royal Marines their first taste of heli-borne assault, although in less than auspicious circumstances. In fact, at the outset the operation looked less than promising.

Ocean carried the Joint Experimental Helicopter Unit, 600 men of 215 Wing, RAF Regiment, half of 45 Commando's men, while *Theseus* had the remaining marines and No. 845 Squadron.

Lieutenant Jack Smith was commander of Z Troop, No. 45 Commando.

'The sea passage from Malta to Port Said took three days, an intense period of briefing, rehearsal and preparation. In HMS *Ocean* these were complicated because there were two types of helicopter, the Army version of the Whirlwind with a load of only five fully-

Sycamore helicopters return to the carriers while destroyers bombard coastal positions. (IWM HU6446)

Also in service for Suez was the Westland Wyvern turbo-prop strike aircraft, which had a short career with the Royal Navy. Here a Wyvern is catapulted off *Eagle*, and the strop can be seen falling away from the aircraft. (IWM A33356)

armed men, and the Sycamore capable of carrying three. Each man, as well as carrying his own ammunition, rations, water, respirator and spare clothing, had to carry some support weapon ammunition . . .

'A loaded Sycamore presented an extraordinary sight. The back seats, side panels and inessential fittings had been stripped to increase the lift. The three passengers sat on the floor, one hunched in the middle with six mortar bombs on his lap, and the other two with their legs dangling over the side, each holding a 106-mm anti-tank shell about three foot long. The man in the middle was responsible for the two outboard members not falling out. The Whirlwind was a little more orthodox, but there were no seats. The five passengers hung on to any handhold available. On approaching the landing zone, the Bren gunner was ordered to put down suppressive fire out of the window if necessary, while the rifleman covered the area of the door. Communications between troops and pilots in both aircraft was either by shouting or tugging at the pilots' legs.'[1]

Not surprisingly, given these loadings, the helicopters could not carry all of the marines at once!

Nevertheless, at 05.45 on 6 November 1956, the men of No. 45 Commando, Royal Marines, were aboard the light fleet carriers *Ocean* and *Theseus*, ready for Whirlwinds of 845 Naval Air Squadron to take them ashore.

The helicopters operated slowly, in waves, before circling over the landing ground and then breaking away to land their marines. One marine jumped out of his helicopter and

[1] Robert Jackson. *Suez 1956: Operation Musketeer*, Ian Allan.

Sea Hawks aboard *Eagle* fire cartridges to start their engines. (IWM A33355)

was immediately hit by a bullet. He was pulled back aboard, and was being treated in *Ocean*'s sick bay twenty minutes later. Another helicopter, from *Theseus*, had to ditch, but there were no casualties.

It must be doubted whether this operation, dubbed a success, would have been so had there been determined resistance by the defending forces. The heavily-laden helicopters would have been an easy target, especially since the men were so encumbered with munitions.

Then, almost as soon as the ground war had started, it was over. Faced with a run on the pound sterling and the franc, and the lack of American support, Britain and France succumbed to international pressure, and accepted first a cease-fire and then the withdrawal of their troops from the Suez Canal Zone.

COMMENT

This was a classic example of the need for the armed forces to be able to act quickly if the operation was to be successful. In this respect, it failed, in marked contrast to the successful campaign for recovery of the Falkland Islands some twenty-five years later. That the Royal Navy could move from peacetime to wartime quickly was shown by the mobilization of *Bulwark*, but this was the exception. There can be little doubt that the helicopters were not up to the role expected of them, and this was a weakness in the naval aspect of the operation. Other major weaknesses lay in the poor capacity of the RAF's transport force. Properly designed ships for an amphibious assault were an essential feature which the operation lacked, and it would have been impossible to mount

British and French losses at Suez were light, but this Sea Venom was damaged by flak, and had to land back aboard *Eagle* without its undercarriage – but it was successful. (IWM A33608)

such an operation with the element of surprise necessary to stop the Egyptians from blocking the canal.

Nevertheless, the one big lesson learnt was the value of the commando carrier, but of a larger size than *Ocean* and *Theseus*. Soon after the Suez Operation, *Albion* and *Bulwark* were converted to become commando carriers, operating Westland S-58 Wessex turbine-powered helicopters. The larger size of both ships and aircraft made these a formidable force. Two amphibious landing ships with a floodable dock, *Intrepid* and *Fearless*, also joined the Royal Navy, and both of these could also operate helicopters from a small deck aft of the superstructure.

NAVAL AIR WAR OVER VIETNAM

1964–1975

CONTINUED INSTABILITY AFTER THE KOREAN WAR

The end of the Korean War had not guaranteed peace in the Far East. Even before the Korean War ended, fighting flared up over the remains of the old French empire. Formed out of part of the former French Indo-China, Vietnam was divided into a northern zone and a southern zone in 1954. The northern zone was dominated by the Communists, while the southern was pro-Western. Meanwhile, Cambodia and Laos, which had also been part of the former French Indo-China, maintained a vague neutrality. From 1957 onwards, communist-backed guerillas started to attack villages and highways, and then towns, in the southern zone, by this time officially known as South Vietnam. While Laos and Cambodia continued to be officially neutral, the guerillas were able to seek refuge in these countries and their supply lines were often run through 'neutral' territory to make it more difficult for South Vietnamese forces to counter-attack.

The North Vietnamese by this time had become a client state of the Soviet Union. South Vietnam had the oddments of equipment donated by the departed French forces, including some light transport aircraft converted for counter-insurgency use. To counter communist influence, the United States began, in 1955, to provide South Vietnam with equipment and training, including military advisers to assist the South Vietnamese forces, which were numerically weaker than those in North Vietnam. Gradually, the number of US advisers grew, until in numbers and rank they were more akin to regular US troops. In 1963, the newly elected President John Kennedy committed American forces to counter the growing menace of Viet Cong guerillas, and encouraged America's allies to help. For the most part, active support came from South Korea and, for a period, Australia.

The role of the aircraft carrier had adapted to a changing world. While maintaining the capability to engage in fleet actions because of the threat of war with the Warsaw pact countries, aircraft carriers were also seeing service in counter-insurgency operations. For these, they brought the security from terrorist attack which shore-bases could not provide. The mobility of the aircraft carrier was also a great asset. A fully equipped airfield with fighter and air traffic control, and its own defences, could arrive in areas where such facilities did not exist.

The United States was actively involved in Vietnam from August 1964 to January 1973, although final withdrawal did not take place until 1975.

SHIPS AND AIRCRAFT

The American carrier fleet had changed considerably since the end of the Second World War, as had most of the aircraft, with the exception of one late arrival at the end of the war, the Douglas A-1 Skyraider. There had been change even since the end of the Korean War, with the early jets having had a relatively short service life.

The main fighter from US aircraft carriers at the outset of the Vietnam War was the Vought, later LTV, F-8 Crusader. (United States Naval Institute)

The aircraft carriers involved were:[1]

America (CVA-66): 4 cruises 1968–73. Naval Air Wings: 6, 8, 9.
Bonhomme Richard (CVA-31): 6 cruises 1964–70. Naval Air Wings: 5, 19, 21.
Constellation (CVA-64): 11 cruises 1964–75. Naval Air Wings: 9, 14, 15.
Coral Sea (CVA-43): 11 cruises 1964–75. Naval Air Wings: 2, 15.
Enterprise (CVAN-65): 6 cruises 1965–73. Naval Air Wings: 9, 14.
Forrestal (CVA-59): 1 cruise 1967. Naval Air Wings: 17.
F.D. Roosevelt (CVA-42): 1 cruise 1966–7. Naval Air Wings: 1.
Hancock (CVA-19): 12 cruises 1964–75. Naval Air Wings: 5, 21.
Independence (CVA-62): 1 cruise 1969. Naval Air Wings: 7.
Intrepid (CVA-11): 3 cruises 1966–9. Naval Air Wings: 10.
Kittyhawk (CVA-63): 6 cruises 1965–72. Naval Air Wings: 11.
Midway (CVA-41): 8 cruises 1965–73. Naval Air Wings: 2, 5.
Oriskany (CVA-34): 12 cruises 1965–75. Naval Air Wings: 16, 19.
Ranger (CVA-61): 7 cruises 1964–73. Naval Air Wings: 2, 9, 14.
Saratoga (CVA-60): 1 cruise 1972–3. Naval Air Wings: 3.
Shangri-La (CVA-38): 1 cruise 1970. Naval Air Wings: 8.
Ticonderoga (CVA-14): 5 cruises 1964–9. Naval Air Wings: 5, 16, 19.

Aircraft types deployed at sea were:[2]

Douglas A-4 Skyhawk squadrons – 107 cruises
McDonnell-Douglas F-4 Phantom squadrons – 84 cruises
Vought F-8 Crusader squadrons – 57 cruises
LTV A-7 Corsair squadrons – 56 cruises
Grumman A-6 Intruder (inc. EA-6) squadrons – 36 cruises

[1,2] US Naval Institute.

North American Rockwell RA-5 squadrons – 31 cruises
Douglas A-1 Skyraider squadrons – 24 cruises
Grumman E-2 Hawkeye squadrons – 24 cruises
Douglas A-3 (all types) Skymaster squadrons – 13 cruises

A total of 432 squadron cruises.

One or two of the the Second World War Essex class aircraft carriers were still in service by the early 1960s, but most had been retired, as had most of the Independence class carriers, other than for odd support tasks or, in one case, loan to the Spanish Navy. The improved Essex vessels, the Hancock class, were also around in small numbers. These displaced more than 40,000 tons, although displacement varied slightly from vessel to vessel, due in part to the modernization which had taken place. Aircraft capacities varied according to the types embarked, but ranged from forty-five to eighty aircraft. Larger still were the Midway class carriers, displacing 51,000 tons, and including *Midway* and the *Coral Sea*, originally entering service in 1945 and 1947, with a capacity of around seventy-five aircraft. These ships had been modernized with angled flight decks, allowing aircraft which missed the arrester wires to 'go around' and try again, rather than risk the dangerous crash barrier. The other big benefit was that aircraft could land on while others were being flown off, or the rate of flying off could be increased as aircraft used the angled flight deck. On many ships steam catapults were also used for the angled flight deck, and when fitted these were usually referred to as 'waist' catapults.

Even larger than these ships were the four Forrestal class aircraft carriers, which had entered service between 1955 and 1959. These had standard displacements of around 60,000 tons and full-load displacements of

Vietnam used a wider variety of aircraft than did Korea, which was primarily a fighter-bomber war. Even so, fighter-bombers such as the Douglas A-4 Skyhawk did much of the hard work. (United States Naval Institute).

75,000 tons or more, depending on the individual ship. More than seventy aircraft could be carried, and surface-to-air missiles were added during their service lives, replacing their 5-in guns. The maximum speed of the *Forrestal* was 33 knots, but the others were slightly faster at 34 knots.

Largest of all the conventionally powered aircraft carriers were the Kitty Hawk class, although at standard displacements of just over 60,000 tons and full load displacements at between 78,000 and 82,000 tons, these were not too much larger than the Forrestal class. The *Kitty Hawk* was commissioned in 1961, along with her sister ship, Constellation, with *America* following in 1965 and *John F. Kennedy* in 1968. These ships had no guns, and could take up to eighty-five aircraft.

Classifications had changed. These carriers were known as large aircraft carriers, or CVB, initially, then reclassified as attack carriers, CVA, in 1952, while still under construction. Later, in 1975, these ships were to be reclassified again, simply as aircraft carriers, CV! Some of the Hancock and remaining Essex class ships were classified as anti-submarine carriers at one time, or CVS.

All of these ships were conventionally powered, using oil-fired steam turbines which powered four shafts. The Kitty Hawk class ships were accompanied by the first nuclear-powered aircraft carrier, the *Enterprise*, which was commissioned in 1961, and initially classed as a nuclear-powered attack carrier, or CVAN, before being reclassified in 1975 as a CVN. *Enterprise* had a development of the Forrestal class hull, but was a few feet longer, at 1,102 feet, and heavier, with a displacement of 75,700 tons standard, and 89,600 tons full load. Aircraft accommodation was for around eighty-five. The big advantage of nuclear power was that the ship no longer needed refuelling for herself, and range could be assessed in years rather than miles, with a need for refuelling every ten to thirteen years. Speed was a high 35 knots.

Just as the aircraft carriers had been through reclassification, so too had the aircraft. In the United States a common classification system

The Essex and Midway class carriers had a distinctive 'pyramid' shape to the island. (United States Naval Institute)

was introduced for military aircraft, regardless of whether they were operated by the USAF, USN, USMC or the Army. This was to prove timely, for in addition to helicopters some fixed wing aircraft were to see service with both the USAF and USN, most notably the McDonnell (later McDonnell Douglas) F-4 Phantom, a rare instance of a carrier aircraft also entering service with air forces.

The Douglas A-1 Skyraider remained operational until 1968, but there were many new aircraft, but the most important being the Douglas A-4 Skyhawk, the North American A-5, the Grumman A-6 Intruder, the LTV A-7 Corsair II, the McDonnell Douglas F-4 Phantom, and the LTV F-8 Crusader. These aircraft were often available in reconnaissance versions as well as the original fighters or attack aircraft. In addition, there were anti-submarine and airborne early warning aircraft, tankers for in-flight refuelling, and carrier onboard delivery aircraft, helicopters for plane guard to rescue pilots whose go-around left them in the water, and for combat rescue, as well as for anti-submarine work and minesweeping.

Here we will concentrate on the most significant of the new combat aircraft.

One of the most successful American military aircraft was the McDonnell (later McDonnell Douglas) F-4 Phantom II, although in practice the 'II' was usually dropped. This aircraft had been developed specifically to give the United States Navy an aircraft capable of countering any shore-based fighter it might have to face. Deliveries started at the end of 1960 to the USN as the F-4B, with the first USAF aircraft being delivered in 1963. In the early versions, two reheated 16,500-lb thrust General Electric J79-GE-8 turbojets gave a maximum speed in excess of Mach 2.0 and a range of up to 2,000 miles. As a fighter-bomber, the aircraft could carry up to 10,000 lb of bombs or air-to-surface missiles on under-wing and under-fuselage strongpoints. Most Phantoms were two-seat aircraft. Developments

included RF-4B reconnaissance variants, operated by both the USN and USMC.

In the early stages of the Vietnam War, most of the carrier fighter duties were carried out by the Ling-Temco-Vought F-8 Crusader. Originating as a Vought design, it had won a USN competition for a supersonic carrier-borne fighter. An unusual feature of this high-wing single-engined and single-seat aircraft was the variable-incidence wing, which reduced the nose-up position during the final stages of the landing approach. Several improved versions entered service, with the later F-8Js using a single 18,000-lb thrust reheated Pratt & Whitney J57-P-20 turbojet for a maximum speed of 1,100 m.p.h. and a range of up to 1,200 miles. Two 1,000-lb bombs could be carried on under-wing strongpoints.

The Douglas (later McDonnell Douglas) A-4 Skyhawk had the distinction of carrying out more raids over Vietnam than any other aircraft type. The aircraft was developed as a simple, lightweight and inexpensive replacement for the Douglas A-1 Skyraider, and was small enough to operate without folding wings from American aircraft carriers. Deliveries of the A-4A had started in 1956, and this version of the single-seat aircraft used a 7,700-lb thrust Wright engine – later versions had improved thrust, with an 8,500-lb Pratt & Whitney J52 on the A-4E of 1961. The later A-4F had 9,300-lb thrust. With external fuel tanks, a ferry range of up to 3,000 miles was available, with a maximum speed of 680 m.p.h., while a fuselage and four under-wing strongpoints could take missiles, rockets, or up to 8,000 lb of bombs.

The A-4 series was also selected by the Royal Australian Navy for operation from their last aircraft carrier, *Melbourne*.

Operations over Vietnam were also conducted by the North American Rockwell A-5 Vigilante, a large carrier-borne bomber with Mach 2 performance and a nuclear strike capability. This two-seat aircraft used two reheated 17,000-lb thrust General Electric J79-GE-8 turbojets, and had a range of up to 3,000 miles. While under-wing strongpoints were provided, the bomb bay was unusual in being a tunnel running the full length of the aircraft, with bombs ejected at the after end. The aircraft was not as successful as some of the others mentioned here, and eventually most were converted to RA-5C reconnaissance aircraft. As a strike aircraft, the A-5 was more suited to all out warfare, and probably nuclear warfare at that, rather than interdiction bombing or counter-insurgency operations.

More important than the A-5 was the Grumman A-6 Intruder, an all-weather strike aircraft which incorporated the lessons of the Korean War. Used by both the USN and USMC, the aircraft, which was two-seat in attack variants and four-seat in USMC electronic reconnaissance versions, used two 8,500-lb thrust Pratt & Whitney J52-P-6 turbofans for a speed of up to Mach 0.95. It was a high-wing aircraft and up to 18,000 lb of bombs could be carried in a semi-recessed bomb bay or on under-wing strongpoints. The first A-6s entered service in 1961, and many remain in USN service today.

Finally, another very important aircraft in the later years of the war was the Ling-Temco-Vought A-7 Corsair II. In common with the Phantom this was another carrier-borne aircraft adopted by the USAF. A development of the F-8 Crusader, the single-seat aircraft was intended to be a replacement for the A-4 Skyhawk. The aircraft first flew in 1965, and a wide variety of powerplants were used. It initially had the Pratt & Whitney TF30 series of turbofans of 11,350 lb or 12,200-lb thrust, but later versions used the Allison TF-41 (a licence-built version of the Rolls-Royce Spey) of 14,240-lb or 15,000-lb thrust. Maximum ferry range was 3,600 miles with external tanks, and the warload was 10,000 lb on two fuselage and six under-wing strongpoints.

In contrast with aircraft during the Second World War, many of these aircraft were also available as trainers, for conversion training. Single-seat aircraft were modified with a second seat for the instructor. Had such variants been available for many of the aircraft used during the Second World War, training would have been more thorough and deck-landing casualties far less common.

ACTION

The Vietnam War was one of the longest-running conflicts of modern times, effectively starting in 1963, although the United States had been involved for most of the preceding ten years, and ending abruptly with American withdrawal in 1975. American warships were operated on what was known to the USN as 'Yankee Station', an area off the coast of Vietnam from which strikes against targets in North Vietnam were conducted. There was relatively little ship-to-ship activity, and that only at the beginning. Air-to-air was against land-based North Vietnamese fighters.

As far as the USN was concerned, the first serious incident was on 21 May 1964, when two RF-8A Crusader photographic reconnaissance aircraft of a light photographic squadron, VFP-63, were launched from the aircraft carrier *Kitty Hawk*, flagship of Rear Admiral William Pringle's task group. Having been given Laotian government approval for reconnaissance flights, these two aircraft flew low over the Plain of Jars in Laos, searching for Pathet Lao and Viet Cong movements. However, flying over Xieng Khouang, one of the Crusaders was caught by ground fire and the port wing caught fire. The aircraft was safely escorted back to the carrier by the other aircraft.

This started a more intensive period of reconnaissance, with additional aircraft joining the *Kitty Hawk* from the *Bon Homme Richard*, at that time in the Philippines. The *Constellation* joined the task group on

Ranged forward on the flight deck of *Independence* were two other very significant Vietnam era aircraft, the Grumman A-6 Intruder and the LTV A-7 Corsair. Note the fully-angled flight deck. (FAAM Independence/224)

6 June. What became known as the Yankee Team flew more than 130 missions over Laos between 21 May and 9 June, while the USAF also conducted missions. The first aircraft to be brought down by Viet Cong AA fire was hit on 6 June, when Lieutenant Charles Klusman's Crusader was flying low attempting to obtain good pictures of ground forces. His aircraft was hit by 37-mm gunfire, and shortly afterwards its systems failed and he was forced to eject. Combat rescue helicopters attempted a rescue, but were forced away by intense groundfire, which led the Americans to ensure that future rescue attempts in communist-held territory were always closely supported by fighter-bombers or attack aircraft for suppression of ground fire. Photographic reconnaissance aircraft also received escorts.

Shore bombardment of North Vietnamese positions commenced on the night of 30–31 July. In retaliation, on 2 August 1964, in what became known as the 'Gulf of Tongking incident', the American destroyer *Maddox* was attacked by three North Vietnamese motor gunboats while she was in international waters. Four torpedoes were fired at the ship, all missing their target, although 14.5-mm gunfire hit the superstructure. In reply, the *Maddox*'s guns damaged one of the attacking craft. Fortunately, four Crusader fighters of VF-53 from *Ticonderoga*, which had relieved the *Kitty Hawk*, were already in the air exercising, and on hearing of the attack raced to the aid of the destroyer. Two aircraft peeled off to attack the damaged MGB, while the other two strafed the other two craft and fired rockets at them, eventually sinking one of them.

On the night of 4 August, another destroyer, *Turner Joy*, was attacked by MGBs with torpedoes, which again missed their target. This time sixteen aircraft from the *Ticonderoga* and *Constellation* came to the aid of *Turner Joy* and *Maddox*.

The order was given for the *Ticonderoga* and *Constellation* to attack the North Vietnamese naval installations at Ben Thuy, Hon Gay, Quang Khe and Lach Chao, as well as the oil storage facility at Vinh. Before noon on 5 August, *Ticonderoga* sent her Douglas A-1 Skyraiders lumbering into the air, to be joined by Crusaders and Skyhawks, and headed for Vinh, en route to Ben Thuy, while other aircraft of Carrier Air Wing 5 headed for Quang Khe.

Hon Gay and Lach Chao were the targets for Carrier Air Wing 14 from *Constellation*. These aircraft were launched at 13.00, and again the Skyraiders were launched first, followed at 14.30 by Skyhawks and the new Phantoms. In all, the two carriers sent sixty-seven aircraft.

The attacks saw Crusaders flying in first using rockets and cannon fire to suppress AA fire, so that the slow and vulnerable piston-engined Skyraiders could then attack. At Vinh, the Skyraiders and some Skyhawks dropped 28,000 lb of bombs onto the fourteen large fuel tanks, before moving on to Ben Thuy, where they sank one naval vessel and damaged three others. At Quang Khe, the attackers sank one naval vessel and damaged five others. A later raid by Skyhawks finished off the fuel storage tanks at Vinh and sank two more naval vessels at Ben Thuy.

At Hon Gay and Lach Chao, the story was much the same. Hon Gay suffered six naval vessels damaged or sunk, and on their way to Lach Chao, the Skyhawks of Carrier Air Wing 14 discovered five enemy naval vessels off Hon Ne island, which they attacked in the face of intense AA fire, leaving the vessels dead in the water.

The final tally was that the North Vietnamese Navy lost seven gunboats, with another ten badly damaged and sixteen hit by cannon fire from the aircraft. This was out of a naval strength of thirty-six gunboats and patrol craft. The USN lost two aircraft, with one pilot dead and another taken prisoner.

Enterprise made six cruises off the coast of South Vietnam; here she has A-7 Corsair, A-6 Intruder and Hawkeye aircraft on one of her later cruises. (United States Navy)

Two aircraft were damaged, but able to return to the carriers.

The full involvement of the US Seventh Fleet started in February 1965, and from then on at least three American aircraft carriers were in operation off the coast of Vietnam, providing support for ground forces whenever necessary, and bombing North Vietnam. At times, efforts where made to negotiate a settlement, and the American effort suffered from protests against the war in the United States. In October 1968, air attacks on North Vietnam ceased, only to restart again in late November 1970, with retaliatory raids from the *Ranger* and *Hancock*.

The early fighter operations during the Vietnam War were dominated by the LTV F-8 Crusader, yet, despite this, the first MiG-17 to be shot down by an F-8 was in fact the fourteenth MiG to be shot down by the American airmen. Already, the USN had decided against free-ranging fighter operations and instead tasked the fighters with close protection of strike aircraft. On 12 June 1966 the naval airmen felt that they were 'knee deep in MiGs'.

That day, Commander H.L. Marr of VF-211 aboard the *Hancock* was flying one of two F-8s when they met two MiG-17s almost head-on, as the F-8s were covering a raid by Douglas A-4 Skyraiders of VA-212 and VA-216. The A-4s were attacking a barracks north of Haiphong in poor weather with a low cloud base.

Marr fired his aircraft's cannon at the first MiG and then at the second, managing to box one of the aircraft into a valley below the clouds. Selecting a Sidewinder missile, he attempted to lock the missile onto the MiG at a range of 2,500 feet, without success. The MiG then broke off the combat, no doubt running low on fuel, and Marr reacted by lighting his aircraft's after-burner and chased the MiG at an indicated airspeed of 500 knots. Closing to within half-a-mile of the MiG, Marr attempted to use his Sidewinder again, and this time the missile locked on. The missile was fired, hitting the MiG, blowing off the tail and the starboard wing.

Elated, on his return to the 'Happy Hannah', Marr made a high-speed pass of the ship, screaming along the port side below flight deck level, and broke standard procedures by finishing with a victory roll, before attempting to land. He forgot to drop his aircraft's tail hook and raced across the, fortunately angled, flight deck!

His enthusiasm must have been infectious, for the *Hancock*'s commanding officer, Captain Jim Davidson, decided that any pilot who shot down a MiG could make a no tail hook pass and that he would pay the customary $5 fine into the party fund![3]

IRON HAND – FIGHTING THE SAM WAR

During the early years of the war, suppression of anti-aircraft measures was achieved by flights of four Vought F-8 Crusaders, but later on the role passed to LTV A-7 Corsairs and McDonnell Douglas F-4 Phantoms.

Suppression was achieved by aircraft flying on the flanks of the strike groups, which would then race ahead of the strike aircraft as they approached the target, planning to arrive over the target some fifteen to thirty seconds before the strike aircraft. In the case of the F-8s, they were equipped with two containers of Zuni air-to-ground rockets, as well as their usual 20-mm cannon. The aircraft would dive at 45 degrees, sighting the target and then firing the rockets from around 4,500 feet. The dive would then flatten slightly and the pilot would use his 20-mm cannon until the ammunition was expended, usually at around 3,000 feet. Although intelligence reports suggested that these techniques were successful, the supply of weapons and manpower for the North Vietnamese seemed to be unlimited.

[3] Barrett Tillman. *MiG Master*, Airlife, 1992.

The anti-SAM sorties were known as 'Iron Hands', and resulted in heavy losses for the American air squadrons during July and August 1967. The technique was to approach the SAM site at below 3,000 feet, because the SA-2 then in service was ineffectual below this altitude. However, this left the American aircraft vulnerable to intense pattern gunfire at its most effective.

Commander John Nichols remembers the Iron Hand sorties.

'The first successful Iron Hands were conducted in October, 1965, but even so, losses continued to mount. ['Success' was defined as confirmed destruction of a SAM site.] In late 1966 my squadron, VF-191, had twelve aircraft and eighteen pilots. In the first four months of combat we lost six planes – three to AAA, one to SAMs, and two in operational accidents. We received no replacement pilots for ten months, although new F-8s arrived. It was an embarrassment of riches, having more airplanes than pilots. In all, Air Wing 19 lost nearly half of its original seventy aircraft, destroyed or damaged.'[4]

The overall commander of American forces in South Vietnam at the time was General William Westmoreland. Of a meeting between General Westmoreland and the Assistant Secretary of Defense, J.T. McNaughton, the commander of the US Seventh Air Force in Vietnam, General William Momyer recalls: 'On a visit to Saigon at a time when my air commander, Joe Moore, and I were trying to get authority to bomb SA-2 sites under construction in North Vietnam, McNaughton ridiculed the need. "You don't think the Vietnamese are going to use them!" he scoffed. "Putting them in is just a political ploy by the Russians to appease Hanoi."'[5]

The ideal way to counter the SAM threat would have been to interrupt the supply of missiles and launchers, most of which arrived through the main North Vietnamese port at Haiphong. Mining the approaches to Haiphong was not allowed for most of the war, with access remaining open until May, 1972. Had this been done from the outset, not only would American losses have been much lower, but the outcome of the war might have been different.

Despite official denials at the time, during the early years of the war the carrier bomber squadrons were often short of bombs. Some aircraft even operated with makeshift weights to ensure that the bomb on one wing did not affect the trim and, in one case at least, an aircraft took off with a toilet bowl on one of its wing strongpoints.

As the war progressed, technical developments were introduced. One of the most effective was the Shrike AGM-45 anti-radiation missile. These first appeared with the USN in March 1966. Shrike homed in on radar beams, following them to their source, and were highly effective in destroying the radar guidance for SAM batteries. The AGM-45A had a range of just over two miles, which meant that the aircraft carrying the missile was vulnerable, but the AGM-45B had a much safer eight-mile range. The effectiveness of Shrike can be assessed by the fact that, in 1965, one out of seventeen SAM missiles shot down an American aircraft, but the following year, the number of missiles fired per aircraft destroyed doubled, and by the end of the war, for every sixty missiles fired, only one aircraft was lost.

One of the most experienced anti-SAM pilots was Bob Arnold, who flew more than fifty missions with VA-164 from Oriskany during 1967–8. 'Half our missile-firing detections came visually – the other half from our AGM-45 electronic listening . . . we got smart and configured our A-4s with two Shrike and two Mk 82s on parent racks – no ejector racks. This gave us the mobility and flexibility to reattack a SAM site with bombs.

[4–9] Commander John B. Nichols, USN (Ret) and Barrett Tillman. *On Yankee Station – The Naval Air War over Vietnam*, Naval Institute Press, 1987.

One of the most significant aircraft of the Vietnam War was the LTV A-7 Corsair II, with an aircraft from VA-147 seen here over the carrier *Ranger* off the coast of Vietnam. (United States Navy)

'We had no practical ways to train in the Iron Hand missions before we deployed in 1967, other than to listen to ECM tapes. Our . . . on the job training for new pilots who joined us during the deployment was to assign them the Iron Hand near Haiphong with a race-track pattern that flew over the water most of the time. That way, if they got bagged they would land in the water and probably be rescued.'[6]

Later, bigger and longer-range anti-radiation missiles, ARM, appeared, including the Standard ARM, which first entered USN service in May 1968.

TOP GUN – FIGHTING THE MIGS

Before long the North Vietnamese started to send MiG fighters against the American aircraft. Alarmed by the fact that the obsolescent F-8s, which were shooting down six MiGs for every one F-8 lost, were having greater success than the supposedly more capable F-4s, the United States Navy instigated their 'Top Gun' air combat courses. The name was ironic, since USN Phantoms, unlike those of the USAF, did not have guns. Nevertheless, F-4 pilots quickly improved their success rate, from two MiGs for every Phantom lost in 1965–8, to twelve MiGs for every Phantom lost in 1972, usually using Sparrow air-to-air missiles. The main threat to American aircraft remained the missiles, often fired wastefully in salvoes, and after that Chinese Air Force MiGs, since the Vietnamese Air Force itself seemed unable to use its MiGs to great effect. The essential discipline for fighter escorts remained exactly the same as it had been for Norman Hanson when flying Corsairs off British Pacific Fleet carriers in 1944–5. The temptation to chase after enemy fighters had to be resisted, the role of the fighter was to protect the strike aircraft, the strike aircraft must never be left undefended, and breaking up an attack by enemy aircraft was more important even than the number of enemy aircraft shot down.

The key to evading SAMs was to see them early, so that they could be out-manoeuvred. The best method was soon found to be a series of hard descending turns, although the pilots found these exhausting and they also lost altitude and risked running into AAA fire. They could also become disorientated, and losing contact with the rest of the strike formation, with its fighter escorts, was another very real risk.

Bob Arnold again: 'I led an Alpha strike to a target six miles outside Hanoi. We approached at 12,000 feet, plus or minus 500, with no AAA or SAMs until two minutes from our time over target. From that point we had thirty missiles and every goddamned gun that could fire. A couple of planes got shot up, all of us were forced down. Only two of us – my wingman and myself – made it to the target. He missed and I laid a string of eight or ten Mark-8s on target. We exited the area at 500 plus knots (no centreline tank) at 50 feet or less, violently S-turning all the way because my ECM gear told me a SAM was tracking me. It turned out to be overly sensitive equipment, but at the time we only knew that the damn things were deadly.'[7]

Pilots concentrating on evading a SAM were easier prey for waiting MiGs, and this was when the fighter escort was most needed.

The pace of the war was intense. The operation known as 'Rolling Thunder' set out to push Viet Cong guerilla fighters north, clearing areas of South Vietnam. The intense aerial activity required could clear the magazines of an Essex-class aircraft carrier in just three days, after which the ship would retire from the firing line to replenish from supply ships. Ships usually spent a total of thirty days on the line, although it could be much longer, before a visit to a safe port, such as Hong Kong, for rest and recuperation.

At its peak, Rolling Thunder saw the carriers launching and recovering aircraft for a ninety-minute flight cycle over a period of twelve or thirteen hours, usually flying from 04.00 to 16.00, or 13.00 to 01.00. Recovering damaged aircraft at such times was difficult, since the commanding officer had to decide whether it would risk damaging the ship or aircraft parked on the deck; often aircraft ranged for take-off on a mission would have to be moved. Rather than risk cancelling a mission or suffering damage to the ship and its aircraft, the order would be for the aircrew aboard the damaged aircraft to eject close to a destroyer or cruiser, which could then pick them up.

John Nichols again: 'Is landing a jet aircraft aboard a pitching, rolling ship "routine"? You cock the aircraft's nose up, play with the few knots of airspeed that science and gravity have granted, and keep the illuminated ball even with the horizontal datum lines on the deck mirror. Adjust rate of descent with power and crunch onto the deck within 160 feet or so from the stern to snag one of the arresting wires. Routine.

'Returning sections or divisions were about 1,000 feet apart, compressing the traffic pattern to the limit. As one plane rolled wings-level on final, the angled deck was probably still occupied by the plane that had just trapped. It took practice, a keen eye, and well-developed judgement for the landing signal officer holding the waveoff switch to determine whether the plane on deck would taxi clear in time for the approaching pilot to get aboard on this pass.'[8]

Of course, amidst all of this activity, aircraft would be prepared for launching while others were struck down into the hangars for maintenance and refuelling. Nor were strike aircraft the only aircraft operated, for in addition to their fighter escorts, tanker, reconnaissance, and airborne-early-warning aircraft all had to be operated, along with helicopters, perhaps for search and rescue.

Aircraft on deck were parked so closely that John Nichols recalls that pilots in adjacent F-8s, with wings folded, could not test their droop flaps without checking with one another first to take turns. If they both happened to do the test at once, the flaps collided.

Despite debriefing after landing on, the individual missions were not documented in the same detail as those of the Second World War.

A major communist spring offensive in April 1972 also saw increased bombing of North Vietnam. On 15 April carrier aircraft joined USAF Boeing B-52 bombers in a raid on Haiphong, the main North Vietnamese port, damaging several Soviet freighters. The following month, the main North Vietnamese ports were mined and blockaded. Defeat for South Vietnamese and American forces at this time meant that bombing was escalated, with the carriers *America*, *Enterprise*, *Kitty Hawk*, *Midway*, *Oriskany* and *Saratoga* in action together during October. The intense bombing was also intended to help strengthen the American and South Vietnamese position during peace negotiations, which resulted in an armistice on 28 January 1973.

The armistice was soon broken by the North Vietnamese, who continued to receive arms from the Soviet Union, while the South Vietnamese continued fighting on their own. Eventually, by April 1975, South Vietnamese defeat was inevitable, and the warships of the US Seventh Fleet were ordered off the coast of Vietnam to evacuate almost 20,000 Americans and South Vietnamese. *Enterprise* and *Coral Sea* provided air cover while *Midway* arrived with helicopters to assist the evacuation, and Task Force 76 comprised amphibious ships.

On 30 April, the final day of the evacuation was marked by a state of near panic among those ashore. Fearful of being left behind, South Vietnamese helicopters

McDonnell F-4 Phantoms played an important part in the Vietnam War, and here an aircraft lands on a carrier, with arrester hook fully extended. (Fleet Air Arm Museum)

and aircraft were commandeered for the short final flight out to the waiting fleet, as indeed were fishing and merchant vessels, pleasure craft and South Vietnamese naval vessels. So many helicopters landed on the waiting warships that many had to be pushed overboard to allow others to land, and in one case a helicopter landed on top of another whose blades were still turning, sending blades flying across the ship's deck. Transport aircraft attempted to land on the big American carriers, and unable to do so, ditched alongside. Altogether, fifty-four South Vietnamese helicopters had to be thrown overboard, although when the Seventh Fleet sailed on 2 May, another forty-one South Vietnamese helicopters were aboard.

The helicopters had been American military aid to South Vietnam. The North Vietnamese demanded their return!

COMMENT

The Americans did not start the war in Vietnam, but their intervention escalated the fighting and intensified the level of the conflict. Despite the heroism of the aircrew, the bomber and strike aircraft were not the means by which the war could have been won. It had to be won on the ground, albeit with USN and USAF assistance. Tackling porters and mules on jungle trails in Laos and Vietnam was neither easy nor effective using bombers. This was not a case of finding and attacking fixed installations such as bridges, metalled highways and railway lines, but of keeping a devious enemy on the move, making it difficult for him to muster in sufficient strength to pose a threat. It was about jungle warfare, and a 'hearts and minds' operation to gain the support of the uncommitted rural dweller, as shown so successfully by the British Army in Malaya.

The failure of the South Vietnamese to hold the enemy was not surprising. It can take upwards of six or seven defending troops to tackle one fast moving guerilla fighter, never knowing where he will strike. The Americans had also been far more honourable in keeping to the armistice than had the North Vietnamese or their Soviet supporters.

On the other hand, the loss of South Vietnam did not have the anticipated effect. The domino theory did not work, and the rest of South-East Asia was not overrun by communism; its days were numbered anyway. The real strategic implication was the loss of American self-confidence, and a desire once again to avoid involvement overseas. This was only reversed with victory in the Gulf War.

THE WINTER WAR – BATTLING FOR THE FALKLANDS

On 2 April 1982 Argentine troops invaded the Falkland Islands, a British colony in the South Atlantic long claimed by Argentina as her own, despite the fact that the local residents were all of British descent. The initial invasion was contested by the small force of thirty or so Royal Marines, the sole garrison on the islands, who managed to

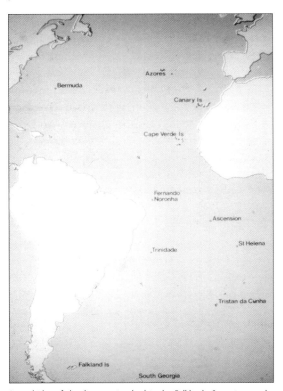

A good idea of the distances involved in the Falklands Campaign can be gathered from this map, making it not just ideal for carrier operations, but making land-based operations for recovery of the islands virtually impossible. (IWM FKD2304)

shoot down a helicopter with an anti-tank missile before bowing to the inevitable and surrendering. The British government immediately raised a task force for the recovery of the islands, and of South Georgia, some distance further south, which had also been seized by Argentine forces.

On 5 April, just three days later, the core element of the task force sailed, including the carriers *Hermes* and *Invincible*.

SHIPS AND AIRCRAFT

The aircraft carrier *Hermes* was a sister ship of *Albion* and *Bulwark*, although with much additional equipment and slightly larger, giving her a displacement of 27,000 tons. The last conventional aircraft carrier to enter service with the Royal Navy, *Hermes* had had a varied career. Originally, she was a light fleet carrier and as such had operated strike aircraft, such as the potent Buccaneer bomber, but eventually she was converted to a commando carrier, intending to replace both *Albion* and *Bulwark*. By the time of the Falklands campaign, *Hermes* had been converted yet again, to a Harrier carrier, designed to operate the versatile Sea Harrier V/STOL jet, and instead of her catapults, she had a large bulge in her flight deck forward intended to provide the 'ski-jump' effect needed to boost the Sea Harrier's performance.

Accompanying *Hermes* was *Invincible*, the leadship of a class of three new carriers designed around the needs of the Sea Harrier, perhaps the first time a warship has been built around an aeroplane since *Campania* in the First World War. Smaller than *Hermes*, at 20,000 tons, *Invincible* was the only ship of her class commissioned at the time, and could carry eight Sea Harriers and twelve Westland Sea King anti-submarine helicopters. At the time of the Falklands campaign, *Invincible* was 'under offer' to the Royal Australian Navy as a replacement for *Melbourne*, after a defence review had decided that the Royal Navy should have just two small carriers, with *Hermes* also likely to be sold or scrapped (in the end, she was sold to the Indian Navy to give them a second aircraft carrier).

Invincible was also the first gas turbine-powered aircraft carrier in the world, using four Rolls-Royce Olympus turbines, marine versions of the same engines used to power the Concorde supersonic airliner. On the way to the Falklands, technical problems resulted in press reports that *Invincible* was unable to move astern, to which one naval officer retorted that: 'the Royal Navy is not going anywhere backwards!'

The Sea Harrier was a development of the Royal Air Force's British Aerospace Harriers, but in this case development went far further than simply adding an arrester hook, which in fact was one naval feature unnecessary in the Sea Harrier. The aircraft had the airframe and engine of the Harrier, but a far more sophisticated navigation system. Radar enabled it to operate as a fleet fighter, rather than as a ground attack aircraft, as was the case with the Harriers of the RAF and the AV-8s of the United States Marine Corps. The RAF aircraft used vertical take-off and landing, but this limited range and warload because the overall weight of the aircraft could not exceed the vertical thrust available on take-off. The 'ski-jump' of the carriers adapted for Sea Harrier operations enabled the aircraft to make a short take-off and vertical landing, known as advanced short take-off and landing, or ASTOVL, allowing a higher gross

One of the successful pilots of the Falklands was Lieutenant-Commander (later Commander) Nigel 'Sharkey' Ward, who commanded *Invincible*'s 801 Naval Air Squadron and shot down three Argentinian aircraft. (IWM FKD541)

weight which could be used for extra range or a heavier warload. The Rolls-Royce Pegasus turbofan produces 21,510-lb thrust, and the aircraft can operate over a radius of up to 500 miles, or carry a warload of 4,000 lb. A wide variety of weapons can be carried, including BAe Sea Eagle anti-shipping missiles.

For the Falklands campaign, the flagship *Hermes* carried twelve Sea Harriers while *Invincible* had eight.

The other carrier-borne aircraft in the Falklands was the Westland Sea King, a licence-built version of the Sikorsky S-61 helicopter, but with twin 1,500 s.h.p. Rolls-Royce Gnome turboshafts, giving the helicopter a maximum speed in excess of 150 m.p.h. and a range of up to 700 miles. The sophisticated anti-submarine equipment aboard the helicopter includes a dunking sonar, and homing torpedoes or depth charges can be carried. In its ASW role, the Sea King normally has a crew of four.

Hermes started life as a light fleet carrier, became a commando carrier and then was converted to a 'harrier carrier' by the removal of her catapult and the substitution of the flight deck bulge to provide a ski-jump effect for the Harriers. In this photograph, a Sea King is moving a bulk fuel container. (FAAM Falk/104)

ACTION

Commander Nigel 'Sharkey' Ward commanded 801 Naval Air Squadron aboard *Invincible*, and was senior air adviser to the commander of the Task Force, Admiral Sir Sandy Woodward. He flew over sixty missions, achieved three air-to-air kills, and took part in or witnessed ten more kills. He realized the enormity of the threat which faced the task force.

'On the way down it was very clear that we were short of air defence, the Air Force couldn't provide it, and we had twenty aircraft against what we were told were two hundred Argentinian aircraft. Our admiral back in Somerset told our wives that . . . 75 per cent of us wouldn't return!'[1]

On 30 April 1982 action was due to commence that night, initially with an attack by Ward's Sea Harriers, but instead 801 Squadron was tasked with combat air patrol and standby duties, before providing fighter cover for the solitary RAF Vulcan bomber flying a 7,000 mile round trip from Ascension Island with twenty-one 1,000-lb bombs. In addition, 801 had to provide fighter escort for the Sea Harriers of 800 Squadron from *Hermes*, which was to send eight aircraft to attack the main airfield at Port Stanley, and four to attack a smaller airfield at Goose Green.

Ward was, and remains, convinced that four of his aircraft could have done as much damage as the Vulcan, which requested, and was given, a 'weapons tight' procedure in the middle of a war zone! One of his fellow officers with Vulcan experience estimated that it must have taken ten Victor tankers to keep the Vulcan in the air for the round trip with such a heavy bomb load, which was equivalent to 1.1 million lbs of fuel, or enough for 260 Sea Harrier sorties taking 1,300 bombs to Port Stanley! His views were reinforced by the subsequent discovery that the Vulcan, an aircraft designed for warfare with either free fall or stand-off nuclear weapons, had done little effective damage to the airfield, with its bombs only reaching the edge of the runway.

[1-5] Commander Nigel 'Sharkey' Ward RN. *Sea Harrier over the Falklands*, Leo Cooper, 1992.

Phase 1 of the Falklands Campaign was to soften up the Argentinian defences, while Phase 2 would be the invasion, with the Fleet Air Arm planning to have six Sea Harriers constantly on low-level CAP to provide air defence for the Army and Royal Marines on the ground.

Waiting to take off that first night from *Invincible*, Ward wondered: 'Were the Argentine pilots as keen to fight as my boys were: and if not, how would they play the game? One thing was certain – the importance of coming out on top in the first few engagements, and the psychological advantage that would be won and that would pay huge dividends.'[2]

These musings were soon interrupted by a message from the ship.

'"003, Flyco. You are clear to start."

'As soon as I was turning and burning, I put the radar to 'standby' to warm up and called "on deck".

'"Roger. Ship's head is 340 degrees; now, now, now! Your position is 55 degrees 05' West and 51 degrees 12' South." The common link between Flyco and aircraft on deck was via a wire, not radio.

'The information passed was necessary for aligning the Navhars platform. My HUD had already showed me that the aircraft was pointing 2 degrees to the left of the ship's centre-line, and so on the third 'now' I entered 338 degrees into the system. Geographical coordinates were also entered, and I was ready for launch.'[3]

'Navhars' was the Sea Harrier Navigation Heading Attitude Reference System, and 'HUD' was the aircraft's head-up display.

'The ski-jump loomed large ahead and then disappeared from view. I was pressed down in my seat for a second, and then I was free. I was airborne and automatically nozzling away into wingborne flight, cleaning up the aircraft as I did so. I left the radar on

Invincible through the haze. (IWM FKD477)

standby, switched off my navigation lights, levelled momentarily at 800 feet, and then, as I throttled back to maintain 420 knots, gently descended to a comfortable 20 feet above the waves . . .'[4]

This first combat air patrol was uneventful, and eventually the aircraft returned to *Invincible*. Landing on with the Sea Harrier marked a big change from conventional aircraft carriers – no tailhook and no arrester wires to worry about, but approaching a carrier in the dark still required skill and strong nerves. Ward again: 'I descended to low level and, using my Navhars, navigated through the briefed safety zone to where I expected *Invincible*'s aircraft marshalling area to be. Switching my radar to transmit, I found what I thought was *Invincible* amidst my neat green radar display and called the Approach Controller: "003 estimating six miles on the approach. 800 feet, gear down and locked. 2,200 lbs." I had stacks of fuel.

'"Roger, 003". It was Tony Walker's familiar voice. "I have you at 5[8F] miles. Ship's head 320 degrees. Wind over the deck 18 knots."

'It was an eerie feeling. There was I preparing to land – but there was only total blackness ahead as I started the descent . . . I called 'lights' and was surprised at the size I assumed as the subdued deck lighting suddenly shattered the darkness. That was much more comfortable.'[5]

Fighting began on 1 May, and the Sea Harrier was soon bombing Port Stanley. Dave Morgan was one of the pilots with 800 Squadron:

'I came round the side of the airfield and at that stage I saw tracer start to come towards me, and realize that someone was trying to shoot down my mum's little boy, and there was a bloody great bang and the whole aircraft started vibrating and I realized that I had been hit. I discovered . . . that a 20-mm high explosive shell had gone through my tail. It made a very small neat entry hole on the left hand side of the tail . . . had the aircraft patched up and flying again the next morning.'[6]

Brian Hanrahan was BBC war correspondent sailing with the task force aboard *Hermes*. He was not allowed to tell his audience exactly how many aircraft from the ship had set off to attack the airfield at Port Stanley, but he gave great peace of mind to many with relatives and friends among the pilots when he broadcast 'I counted them all out and I counted them all back'.[7]

The Sea Harrier was pitched against one of the classic jet fighters, the Mirage III, Israeli-built 'Dagger' developments of the Mirage V strike aircraft, and Mirage Vs themselves. The Mirage was twice as fast as the Sea Harrier.

'For our tactics of fighting against the enemy, we used a manoeuvre called the 'hook manoeuvre', which was quite simply sending one aircraft in ahead and one behind . . . putting the enemy in a problem, they're in a sandwich, somewhat like the Army pincer movement. It's commonsense, good strategy, good tactics, and it worked,' explained Ward. 'On day one we shot down two aircraft using this method.'[8]

The tactic had worked well. On that first day of the air campaign, 1 May, two Sea Harriers of 801 Squadron confronted two Argentine Mirages. One of the Sea Harriers, flown by Lieutenant Steve Thomas, attempted to lock on a Sidewinder air-to-air missile, but without success. As Thomas' aircraft passed between the two Mirages, two missiles from one of the Mirages shot past his aircraft! Meanwhile, the other pilot, Lieutenant Paul Barton, locked his missile on to a Mirage, fired, and had the satisfaction of

[6] *Decisive Weapons: Jumping Jet Flash*, BBC/A&E network co-production, 1997.

[7] Brian Hanrahan and Robert Fox. *I counted them all out and I counted them all back*, BBC Publications, 1982.

[8] *Decisive Weapons: Jumping Jet Flash*, BBC/A&E network co-production, 1997.

Dave Morgan of 800 Squadron back safely aboard *Hermes* with his Sea Harrier, proudly showing the hole shot in his tail on a sortie over Port Stanley.

Keeping a carrier's flight deck and hangar deck clean during operations is a demanding task, but vitally important for efficiency and safety of both personnel and aircraft.

seeing the Argentine aircraft blow up. Lieutenant Thomas by now had turned and fired a Sidewinder at the remaining Mirage, but the aircraft raced into cloud before the missile could hit it, and so Thomas decided that he could not claim a kill. What he did not see was that his missile was proximity fused, and damaged the Mirage. Nevertheless the aircraft remained flyable, so the pilot decided to nurse it back to base. To lighten the aircraft, he dumped his warload but, unfortunately for him, this fell on Argentine troops, who, convinced that they were being bombed, shot down his aircraft!

Ward and his fellow pilots found the Argentine Mirages playing cat and mouse with them – reluctant to engage at first, they would advance towards the warships and then turn to fly away again as the aircraft on CAP moved to intercept. Whether this was nervousness on the part of the Mirage pilots, or an attempt to waste the fuel of the Task Force's aircraft, can only be surmised.

The other enemy was the weather, and during the early hours of 6 May, two Sea Harriers collided, with the loss of both pilots. The force was now down to just eighteen Sea Harriers, which as one commentator has since pointed out, can be viewed against RAF losses of twenty-seven aircraft a day during the Battle of Britain. It says much about the high standards of pilot training that losses due to bad weather were as low as they were. The campaign was fought in the southern winter, with just three hours of daylight each day. The weather was so bad that heavy seas broke over even the huge bulge at the forward end of the flight deck on *Hermes*.

The Sea Harriers were not the only casualties. Captain Chris Craig, a former Fleet Air Arm officer, was commanding officer of the Type 21, or Amazon-class, frigate *Alacrity*.

He recalls being ordered to destroy a ditched Sea King helicopter: '. . . on 16 May.

Hermes had a Sea King helicopter ditch with a major malfunction, but her crew recovered safely. We were then invited to send the persistently floating hulk to the bottom – but there was a twist. As we approached the bobbing fuselage, we saw two live homing torpedoes still strapped to the inverted belly. Only in retrospect was the next hour hilarious, as I moved the ship gently back and forth from as far away as possible, carefully directing small arms fire in an attempt to perforate the helicopter without exploding the warheads. And all the while, I could imagine the small talk in naval bars for years to come.

'"Remember Craig? Silly bugger who blew up his ship with our own torpedoes. Should have been certified."'[9]

Fortunately for Captain Craig's reputation, his gunners succeeded in sending the Sea King to her watery grave without any damage to his own ship.

As a former pilot, Craig could well imagine the procedures the attacking Argentine Air Force and Navy pilots had to go through when attacking the task force ships, and especially how an Exocet missile firing Dassault Etendard would attack.

'I imagined myself in the cockpit of one of the incoming jets. Depart Rio Grande, aircraft heavy with fuel and Exocet, briefed on the latest enemy position. Medium-level transit 400 miles east, rendezvous with the airborne tanker, suck fuel, turn south towards the Malvinas. Fast descent with 200 miles to go – no radar on. First faint interception of British radar signals, hard descent again, right to the wave caps, tucked in beneath the enemy radar beams. Keep boring in on a timed run, until within 50 miles. Zoom to several hundred feet and a quick transmission on radar. Relief at being above the sea spray and the buffeting turbulence below. Target selection: big echo must be *Hermes* or *Invincible*. Sharp descent again to avoid

[9, 10] Captain Chris Craig. *Call for Fire*, RN Pub: John Murray, 1995.

giving a single paint on British radar screens. Pop up for the final time. At last; let go the damned missile. Aircraft bucks with relief. Bank away and start the long, long run for home. Think fuel.'[10]

Fortunately for the task force, which lost the Type 42 destroyer *Sheffield* to Exocet attack on 4 May, the Argentines had just five Exocet missiles. The Argentine Navy's sole aircraft carrier, *Veinticinco de Mayo*, played no part in the operations. At the time, many believed that she ran for port as soon as the cruiser *Belgrano* was torpedoed and sunk by a British submarine, but it seems that she never left port. A British Colossus class light fleet carrier, *Veinticinco de Mayo* went to Argentina via the Royal Netherlands Navy, where she was called *Karel Doorman*, after the Dutch admiral lost in the Battle of the Java Sea. Subsequently it emerged that *Veinticinco de Mayo* was suffering from boiler problems, while her catapults were also in poor shape and may have been unable to launch Etendards, which were designed for the larger French carriers, *Clemenceau* and *Foch*.

Nevertheless, life aboard the warships had to change in recognition of the possibility of attack. Brian Hanrahan reported on the changes for those in *Hermes*.

'When *Hermes* steamed from Portsmouth, her officers dined in traditional normal splendour. They wore cummerbunds and evening dress, sat at tables laid with a silver service, and ate by the light of candelabra.

'Now these tables are frequently overturned in the middle of the floor, tied down firmly by thick rope, the chairs locked on top like barricades in a Belfast street. Around them men in grubby overalls eat snack meals, taking ten minutes away from their action stations. At their waist . . . blue webbing belts. On each is clipped a gas mask, a life jacket and a survival suit – an all-embracing garment made of dayglo orange

rubber. It looks like a pair of baggy pyjamas, but wearing it in the chilly waters of the South Atlantic increases survival time from minutes to hours.

'Like the men, the ship is wound up tight. Every watertight door is closed and walking around the ship means constantly knocking off the metal clips which hold the doors in place and ramming them back after passing through. To pass from one deck to another means scrambling through tiny manholes, twisting and turning to get through with all the survival kit at your waist: groping for the heavy metal hatch to bolt it down over your head. Every hatch is marked with a Z, the last letter of the alphabet. This is condition Z alert, the Navy's highest level of preparedness.'[11]

The tedious and exhausting business of moving around a ship closed up for action stations would have been familiar to both Hanson and Fuchida during the Second World War. Had they been available at the time, the survival suits would have saved many more lives from the ill-fated *Glorious*, not least because patrolling aircraft had missed many men on the grey Carley floats, which merged with the grey northern seas when viewed from above.

Later, on 21 May 1982, the day of the British landings on the Falklands, when the Sea Harrier squadrons were at full stretch protecting the beachheads, Lieutenant Steve Thomas shot down two Argentine Daggers on one sortie. The Argentine pilots called the Sea Harrier, 'La Muerte Negra', 'the Black Death'.

Ward had three confirmed kills to his own credit and one of these was a Pucara twin-engined ground attack aircraft.

'I saw one of the Pucaras. Steve was closing in . . . I decided to attack the same aircraft from astern . . .

'I had a lot of overtake, centred on the Pucara at the end of my hotline gunsight in

---

[11] Brian Hanrahan and Robert Fox. *I counted them all out and I counted them all back*, BBC Publications, 1982.

The Fuerza Aerea Argentina Mirage IIIs and Vs were supposed to be far superior to the Sea Harrier, but fared badly when confronted with the naval aircraft. (FAAM Falk/240)

the HUD, and squeezed the trigger. The aircraft gave its familiar shudder as the 30-mm cannon shells left the two barrels. They were on target.

'The Pucara's right engine burst into flames and then the shells impacted the left aileron, nearly sawing off the wingtips as they did so. I was very close, and pulled off my target.

'I was amazed that the Pucara was still flying as I started my third and final run . . . Pieces of fuselage, wing and canopy were torn from the doomed aircraft. The fuselage caught fire . . . as I raised my nose off the target, the pilot ejected.'[12]

Later Ward was to explain that it was basically 'a no hope position for the Pucara for I was firing at him from six o'clock – right behind him!'[13]

The pilot was Major, later Comodoro, Carlos Tomba of the Fuerza Aerea Argentina, who was taken prisoner of war, and spent

part of his time as a PoW acting as an interpreter for his fellow countrymen in a British field hospital. Some years later in a television interview, Tomba recalled the attack by the Sea Harrier: 'My comrade shouted to me that Harriers were coming in to attack. We began our defence and within an instant I felt the plane tremble . . . the plane trembled again and began to shudder, I lost control.'[14]

The courage of the Argentine pilots was never in doubt but their briefing and the Fuerza Aerea Argentina's strategy combined to fail them, since the emphasis was on destroying the warships and troopships. Instead, they should have concentrated on gaining aerial superiority. As one naval officer put it, 'had they lost five of their aircraft for every Sea Harrier shot down, they could then have picked off the task force vessels at will.'

[12] Commander Nigel 'Sharkey' Ward RN. *Sea Harrier over the Falklands*, Leo Cooper 1992.

[13, 14] *Decisive Weapons: Jumping Jet Flash*, BBC/A&E network co-production, 1997.

Ward later went on to shoot down a Dagger strike aircraft and a Fuerza Aerea Argentina Lockheed Hercules transport. He recalls the shooting down of the Dagger.

'Adrenalin running high, I glanced round to check the sky about me. Flashing underneath me and just to my right was the beautiful green and brown camouflage of the third Dagger. I broke right and down towards the aircraft's tail, acquired the jet exhaust with the Sidewinder, and released the missile. It reached its target in very quick time and the Dagger exploded in a ball of flame. Out of the flame ball exploded the broken pieces of the jet; some of which cartwheeled along the ground before coming to rest, no longer recognizable as parts of an aircraft.'[15]

This was a low altitude war, and the Sea Harrier was to prove almost unbeatable at such altitudes, where atmospheric pressure prevents even supersonic aircraft from realizing their full potential.

On 5 June a flight of four Douglas A-4 Skyhawks attacked. Dave Morgan's was one of two Sea Harriers sent to intercept. He fired one Sidewinder missile which he saw disappear into the jet pipe of a Skyhawk, followed by a very big explosion which left only small bits. He shot down a second Skyhawk, and his wingman shot down a third. The fourth Skyhawk escaped, and it was only later that he learnt that he had flown past the aircraft at high speed and for an instant had been in the aircraft's sights, but the firing mechanism on the Skyhawk's guns had failed.

After the arrival of RAF Harriers of No. 1 squadron, the RAF took over ground attack, leaving the Fleet Air Arm free to concentrate on air defence. This did not ease the burden on the Fleet Air Arm, however, since with six aircraft and eleven pilots left aboard *Invincible*, one aircraft was always ready with the pilot sitting in the cockpit, with another pilot ready below decks. Then the aircrew would be expected to fly during the day after spending half the night on alert.

Argentine forces surrendered on 14 June. The Fleet Air Arm had shot down twenty-three Argentine aircraft and destroyed another nine on the ground. Not one Sea Harrier had been shot down by Argentine fighters. No less important, they had forced the enemy to make limited use of Port Stanley's airfield, so that Argentine fighters were at the limits of their range once over the islands.

The war had placed a great strain on the limited resources of the task force, operating far from its bases and exposed to extremely poor weather, with just three hours of watery daylight. In early June Captain Chris Craig was ordered to return to the UK with *Alacrity* on roulement as operations began to wind down, but he decided to visit *Hermes* in his ship's Westland Lynx helicopter to ask the commander of the task force, Admiral Sandy Woodward, for permission to stay to see the final defeat of the Argentine forces.

'The vast darkened bulk of superstructure towered over the Lynx as we landed on the rust-stained deck of *Hermes* and I reflected ruefully that the flagship too was exhausted. Ancient boilers were in desperate need of repair but there was certainly no way she could return home yet. As I was escorted down to the Admiral's fighting quarters, I was shocked at how tired his personal staff looked in the dim red lighting. I hope to God that the Admiral did not view me the same way, otherwise my chance of a stay of execution was nil. He was gracious, charming and terribly patient: he too looked gaunt and weary.'[16]

He also said 'no'!

ACES

Apart from Ward himself, Lieutenant Steve Thomas, with a Mirage on the first day of the air war and two Daggers on one sorties later,

---

[15] Commander Nigel 'Sharkey' Ward RN. *Sea Harrier over the Falklands*, Leo Cooper, 1992.

[16] Captain Chris Craig. *Call for Fire*, RN Pub: John Murray, 1995.

emerges as the leading British ace. Dave Morgan managed to shoot down two Skyhawks in one sortie, but the Skyhawk and the Sea Harrier would have been regarded as well matched in combat, before the Falklands campaign showed the Sea Harrier's ability to shoot down much faster aircraft in low altitude combat.

While none of the British aircraft were shot down by Argentine fighters, the bravery of Argentine Air Force and Navy pilots in pressing home their attacks cannot be ignored.

The Royal Navy lost four ships with many more damaged, and 87 out of 255 dead were lost at sea. The Argentinians lost 780 men, and more than 100 aircraft against 34 British. 12,978 prisoners were taken.

COMMENT

In marked contrast to the débâcle at Suez, the British armed forces managed to organize themselves quickly, and were on their way within a few days, adding military pressure to diplomatic pressure as the United Nations and the United States attempted to obtain Argentine withdrawal. The campaign probably saved the Fleet Air Arm, which was distinctly out of favour under a Secretary of State for Defence, John Nott, who claimed to have been amazed at how much effort had to be devoted to the fighter protection of the fleet. The problem was that the RAF could never guarantee fighter protection of shipping outside territorial waters, given the constraints on range of even the best fighter aircraft. Equally, the RAF was unable to provide interdiction unless suitable bases were close enough to the target.

In the spirit of Taranto, the Fleet Air Arm managed to pull off the impossible, doing a great deal with not very much against overwhelming forces. The Sea Harrier proved

itself to be one of the classic naval fighters of all time, and in handling bombing and fighter work, also proved to be that rarity, the true multi-role aeroplane. According to Admiral Sir Henry Leach, the First Sea Lord, 'Without the Sea Harriers, there could have been no Task Force'. Without a task force, the Argentine invasion of the Falklands and South Georgia could not have been reversed, sending the wrong signals to other regimes with ambitions on their neighbours' territory. Despite all of this, the RAF Vulcan pilot received a DFC, but Sea Harrier pilots with sixty sorties got nothing.

Some members of the Fleet Air Arm believe that some of the task force's senior officers blamed them for the loss of the *Sheffield*. The problem was that the combat air patrol Sea Harriers were ordered to investigate a suspicious surface craft. Had this order not been given, *Sheffield* might have been saved from attack, or she might not. No one can tell, but it is a reflection on the inability of many naval officers even today to use air power effectively, especially when there is very little of it available. A Sea King helicopter or a frigate could have investigated the surface vessel, more slowly perhaps, but without dropping the task force's guard against air attack.

Nevertheless, the recovery of the Falklands would have been far easier, and losses far less, had the Royal Navy had its strength of seven aircraft carriers, two of them commando carriers, of twenty years earlier. The fighters and bombers apart, the fleet then had its airborne early warning Fairey Gannet aircraft, which would have extended the eyes of the fleet far over the horizon, saving many of the task force's ships. Adequate defence does not come cheaply, but like a good insurance policy, it is the best value when things go wrong.

271

WAR IN THE GULF – RECOVERING KUWAIT FROM IRAQ

2 AUGUST 1990 – 26 FEBRUARY 1991

IRAQ INVADES KUWAIT

Iraq had long maintained that the small Arab state of Kuwait was Iraqi territory, and this had from time to time led to tension in the Persian/Iranian Gulf. As long ago as 1961, tension between Iraq and its much smaller neighbour had led to British forces being deployed in the area, with the commando carrier *Bulwark* arriving with

The United States Navy played a major role in the Gulf War, and here ordnancemen aboard *Saratoga* handle a Phoenix air-to-air missile. The F/A-18 Hornets in the background earned their spurs in this conflict. (IWM GLF992)

Royal Marine Commandos and shortly afterwards being joined by the carrier *Victorious*, with her fighters and bombers. The situation was rapidly defused by these two ships, with *Victorious* also providing fighter control for RAF aircraft deployed to Kuwait.

A prolonged and bloody conflict between Iraq and Iran in the Gulf throughout the 1980s, now usually referred to as the 'First Gulf War', was generally regarded as having left both countries weakened, but this was not the case. By 1990 Iraq was able to turn its attention to Kuwait again, making a surprise invasion of the 'city state' during the early hours of 2 August 1990. The Kuwaiti armed forces were taken by surprise, but in any event there was insufficient land area for a defensive battle and Kuwait's defences were heavily outnumbered by those of its larger neighbour.

International anger at Iraq's action, and the break-up of the former Soviet Union, together meant that for only the second time in its history, the forces gathered to recover Kuwait were operated under the banner of the United Nations. Nevertheless, the command and control mechanisms necessary to turn a vast multinational force into an effective operation were based on those of the North Atlantic Treaty Organisation, NATO, countries, who alone had experience of combined and multinational military operations. The backbone of the air, land

and sea operations was provided primarily by the United States, but with strong support from the United Kingdom and France. Many Arab states also made significant contributions to the forces deployed, although even the larger and wealthier Arab countries, such as Saudi Arabia, were limited to some extent by their comparatively small populations.

The one-off alliance of nations involved in the operation became known as the 'Coalition'.

The operation was in two stages. The first stage concerned the protection of Saudi Arabia, and this was known overall as 'Desert Shield', although within that the British armed forces described their contribution as 'Operation Grandby'. Liberating Kuwait was the second stage, and this became 'Desert Storm'. The resultant conflict is now known to historians as 'The Second Gulf War', recognizing the earlier Iraq-Iran conflict.

SHIPS AND AIRCRAFT

The United States was the only country to deploy aircraft carriers in the Gulf, although Royal Navy warships carried their helicopters, and the Royal Fleet Auxiliary *Argus* transported Royal Navy helicopters, Sea King HC.4 troop-carrying aircraft of 846 Naval Air Squadron, to the Gulf in support of the forces ashore.

At its peak, the United States Navy carrier strength in the Gulf reached six aircraft carriers. Some of these were veterans of the Vietnam War, but the most significant were the large carriers of the Nimitz class, including *Dwight D. Eisenhower* (CVN-68) and *Theodore Roosevelt* (CVN-71), as well as the older *America* (CV-66), *Saratoga* (CV-60), *Independence* (CV-62) and *Midway* (CV-41).

The Nimitz class vessels remain the largest warships in the world, at 81,600 tons standard displacement, and up to 98,000 tons full load displacement, with a hull 1,092 feet long and a flight deck 252 feet wide. The first ship was commissioned in 1975, and these vessels usually carry between 80 and 90 aircraft. Capable of more than 30 knots, the ship's company totals some 6,000 men, about half of them for the embarked carrier air group. Defence against air attack is provided by Sea Sparrow point defence missile systems. Since *Nimitz* herself, another seven vessels of this class have joined the United States Navy, and another is being built.

Most of the aircraft operated by the United States Navy have changed since the end of the Vietnam War, although Operation Desert Storm was to be the final conflict for the LTV A-7 Corsair strike aircraft. The Grumman A-6 Intruder was also described in the Vietnam War chapter, and it may well prove that Desert Storm will have been the last occasion for operations by this aircraft as well.

Largest and fastest of the USN aircraft was the Grumman F-14A Tomcat, which first entered service in 1975. A twin-seat, twin-engined variable-geometry, or 'swing-wing', aircraft, the Tomcat follows in the great tradition of Grumman carrier fighters, with its Pratt & Whitney TF30 turbofans each providing 41,850-lb thrust with reheat and a maximum speed in excess of Mach 2. Although the aircraft has just a single 20-mm cannon, its main armament consists of a mixture of air-to-air missiles. More than 600 of these aircraft have been put into USN service.

The high cost of the Tomcat air superiority fighter led the USN to match this with a less expensive aircraft, the McDonnell Douglas F/A-18C Hornet, a single-seat fighter-attack aircraft, with two General Electric F404 reheated turbofans, each producing almost 32,000 lb of thrust with reheat. With a maximum speed in excess of Mach 1.8, the Hornet is versatile, and in addition to its four air-to-air missiles and single 20-mm cannon, can carry up to four 2,000-lb bombs. The Hornet first entered USN service in 1980, and was based on the Northrop YF-17 experimental fighter design.

The other significant new aircraft, which was to play a major role in warning the fleet of impending air attack, was the largest aircraft ever to operate from aircraft carriers, the Grumman E-2C Hawkeye airborne-early-warning aircraft. Powered by two Allison T56-A-427 turboprops, this aircraft can fly at up to 340 knots and remain on station for up to 4 hours.

During their deployment to the Gulf, *Saratoga*, *Independence*, *America* and *Eisenhower* each operated 80–85 aircraft in their carrier air wings (CVW), while *Roosevelt* had a new style of air wing with her Tomcats and Hornets reduced to allow an extra squadron of A-6E Intruders. *Midway*, the smallest and oldest of the carriers, operated 36 Hornets, 20 Intruders, of which 4 were electronic warfare EA-6Bs, 4 Hawkeyes and 6 SH-3H helicopters for plane-guard duties.

One commentator has since explained that the Royal Navy could not send its newest carrier, *Ark Royal*, to the Gulf because of the estimated £20 million cost of modifying the ship which had been designed for all out nuclear warfare against the Soviet Bloc. This seems to be an unlikely explanation, since the same applied to *Invincible*. The real reason was that, with so many large American carriers available, and air bases ashore provided by a sympathetic Saudi government, there was no need. The larger American carriers with their longer-range aircraft could also operate further away from the threat of Iraqi air and surface-to-surface missile attack than could *Ark Royal* and her Sea Harriers.

ACTION

The Coalition naval forces were under the command of Vice-Admiral Stan Arthur, USN, aboard the *Blue Ridge*, an amphibious command ship, since it was originally intended to retake Kuwait through an amphibious assault by the United States Marines; in the end this was not necessary. The carrier force was led by Rear Admiral Dan March aboard *Midway*. *Midway* had been operating in the Pacific and had been diverted to the Gulf, but she was soon joined by *Saratoga*, which had to transit the Suez Canal. The arrival of *Saratoga* was more important than simply providing another carrier, since it was felt that *Midway*'s officers might not be too familiar with standard NATO procedures. *Roosevelt*, *America* and *Kennedy* followed soon after, as did *Ranger*.

The carrier *Kennedy* (CV67) had left Norfolk, Virginia, on 15 August 1990, leading a carrier group. The embarked Air Wing, CVW-3, had two squadrons of A-7s (VA-46, VA-72), with the Gulf deployment interrupting a planned conversion to F/A-18 Hornets.

Kennedy's carrier group was commanded by Rear Admiral Riley D. Mixson, who recalls that 'All I had time to do was to get my philosophy on the street. My philosophy about winning, about the things we had to prepare for in short order, and essentially what most battle group commanders would say. . . . Rather than just going on a Mediterranean deployment, I felt we would be at war within 20–30 days. As it turned out, we had longer than that . . .

'For the Air Wing, we had to plan not only the usual contingencies for the Med, but also for the Iraqi theater of operations once we got the targets. It was a very intense time. I don't remember a time in my Navy career that was as intense as the 60 days beginning with that Friday when AIRLANT told us we

Aboard *Saratoga* with an A-6 Intruder in the background. The flight deck crew can be identified by different coloured shirts, with yellow for the plane director (middle), red for ordnancemen (left), and green for the catapult crew (right). (IWM GLF993)

were going to sea to when we arrived in the Red Sea, and some time after that.'[1]

The initial objective was to blockade Iraqi ports, stopping ships carrying supplies. This task was supported by the carriers, but carried out by frigates and destroyers. In the months leading up to Desert Storm, 165 ships from 19 navies challenged 6,920 ships, with 832 boardings, and diverted 36 embargo breakers.

Aboard one of the ships, the British frigate *London*, was Captain Chris Craig. He remembers the American carriers making a big impression.

'As we re-entered the Gulf, I helicoptered into *Midway* and *Bunker Hill*. Though they originated from different eras, they were the pick of all the allied ships I had seen. A huge grey city of 67,000 tons, *Midway* carried 2,500 men and more fixed-wing aircraft –

F-18 Hornets for air defence and A-6 Intruders for attack – than we had been allowed to retain for the whole of our navy. Having watched camouflaged Hornets being punched off the flight deck at a rate of well over one a minute, Dan March took me into his command centre to view his coloured screen, where all one hundred US ships currently positioned in the Gulf were on display. I was envious of such an accurate surface picture, but noted that many allied ships were not shown – a somewhat symbolic omission.'[2]

The air war began on 17 January 1991, and as in the Pacific War and the Falklands Campaign, the role of air power was to break the enemy's air power and also deny him the use of his port facilities. The big difference on this occasion was that the first shots were fired by helicopters, as twelve United States Army McDonnell Douglas Apache approached two

[1] Stan Morse (ed.). *Gulf Air War Debrief*, Aerospace Publishing, 1992.

major Iraqi radar installations, flying low and slowly to evade detection, and fired laser-guided missiles to destroy the radar stations. This gap in Iraqi defences was almost immediately exploited by some 700 Coalition aircraft, including those from the American carriers. The first hectic day of air operations was to be typical of many, with 67,000 sorties between 17 January and the start of the ground war on 23 February.

Lieutenant-Commander Gil Bever was flying one of VA-35s Grumman A-6 Intruders off *Saratoga* during the early hours of 17 January. His target was to the west of Baghdad.

'We had a huge support package going in with us. We had planes dropping decoys, shooting HARMS, as well as fighters for escort doing this two-stage attack on this airfield for MiG-29s.

'We rolled in from 25,000 feet, and released at 15,000 feet, high altitude. We decided later that wasn't high enough because there was still too much stuff going over us. Each of our four A-6s carried four 2,000-lb bombs, one on each wing strongpoint. That was a pretty good load for us, although we had other loads, depending on our missions . . . although when we carried a big load, we lost a lot of manoeuvrability and speed, naturally.

'We went in, and there was stuff flying around. Then we heard that there was a MiG-25 in the air . . . he launched against us, and everyone was manoeuvering around . . .

'We came up to the north, right along the river, and followed it to the target, made a left turn, and egressed, right down to the deck, low, almost the way we came in. It was busy, like the Fourth of July.'[3]

The raids continued after daylight when F/A-18C Hornets from VFA-81, part of CVW-17 embarked aboard *Saratoga*, accompanied aircraft from CVW-3 off *Kennedy* on the first daylight raid of the Desert Storm, maintaining the pressure on Iraqi defences started by the previous night's interdictor strike by hundreds of Allied aircraft. The four F/A-18Cs each carried four Mk.84 2,000-lb bombs, a heavy load for a single-seat aircraft. They approached their target, an airfield in western Iraq known to the Allies as H-3, operating as a 'wall' flying abreast. The pilots were Commander Bill McKee, VFA-81's executive officer, Lieutenant-Commanders 'Chuck' Osborne and Mark Fox, and Lieutenant Nick Mangillo.

As they approached their target, they had the support of a Grumman E-2 Hawkeye from *Saratoga*, which provided additional early warning and control to that being offered over a wider area by Boeing AWACS observation aircraft. *Kennedy*'s strike aircraft went in first and after leaving the target area were tracked by Iraqi MiG-29 Fulcrums, but the Iraqi aircraft were promptly despatched by a flight of USAF McDonnell Douglas F-15 Eagle interceptors.

Suddenly, the VFA-81 Hornets were warned of approaching MiGs by an air control officer aboard the E-2, Lieutenant John Joyce, one of three navy flight officers in the back of the aircraft: 'Hornets, bandits on your nose, 15 miles!'[4]

The four pilots in the Hornets thumbed the knurled knobs on the aircraft control columns which selected missiles and switched their aircraft to air-to-air combat mode. They locked on to two MiGs at ten miles.

'It all happened very quickly,' Lieutenant-Commander Mark Fox recalls. 'I switched back to air-to-air and got a lock on one of them. I had the MiG on the right while the second Hornet in our formation – Lieutenant Mangillo – took the MiG on the left. . . . The MiGs approached us, supersonic at Mach 1.2. Our relative rate of close was more than 1,200 knots. They weren't manoeuvering.

2 Chris Craig, Capt. RN. *Call for Fire*, John Murray, 1995.

3–6 Stan Morse (ed.). *Gulf Air War Debrief*, Aerospace Publishing, 1992.

'I shot a Sidewinder first. It was a smokeless missile and I thought, at first, that I had wasted it because I couldn't see it tracking towards the MiG. I fired a Sparrow. The Sidewinder hit, though, followed by the Sparrow. The first missile actually did the job, and the Sparrow flew into the fireball. The whole event, from the E-2's call to missile impact, took less than forty seconds.'[5]

While this was happening the second MiG was shot down by Mangillo firing a Sparrow.

Despite being engaged in air-to-air combat, the four Hornets did not drop their bombs, and after disposing of the Iraqi aircraft they then flew on to make a successful strike against the Iraqi airfield. Rather than risk losing their aircraft and pilots in aerial warfare, the Iraqi Air Force soon moved the remainder of its combat aircraft to safety in neighbouring Iran!

Even if the Iraqi Air Force had moved to safety, the need to soften up the Iraqi defences meant that the pressure on those aboard the ships and flying the aircraft was relentless. The weather was good enough for continued air operations, and modern carrier aircraft could operate at any hour of the day or night.

Captain Warren was *Kennedy*'s air boss, the equivalent of 'Commander Air' or 'Commander Flying' on British carriers.

'The daily operations, unfortunately, made it hard to maintain the catapults and arrester gear, as well as to keep the flight deck petroleum-free. Without a good non-skid base, the flight deck becomes very hazardous. The flight deck and hangar crews quickly became experts on how to manoeuver aircraft under these conditions, especially during a launch. They kept the planes in a sequence so that we

F/A-18 Hornets and an A-6 Intruder share the flight deck of *Independence*. (IWM GLF1004)

An eye-in-the-sky Grumman E-2C Hawkeye AEW aircraft takes off from a carrier's angled flight deck. (IWM GLF1006)

didn't have too many aircraft in the same spot, allowing room for a plane to slide.'[6]

Inevitably, there were casualties, but no war before had the search and rescue support seen in Desert Storm, and, as Chris Craig recalls, it could be almost too much: '. . . as *London* held her slow patrol position north of Bahrain, an F-18 fighter pilot, returning to *Midway*, ejected from his failing aircraft into the sea eight miles ahead of us. Our Lynx, two Sea Kings from *Argus* and the USN rescue helicopter all sprinted for the lonely airman. I urged caution; it was a classic formula for mid-air collision. I needn't have worried: our young helicopter controller was already directing height separations as all the radar blips converged.

'"The combined helicopter downwash will probably kill him anyway," morosely commented the Petty Officer at my elbow. The USN won by a short rotorhead . . .'[7]

The biggest strike against Iraqi naval vessels was on 31 January, but carrier aircraft were not involved. Instead, a Westland Sea Lynx helicopter from *London* attacked seventeen landing craft with her Sea Skua anti-shipping missiles, while Royal Air Force Jaguar strike aircraft joined in, so that out of seventeen Iraqi vessels, four were sunk and another twelve damaged. The Sea Lynx were in action again on 8 February, destroying Iraqi patrol craft in the northern Gulf.

COMMENT

Many believed that the Gulf War was too long in starting, but while naval and air forces were soon in position, it took time to

[7] Chris Craig, Capt. RN. *Call for Fire*, John Murray, 1995.

move the heavy armour and artillery which the armies required to overcome Iraqi defences. The air element also required a substantial stock of munitions for the intensive operations when these started.

Even in retrospect, this was a well-organized operation, the more so because of the many nations involved. It showed the speed of response and flexibility of the aircraft carrier, although this was not as prominent as it might otherwise have been because of the availability of well-equipped Saudi air bases.

While the main media event of the Gulf War was the accuracy of American cruise missiles, other weapons also showed remarkable progress. The F/A-18 Hornet was a potent aircraft, both as a bomber and as a fighter. From the Iraqi perspective, it also showed that having substantial weaponry is an absolute waste if it cannot be used when needed. One suspects that the Coalition forces would have welcomed a worthier opponent!

BIBLIOGRAPHY

Brooke, Geoffrey. *Alarm Starboard: A remarkable true story of the war at sea*, Patrick Stephens.

Craig, Captain Chris RN. *Call for Fire*, John Murray, 1995.

Cunningham, Admiral of the Fleet Sir Andrew. *A Sailor's Odyssey*, Hutchinson, 1951.

Cutler, Thomas J. *The Battle of Leyte Gulf*, Pocket Books.

Davis, Larry. *MiG Alley: Air-to-Air Combat over Korea*, Squadron/Signal Publications.

Gelb, Norman. *Desperate Venture*, Hodder & Stoughton, 1992.

Hanrahan, Brian and Fox, Robert. *I counted them all out and I counted them all back*, BBC Publications.

Hanson, Norman. *Carrier Pilot*, Patrick Stephens 1979.

Hastings, Max. *The Korean War*, Michael Joseph, 1987.

Hickey, Des and Smith, Gus. *Operation Avalanche: Salerno Landings 1943*, Heinnemann.

Hobbs, Commander David RN. *Aircraft Carriers of the Royal and Commonwealth Navies*, Greenhill Books.

Hoyt, Edwin P. *Japan's War*, Hutchinson, 1987.

— *The Kamikazes*, Robert Hale, 1983.

Jackson, Robert. *Suez 1956: Operation Musketeer*, Ian Allan.

— *Suez: The Forgotten Invasion*, Airlife.

Johnson, Brian. *Fly Navy*, David & Charles, 1981.

Johnson, Stanley. *Queen of the Flat Tops*, Dutton, 1942.

Kennedy, Ludovic. *Menace: The Life and Death of the Tirpitz*, Sidgwick & Jackson, 1979.

Lamb, Charles. *War in a Stringbag*, Cassell, 1977.

Masters, A.O. 'Cappy'. *Memoirs of a Reluctant Batsman*, Janus.

Morison, Samuel E. *The Liberation of the Philippines*, Little Brown & Co, Boston, 1959.

Morse, Stan (ed.). *Gulf Air War Debrief*, Aerospace Publishing, 1992.

Nichols, Commander John B. USN (Ret) and Pack, S.W.C. *Cunningham the Commander*, B.T. Batsford, 1974.

Prange, Gordon W. with Goldstein, Donald M. and Dillon, Katherine V. *God's Samurai*, Brassey's, US.

Sauter, Jack. *Sailors in the Sky*, McFarland & Co.

Smith, Peter. *Pedestal: The Malta Convoy of August 1942*, William Kimber, 1970.

Tillman, Barrett. *MiG Master*, Airlife.

— *On Yankee Station – The Naval Air War over Vietnam*, Naval Institute Press, 1987.

Vian Admiral Sir Philip. *Action This Day*, Muller, 1960.

Von Mullenheim-Rechberg, Baron Burkard. *Battleship Bismarck*, Triad, Grafton Books, London, 1982.

Ward, Commander Nigel 'Sharkey' RN. *Sea Harrier over the Falklands*, Leo Cooper, 1992

Winton, John. *Carrier Glorious*, Leo Cooper, 1986.

— *The Forgotten Fleet*, Coward McGann, 1970.

Woodman, Richard. *Arctic Convoys*, John Murray, 1974.

INDEX

Illustrations are shown in italics.
British and American aircraft are indexed by name rather than designation, unless no commonly used name is in existence, to avoid confusion between British and American designations, or changes in designations when the United States armed forces standardized these.